INTOXICATED IDENTITIES

Alcohol's Power in
Mexican History and Culture

Tim Mitchell

ROUTLEDGE

NEW YORK AND LONDON

Published in 2004 by
Routledge
29 W 35th Street
New York, NY 10001
www.routledge-ny.com

Published in Great Britain by
Routledge
11 New Fetter Lane
London EC4P 4EE
www.routledge.co.uk

10 9 8 7 6 5 4 3 2 1

Library of Congress Cataloging-in-Publication Data

Mitchell, Timothy (Timothy J.)
   Intoxicated identities : alcohol's power in Mexican history and culture /
Tim Mitchell.
      p. cm.
   Includes bibliographical references and index.
   ISBN 0-415-94812-6 (alk. paper) -- ISBN 0-415-94813-4 (pbk. : alk.
paper)
   1. Drinking of alcoholic beverages--Mexico. 2. Alcoholism--Mexico. I.
Title.

HV5313.M57 2004
394.1'3'0972--dc22
                                                          2003063602

Dedication

*This book is dedicated to
Karla Ysabel Cavazos and to all the people
who loved her and believed in her*

Acknowledgments

My drinking research began during the 1998 Faculty Abroad Seminar at the Texas A&M University Center in Mexico City. A Faculty Development Leave Award kept the project going and a 2002 Summer Development Grant was crucial to its completion. I greatly appreciate the support or advice of Ben Crouch, Charles Johnson, Craig Kallendorf, the Office of the Vice President for Research and the Office of Latin American Programs at Texas A&M, Phil Bock, Jeannette Marie Mageo, Mónica García Romero and Mónica Vega, Phyllis Mitchell, Bill and Darrah Plank, Padre Rubén of the Universidad Iberoamericana, and my beloved *cuates* on both sides of the border who shall remain nameless for their own good.

Special thanks to CRC project editor Joette Lynch for an organized and smooth production phase and to Daniel Montero for an outstanding copyedit.

Contents

Introduction

When an intoxicated human being from another culture or another century speaks (or shouts or sings or weeps), should we even listen? And if so, how should we listen? Every system ever devised for disciplining meaning is rendered suspect or vulnerable by liquor's peculiar psychology. In the right excessive quantities, alcohol seizes personalities or local cultures and shifts them into radically different zones, cycles, and wavelengths. Binge drinking should not be seen as just another item in a behavioral inventory, still less as mere pathology, but as a frightfully efficient meaning-generation machine, one that taps into an abused group's immense stores of psychic "dark matter." To study the workings of this somatic/semiotic machine yields priceless insights into the social construction of selves and identities.

Our overfamiliarity with alcohol is the initial handicap to overcome. Every country has its own heavy drinkers, light drinkers, nondrinkers, binge drinkers, even "alcoholics." Every country ever introduced to fermented or distilled beverages developed its own love-hate affair with them, the United States most notoriously. If we look at other nations, we find that certain cultures or subcultures within them consume alcohol in less conflicted, more visionary ways. Some have cultivated a taste for embodied temporal experimentation. Some venerate their hard-drinking ancestors in newer, wilder bacchanals. Certain communities, in consequence, have reaped the whirlwind of alcohol's hedonic, philosophical, and stupefying powers. Enter Mexico, home to hundreds of such communities as a matter of ethnographic and historical fact.

The omnipresence of alcohol in Mesoamerican lifeworlds has long been confirmed. The "muse" role of alcohol in Mexican artistic and literary production has long been suspected. The seductive influence of heavy-drinking role models in Mexican popular culture has been decried. Tequila's role in gender battles waged from Chiapas to Chicago is getting more attention in recent times. Yet there is still a great deal to learn about Mexico's heavy drinkers, and even more to learn *from* them, if we can only

1

narcotize our prejudices. Culturally oriented drinking histories seek to be "policy-relevant" without falling into the traps that characterized older modes of alcohol-knowledge production — scientific protocols that kept drunkards at arm's length, with research rationales rooted in cultural blindspots or positions on the social map. The damage done to a body politic by alcohol is not a figment of the clinical imagination, however. This damage must be fully acknowledged and faced at the outset, so I proceed with statistics that might strike anyone as alarming. A 1998 study undertaken at the federal level to determine the connections between ethnicity and substance abuse found Mexican-American men to have the highest rates of heavy, problem drinking — downing five or more drinks in one sitting at least five times a month. The rates were a third higher than any of the eleven groups surveyed, including American Indians. Nationwide, Mexican Americans are nearly twice as likely to be arrested for drunken driving as whites or blacks. In Los Angeles, cirrhosis of the liver kills Mexican-American men at double the rate of white and black men (Nazario 1999, 24).

Public health expert Raúl Caetano notes that "The profile of a drunk driver in California is a young Hispanic male, and you have a similar situation all over the Southwest" (Osborn and Alford 2003,13). In Austin, Texas, men of Mexican culture comprise just 11 percent of the driving population, but account for 43 percent of drunken driving arrests. "One thing I have noticed," says an Austin policeman, "is that the Hispanics I arrest for DWI, 90 percent of the time, are more drunk than the white and black people I arrest" (12). This is not the kind of diversity that gets celebrated at universities. In Sonia Nazario's study, Mexican-American women more than made up for the misbehavior of their men — "resulting in the greatest gender gap in drinking problems of any ethnic group studies" (1999, 24). She points out the obvious: we are in ethnically sensitive territory. "Although many Mexican-American public figures and groups privately acknowledge the harm inflicted by alcohol, few have tackled the problem publicly, in part from fear that it would cement ugly stereotypes. But doing nothing, many health officials warn, will hold back the nation's largest Latino group."

What we see in the United States is the tip of an iceberg; the rest of the iceberg is in Mexico. In the Western hemisphere as a whole, Mexico ranks number one in deaths from cirrhosis. In 1985 it was the fourth leading cause of death in Mexican males aged 15 to 64; by 1995 it was the second leading cause of death for this gender and age group (Narro 1999, 101). In Mexico we find a statistically constant increase in cirrhosis deaths since 1929. In men aged 45–64 it is the leading cause of death, with the majority of those deaths coming from the lower socioeconomic levels. It is the number one cause of death in most rural areas. The regional distribution of cirrhosis deaths has shown a remarkably consistent pattern for forty years.

TABLE 1.1

Rank	States
1	Hidalgo, México, Puebla, Taxcala
2	Querétaro, Quintana Roo
3	Distrito Federal, Campeche, Veracruz, Yucatán
4	Baja California, Colima, Jalisco, Morelos, Oaxaca
5	Aguascalientes, Chiapas, Guanajuato, Nuevo León, Tabasco
6	Baja California Sur, Coahuila, Chihuahua, Michoacán, Nayarit, San Luis Potosí, Sonora, Tamaulipas
7	Durango, Guerrero, Sinaloa
8	Zacatecas

(Source: Mexico's *Dirección General de Estadística*)

As table 1.1 makes clear, states in central Mexico are at the center of the biocultural maelstrom. This has been an area of intense consumption of fermented maguey juice — *pulque* — since pre-Hispanic days. If one had to pick an epicenter, it might be the town of Ixtenco in Tlaxcala, with a cirrhosis mortality rate six times the already high national average. Investigators suspect that pulque production and distribution practices make it vulnerable to bacterial contamination, but detailed studies have yet to be completed. It must also be mentioned in this context that possibly one out of every three bottles of distilled liquor sold in Mexico is adulterated in some way (Blomberg 2000, 51).

Cirrhosis is one of the top five health problems Mexico faces today; it is epidemic as of this writing. Contrary to popular belief, however, only a fraction of drinkers develop serious levels of liver disease; the statistics above would thus suggest that very large numbers of Mexican men engage in heavy drinking. A number of studies carried out in the 1970s calculated that anywhere from 29 to 36 percent of rural men could be classified as "excessive" or "problem" drinkers; recent studies place the average number of men who drink regularly, rural or urban, at between 70 and 82 percent depending on the region (Narro 1999, 103). Emergency room patients in Mexico tend to have much higher levels of blood alcohol than in other countries (Medina 1999, 264). Two Mexican psychiatrists found that in one sanitarium run by the government, 107 of 161 patients admitted for the first time were there for "alcoholic psychosis" (Cortés 1992, 105). Along with such physical or mental consequences of heavy drinking we must include the indirect social consequences, insists medical anthropologist Eduardo Menéndez (1991, 29). In 1997, 25 percent of all people sentenced for crimes committed them while intoxicated. The number is significantly higher in the states of San Luis Potosí and Sonora, higher still in Nuevo León, and in the state of Querétaro it reaches 47 percent. In Mexico City, 49 percent of people sentenced for homicide had been drinking beforehand; in the same megacity, 37 percent of all suicides were completely drunk when they did the deed (De la Fuente et al. 1997, 278). If the role alcohol plays in accidents and violent incidents of all types is brought into the equation, then it necessarily constitutes the number one cause of mortality for Mexican society as a whole. Even when *nondrinkers* decide to end their lives, they get as drunk as possible first (Medina 1999, 276).

The cultural pattern of drinking that emerges from the statistics cited above differs significantly from the American "norm." In Mexico the issue is not so much the *frequency* of drinking (Americans generally imbibe more often) but the *amount* of alcohol consumed on a particular drinking occasion. De la Fuente and his team find plenty of evidence that this is indeed the characteristic pattern of drinking in Mexico, applicable to some 75 percent of all alcohol consumers (1997, 274). Mexicans who migrate to the United States "maintain the pattern of consuming large quantities in a short time" (274), exactly the data confirmed by Dr. Caetano (Osborn and Alford 2003). Dr. Medina and her team deem alcohol the chief addictive substance used in Mexico, an addiction satisfied not so much on a daily basis as on a "special occasion" basis (1999, 264). The Spanish word for a binge — *borrachera* — encapsulates its episodic nature, its status as a special event. The borrachera patterns that concern epidemiologists were already well established by the end of the eighteenth century. Heavy drinking was promoted by powerful vested interests, both rural and urban. "Some of the wealthiest and most influential families [of Mexico City] were pulque producers, more than five hundred shopkeepers sold wine and spirits as well as sundries, and the tax revenue from liquor was a prime source of municipal funds" (Taylor 1979, 68). But whence the unusual demand? Was it a response to ethnocidal colonial politics? To poverty, oppression, or racism? Was it some sort of irrepressible love of the fiesta that persists to this very day? Although Medina and her colleagues consider alcohol to be the number one Mexican addiction, they do not maintain that the addiction paradigm suffices to explain it. Rather, they cite the urgent need for new studies focusing on the "cultural definition" of alcohol use in Mexico, including the powers and properties it is believed to possess (1999, 271). This is exactly the objective of my own study, which by necessity draws methods and ideas from anthropology, ethnohistory, cultural history, cultural psychology, literature, sociology of the arts, ethnomusicology, and many others.

Some scholars are strict supply-siders. For Eduardo Menéndez and his team, the key concept to grasp is "alcoholization," the historical structuring of the alcohol supply by powerful groups or entities. The Mexican custom of "drinking and dying" is not a bizarre quirk of the collective unconscious, Menéndez maintains; rather it is inseparable from a massive for-profit agroindustry that has grown up around alcohol use, the tax benefits that accrue to the Mexican State, and the ideological manipulation of subaltern groups (1991, 29). Public health experts in the United States have been sharply critical of companies like Anheuser-Busch. The company aggressively pursues Mexican and Mexican-American drinkers, as evidenced by its marketing of Azteca beer in Southern California, by its Bud Light product — the number one choice of Hispanic drinkers in the United States — and by the strategic use of Mexican nationalist slogans in its advertising campaigns (Nazario 1999, 25). The Miller Brewing Company is the major and sometimes the only sponsor of "Fiestas Patrias" celebrations every September Sixteenth in scores of U.S. towns and cities with significant Mexican populations. Other major brewing companies are pouring money into Spanish-language advertising to ensure that any emerging Latino identity retains a strong alcohol-friendly component.

Patriotic alcoholization is a very old game indeed. Mexican liquor companies were the first to link nationalism with their products, and they had the kind of governmental support that American brewers and distillers would envy. Nowadays, in any country, the alcohol industry makes use of cultural identity symbols in its advertising or marketing. What demands further exploration is *demand*, that is, the extent to which those cultural symbols achieved preeminence precisely *because* they involved heavy drinking long before modern advertising came into the picture. The cognitions that support the demand for alcohol are as much a product of social history as the alcohol supply itself, after all, and some of the cognitions relate to the specific intoxicating beverage in use. Archaeologists of the ancient world routinely distinguish the "wine civilizations" of regions blessed by wild grapes from "beer civilizations" — everywhere else (McGovern 2003). Boris Segal (1986), a specialist on Russian and Irish alcoholisms, insists that we look at the drinking habits of the whole culture over time, especially at formative periods of the national cultural identity, and pay close attention to any historical shift from low alcohol content beverages to high ones. Distilled spirits alter consciousness more severely; some ethnic groups never could or never wanted to modify their "wild" drinking styles and the ethnophilosophies that supported them.

In any case, to think in terms of massive sociocultural demand or global marketing strategies disrupts our habitual view of alcoholism as one pathetic individual's weakness. There can be no drinkers of polluted water without prior industrial pollution; there can be no alcoholics without prior national, or deliberately nationalistic, alcoholization. Although I am not a supply-sider, it is tempting to speculate that binge drinkers are the hapless victims of "soft" or symbolic violence, defined by Pierre Bourdieu as a form of violence "exercised upon a social agent with his or her complicity" (Bourdieu and Wacquant 1992, 167). This strange complicity or vulnerability could presumably take as many different forms as we have drinking cultures. Might it relate in some way to posttraumatic cultural adaptation? The social trauma paradigm is not a disease or a mental illness paradigm; it does not pathologize; it deals with real social history and the meanings people attach to historical catastrophes, as well as collective modes of self-medication. "Alcohol is probably the oldest medication for the treatment of posttraumatic stress" (Van der Kolk 1996, 191). In recent years, citizens in several Latin American nations have struggled to recover from episodes of state terror and "Recovery begins with memory, and memory is a key slogan and project for most of the continent's human rights movements" (Brysk 2003, 239). Thus it is intriguing to discover that, long before the emergence of support networks and "truth commissions," Mexico's heavy drinkers organized their mental lives around trauma and deployed their own mnemonic traditions that went against official or institutionalized norms of remembrance.

People are not mere pawns somehow incapable of noticing alcohol's dark side; their readiness to keep drinking in spite of (because of?) the risks is the enigma to be unravelled. We cannot stop at the initial explanations or popular justifications for alcohol use, that is, "I'm getting drunk because I can't stop loving you" — a rationale repeated endlessly in Mexican music. How many of the cognitions or emotions that support the demand for drink are even conscious? I believe we are dealing with a labyrinth of subterranean motivations not accessible to traditional methods of investigation — least of all to pathologizing methods. It is essential to begin from inside this Mexican labyrinth, therefore, plausibly to reconstruct the existential parameters of a *borrachera*, its cognitive and emotional templates, its uncanny ability to conjure up a deeply desired self. Only then can we presume to gauge the societal and cultural impact of the selves constructed thereby. Alcoholization and Spanish imperialism went hand in hand, as we will see, but only because alcohol possessed a number of subversive powers, for the indigenes, that the colonizers did not anticipate: the power to unleash ecstatic self-experiencing; the power to assuage or numb distress of all kinds; the power to help people cope with loss of life from disease and exploitation, perhaps to keep survivors from sliding into full-blown dissociation; and, most striking of all, the power to serve as a continuing template for the emergence of new cognitions, new identities, and rekindled hopes for the eventual redress of grievances. It seems very likely that Mexican "problem drinking" began as *solution* drinking.

Alcoholization is strategic by definition, serving the interests of large daytime business concerns; alcoholic creativity is tactical, clandestine, and nocturnal, pitting time against space in Certeau's sense (1988, 41). For some groups drinking is the continuation of politics by other means, a strategy of subversion, a sui generis set of counterhegemonic practices and beliefs. Old data take on new significance within this social resistance paradigm. In 1959, for example, when the people of one Mexican village were organizing their traditional Holy Week play,

> the bishop and head priest of the municipality opposed it on the grounds that village plays were poorly done and were comic and

disrespectful, often involving obviously drunk actors in central roles. According to the priest, in one village Christ staggered more from intoxication than from the weight of the cross. (Romanucci-Ross 1973, 161)

Did this local *via crucis* have anticlerical implications? A great many officially decried behaviors, traits that to an earlier generation seemed mere vices or symptoms or supports of false consciousness, may be nothing less than "the arts of resistance" (Scott 1990). The concept of "adaptive resistance" is familiar to students of Mexican cultural history from such works as *Everyday Forms of State Formation* (Joseph 1994) or *Power and Persuasion* (Brandes 1988). This approach has its enemies (Brass 2002), but it does make sense to see wild proletarian drinking as a kind of resistance to the powers-that-were, even if the spaces and opportunities for it were sketched out in advance or "enabled" by domination. Sometimes, in some places, the drinking was simultaneously hell-bent and rational. Who could blame the miners of Chiuhuahua, for example, threatened with death every workday, for crowding the cantinas and striving to make every Dionysian second count?

The ansiolytic or stress-reducing powers of alcohol work in tandem with its psycholytic or "mind-expanding" powers. Alternative states of consciousness are sought after in every known culture. Dreamtime creation epochs captivate the human imagination; time-erasing rituals are found in ancient and modern times; all manner of substances are employed to "break on through to the other side." Not to include alcohol on the psychotropic list would be cultural blindness of the worst sort. Following cultural psychologist Richard Schweder, we must also admit the possibility that, for some intentional space-times, drinking to excess may be the most civilized thing one can do (cf. Shweder 1991,108–10). Could certain indigenous or mestizo groups be virtuosos at allowing themselves to be creatively transformed by a toxic substance? Could the drunkards of Mexico know something we forgot or never learned in the first place? Why do they make such a show of their eagerness to confront the powers of death? Are we dealing with a whole nation of amateur shamans? One thing we do know: in Mexico, the way of the cross was lined with cantinas. While Catholic clerics administered the sacred within a stationary, fixed realm of representations, the marginalized peoples they sought to control preferred more direct contacts inside the numinous realm of alcoholic becomings. Rum-fueled mourning rituals, for example, constituted a viable system of portals to the spirit world. There was an ongoing battle in the eighteenth century between the ruling classes of Mexico City and the masses who crowded into the burial ground of the Royal Indian Hospital every Second of November to get drunk and talk with their dead personally. "But this festivity, which blurred the line between the living and the dead, necessarily scandalized and even horrified the enlightened elites.

These intellectuals were increasingly devoid of any rites and beliefs that helped them confront the reality of death. They sought to separate it strictly from life, to exile it from society, and to forget its existence" (Viqueira 1999, 117). A very similar struggle took place in Veracruz during the same time period (Voekel 2001). Flash forward two centuries and listen to a popular *norteño* song in which the dying singer begs his friends to sprinkle tequila on the four corners of his sepulcher or attend wakes in the state of Nuevo León where mourners sit by the corpse and drink coffee spiked with mezcal until dawn's early light (Durazo 1998, 322–25). In *Human Mourning* (1943), José Revueltas portrays a priest joining with two peasants in just such a ritual:

> And he was then able to understand, with enlightening clarity, that those two beings and the hundreds and thousands who populated the contradictory land of Mexico, always drank their savage, impure alcohol, their bottle of sorrows, silently and lovingly when they were beside their dead. (Revueltas 1990/1943, 23)

Screen idol Jorge Negrete's death from cirrhosis in 1953 led to the first example of a mass-mediatized mourning ritual: five minutes of silence were solemnly observed in every movie theater in the country (Moreno 1989, 221). Have ordinary rural or urban Mexicans given up their liquid conduits to the sacred? In general, no.

The living have discovered that alcohol satisfies many other demands as well, at least temporarily. The liquefaction of bittersweet memories remains a major mode of Mexican alcoholic creativity. Binge drinking grants access to sources of deep inspiration or authorization; the regimes of truth-production thereby installed mirror a person's position on the social map — possibly in a less distorted way. So-called anti-social drinking, moreover, can be very innovative. It is inseparable from the whole system of bodily aesthetics and identity reconstruction that bestows nicknames and makes them stick forever (Vergara 1997). In Tepito and other bad neighborhoods of Mexico City, a cleverly evasive slang system evolved in intimate acquaintance with drunktalk; the movie character known as Cantinflas personified this elaborate form of somatic semiotic resistance that forever changed the way Mexicans use Spanish.

As many have noticed, the *borrachera* is often a stage for the performance of male gender identity, but let us avoid the cliché associations. The main point of having a gender, we sometimes forget, is to facilitate mating. One does not have to be Schopenhauer to see how "the will-to-life" stands ready to exploit any functional or dysfunctional human practice for its own purposes. Sex is alcohol's strongest anchor all over the world, no question. In Mexico and in Greater Mexico, the extent to which men live their courtship emotions through the medium of alcohol is extraordinary, and the folk-urban cultural continuum remains quite old-fashioned in consequence. Girls are still being awoken by *serenatas* at four in the morning, in and out of big cities. Once the suitors or gallants have imbibed enough liquid courage, they can choose from a large traditional corpus of alcoholized love songs. Male insecurity and compensatory drinking walk arm in arm through the plaza, and the combination can acquire much intensity from another source of worry about the body: its color. This fundamental anxiety "is the result of a colonial heritage that has permanently saddled a fundamentally Mestizo-Indian society with standards of appearance, beauty, and behavior that are not its own" (Nutini 1997, 236). Almost any item in the cultural inventory supports Nutini's diagnosis. If we look at vintage Mexican calendar art, for instance, we feel aesthetic pleasure tinged with guilt — almost every "Mexican beauty" depicted has been bleached and Europeanized. Now let us add worries over status and power to the picture, recognizing, with James Fernández, "the centrality to our consciousness of managing and manipulating or being managed and manipulated" (1995, 36). So we have power, gender, racial, and sexual anxieties: small wonder that men eagerly cultivate alcoholic identity stylizations designed to master all manner of past and potential humiliations and perpetuate those genes.

Sometimes the magic works, sometimes it doesn't. Either way, women get the worst of it once courtship has turned into cohabitation. In colonial times, most wife-beaters or wife-killers *claimed* to be intoxicated at the time; they knew it was a mitigating factor recognized by the legal system. Yet Felipe Castro holds the claims to be fundamentally true, noting that the vast majority of beatings "occurred in contexts where tepache and pulque flowed prodigiously. . . . In some way, the husbands felt that striking their wives was not something that could be done in a 'normal' space, in their daily and habitual conduct, but that in order to do it they should enter into an altered state of behavior" (1998, 17). Not every binge drinking tradition of Mexico is a tradition of spousal assault, but many are, and for good reason: "Recent research across a number of countries has suggested that involvement in alcohol-related aggression is more likely among people who are heavier drinkers, especially those who have a drinking pattern characterized by drinking large amounts per occasion" (Wells and Graham 2003, 34) — just the pattern explored in this book. Aggression, transgression, and marital instability are directly related to masculinist drinking bouts to this very day, as is many a terrified Mexican woman's image of man as irresponsible or arbitrarily cruel, as is many a frightened child's understanding of the world. The whole phenomenon is distressing, yet fascinating, and in chapter 7 I discuss some promising new approaches.

Inebriation is never apolitical and it only looks apathetic to judgmental tourists. Men who deliberately drink with a vengeance breed and multiply in the cracks of power's edifice; under the right circumstances, they can bring down the whole mansion and loot its treasures. The Mexican Revolution took the traditional *borracheras* of peasants, miners, and rancheros to new extremes. Throughout the twentieth century, Mexicans seeking to understand their "fiesta of bullets" were extraordinarily dependent on binge drinking for metaphors, for concepts of time, for ideas about death, for modes of memory and representation. The one-party regime that emerged out of social chaos discovered a rich source of legitimation in alcoholic praxis, once the Callista-Obregón attempts at Prohibition proved a dead end. Cantinas were as important to Mexican nation-building of the twentieth century as taverns had been to American settlers and revolutionaries of the eighteenth century (Barr 1999; Rorabaugh 1979; Smith 1998). In the imagined *communitas* of the cantina, we find a magically intense restoration of Revolutionary psychology itself — yet another case of self-construction in the midst of self-destruction, a collective, alcohol-assisted birth of a nation. The Mexican one-party system survived for seventy years because it accomodated alcoholized Catholic "recalcitrance" (Knight 1990, 243–45). If a Mexican writer's work is to have some credible relation to Mexican society, it cannot fail to include binge drinking episodes. I analyze a number of writers (Azuela, Guzmán, Revueltas, Rulfo, Lowry, Paz, Fuentes) who helped to create literary images of a pervasive death-wish culture inseparable from heavy drinking. But I do not give famous authors precedence over the lifeworlds of Mexico that they skillfully milked, recreated, or falsified.

It is always possible to parrot the paradigms with which alcoholism is understood and treated north of the border. Dr. Ernesto Lammoglia, for example, considers the total lack of originality in his recent work as beneficial: "This book does not attempt to modify, adulterate, or change anything that has been expressed, for almost 70 years, in the first publications of Alcoholics Anonymous" (2000, 17). This benign kind of colonization began with a small group of anonymous alcoholics who met in Mexico City in 1947; by 1993 there were some 14,000 groups in existence in the country as a whole (Musacchio 1999, 106). Although my research has to do with recalcitrant drinkers rather than repentant nondrinkers, I did attend several AA meetings in Guadalajara and Mexico City. It was my impression that men of diverse economic and racial backgrounds easily adopt the jargon and learn to recast their drink and recovery experiences into narrative formats made in the United States. In general, AA methods of truth production elicit a curiously reductionist recalling of drinking days, a peer-enforced devaluation of inebriate experience, the better to allay temptation and facilitate sobriety in the real world. The Mexican ex-drinkers studied by Stanley Brandes "very much believe in and advocate bodily discipline as a route both to sobriety and professional advancement" (2002, 188). In the end, Brandes finds, they get the discipline without the advancement. I salute all members of AA anywhere, but I cannot grant them the last word on Mexican *borracheras*, for reasons clarified in chapter 2.

Alcohol-supported beliefs and practices are very much alive, and they have crucial, ongoing psychopolitical and demographic ramifications for

Mexico and for all areas inhabited by people of Mexican culture north of the border. In the cities of the United States, workaholics fearful of losing control confront more playful personality styles "characterized by under-distanced emotion" (Scheff 1979, 207). People do not resign themselves so easily to powerlessness; they seek out alternatives. Alcohol is at its most "magical" in environments that do not offer sufficient real-life outlets for power assertion (Boyatzis 1976, 279–80). What Victor Turner found in rituals goes double for ritual drinking: "It is not merely that new knowledge is imparted, but new power is absorbed, power obtained through the weakness of liminality" (1974, 258). Michael Taussig, an authority on rituals of magic power in Latin America, insists that "it's not Force in some vitally crude sense of force of arms that is appealed to, but Confusion. For all the masculine stress on heroism in both state and popular culture, it would seem that *confusion*, the tool of the fox and the weak, is the primary tool to deploy against persecution" (1997, 123). For hundreds of Mexican subcultures, sedentary and nomadic, alcohol has been key to the magical reversal of the state's violence, and therefore quite useful in the preservation of social sanity, paradoxical though it may seem. Mexico's heavy drinkers are not without ethics, nor blind to personal and social consequences, but they do have urgent priorities. Deliberate interference with the stream of time is one of them, the replacement of clock-time with a more ecstatic event-time (similar to the *kairos* of the Greeks). Another is the quest for sources of power that we might call magical. Another is the ambitious search for truth, with embodied humanistic methods rather than disembodied scientific ones. In highly localized formats and sometimes with very meager resources, people count on alcohol — not mushrooms, not marijuana, not mescaline — to reveal meanings that are cosmic in scope. How can the urgency or the criteria of this search be communicated in a sober way without betrayal, without falsity? What methodology should we use to truthfully render how truth is or was produced in cantinas and *pulquerías*? To clear out a space for the truths of Mexican drunkards, I have been obliged to hack away at a number of pesky scholarly dandelions (Bartra 1987; Bonfil 1996; Careaga 1984; Corcuera 2000; Gruzinski 1989; Monsiváis 1999; Paz 2000; Vasconcelos 1997). Once these influential sources of bias have been weeded out, we are free to fall under the influence of Mexico's alcoholic lore and the many writers who appreciate it. As we will see, Mexican selves constructed through alcohol have more to do with mental health than with mental illness, more to do with creativity than with nihilism (although there is plenty of the latter). These alcohol-constructed selves possess a cultural weight so great that it defies measurement. Euphoric forms of communitas really do give birth to "complex semantic systems of pivotal, multivocal symbols and myths which achieve great conjunctive power" (Turner 1974, 259). Access to these networks is always achieved at the level of an individual brain, one after another, but they are still cultural and collective in nature.

"Intoxicated" does not mean receptive, easily brainwashed, or forgetful of past humiliations. Quite often it means the deliberate cultivation of oneiric-confusional states that enable persecuted subjects to engage in disappearing acts and *bide their time*.

Apart from physical exhaustion, there is a stiff social price to pay for this magical power. Drinking undertaken to recreate a desired identity makes the drinker vulnerable to the attribution of an undesired identity. This attribution can take the form of malicious gossip or a nickname, and can even find its way into an erudite essay on "the Mexican." Literary elites have an uncanny knack for distorting modes of creativity that express non-elite concerns and priorities. In this book, I seek to move away from stigmatizing oracles like Octavio Paz and back to the kinds of self-construction actually practiced by flesh-and-blood Mexicans with names and addresses (withheld by request). It is intriguing to learn, moreover, that the most important composer of Mexican popular music in history was a solution-drinker who never renounced his alcoholic muse, never attended AA meetings, and died of cirrhosis at age forty-seven. The songs he composed combine symbolic mastery of status anxieties with mastery of sexual anxieties. Drinking to excess while listening to José Alfredo Jiménez authenticates the encoded mastery, temporarily, and reinforces Mexican Romance Catholic ideology itself, permanently. This thoroughly alcoholized cultural system is being recreated throughout the United States at this very moment; therefore it is "policy-relevant" and cries out for an empathic exploration.

Chapter 1
Time-Warping in Tenochtitlán

In the beginning was the agave, also known as *el maguey*. Mexico is home to several hundred species of this giant plant, which is not a cactus despite its finger-slicing spines, and it had played a crucial role in scores of cultures, great and humble, for at least three thousand years prior to the arrival of the Spaniards. In every village daily drinking of *pulque* (fermented maguey juice) provided proven nutritional, medicinal, even anesthetic qualities. Pulque alleviated stomach problems, menstrual cramps, constipation, diahrrea, or just thirst; numerous ethnicities short on fresh water considered pulque to be the milk of Mother Earth herself. Not only alcohol but dozens of other lifeworld needs were supplied by the agave and the commoners who knew its secrets. Agave cultivation techniques predate the "higher" civilizations of Mesoamerica; the hardy maguey, moreover, was not to be affected by plant diseases from Europe (Parsons and Parsons 1990: Blomberg 2000: Bruman 2000: Salinas Pedraza 2000). Spanish missionaries were astounded by the natives' ecological ingenuity, and perhaps they blushed at the legends of the maternal divinity who had first given *pulque* to the people: Mayahuel, the goddess with four hundred breasts, perfect for suckling four hundred divine rabbits, each a kind of sponsor or illustration of a different behavioral outcome of binge drinking. José Luis de Rojas sees this folklore as proof that Nahua villagers were intimately acquainted with alcohol and its myriad disorganizing effects (1998, 250). "He has become his rabbit," people would say of a drunkard's surprising or bizarre behavior. This tradition of expecting the unexpected set the stage for a rapid acceptance of the Spanish notion that drunkenness mitigated responsibility for even the gravest sins.

Fernando Benítez, author of a five-volume work on the Indians of Mexico, called alcohol "*la razón suprema de la vida indígena,*" "the supreme rationale of indigenous life" (1967, 149). He stressed that agaves and pulque were intimately connected to the moon, and thereby "symbolized the totality of sacralized life in ancient Mexico" (Benítez 2000/1977, 9). When tribes all over Mexico and Central America looked at the moon, they did not see a man but the figure of a *conejo*, a rabbit. The feast day of the pulque patron god Tezcatzóncatl was celebrated (every Nahua calendar year) on the Second of Conejo. Alfredo López Austin speculates that "the ancient Maya had, among the fears that impelled them to explore the realm of celestial irregularities, a fear of the lunar rabbit's influence" (1996, 66). The liquid fecundity of the moon was associated with natural process — lactation, menstruation, fermentation. López Austin reproduced a Late Classic Maya vessel of the moon goddess holding a smug rabbit on her lap; pregnant women were strongly cautioned to avoid gazing at the full moon, lest their babies be born with harelips (67). Elsewhere, in regions where the agave abounded, the influence of the lunar rabbit was not feared but deliberately sought out. Even today, among the Otomí, to wander into the desert after ingesting five liters of pulque is to *aconejarse* — to become a rabbit (Benítez 2000, 15). Metamorphosis into an animal is an element common to many alternative states of consciousness; it can happen in the Amazon or in San Francisco. "There is an entire politics of becomings-animal, as well as a politics of sorcery, which is elaborated in assemblages that are neither those of the family nor of religion nor of the State. . . . We do not become animal without a fascination for the pack, for multiplicity" (Deleuze and Guattari 1987, 247, 239). Again, there were *centzon totochtin*, four hundred (meaning innumerable) rabbit numens, a potentially infinite number of pulque-induced becomings.

Civilizations are not built on coercion alone; the dominant know they must return at least a small portion of the energies they capture. In any number of ancient urban cultures, the monopolization and timely redistribution of alcohol supplies figured as importantly as religion itself in establishing new power relationships and hierarchical mindsets (Joffe 1998, 298). The Aztec elites were certainly capable of this pragmatism, but no-holds-barred binge drinking was their own jealously guarded prerogative. Heavy drinking by the hegemons was on a par with their other tools of legitimation: ritual anthrophagy, military propaganda, architecture, and time-marking. It was their version of something observed by anthropologists around the world — "sacrally legitimated shamelessness" (Schneider 1977, 125). In this and in other empire-building concerns, they were clearly overcompensating: "Faced with the overwhelming evidence of their predecessors' monumental achievements, sacred genealogies, and complex social structures, the Aztecs felt immensely inferior and strove to construct a city, mythology, and destiny in order to impress and intimidate others and to legitimate themselves" (Carrasco 2000, 160). The adventitious Aztec hierarchs would never be as "numerate" as the Maya (few civilizations were), but they certainly learned to distrust lunation. The rabbit moon was a reminder of the passage of time, water, female cycles, eroticism, decomposition, and, above all, the regime-threatening ambiguity of gods like Tezcatlipoca or Quetzalcoatl. The Mexica-Tenochca overlords identified their prerogatives not with the inconstant moon but with the never-changing sun; even though they took over management of older pyramids, their own temples were designed for spectacular solsticial lighting effects. The Aztecs subordinated the four hundred rabbits of lunar lore to a solar energy-capture model of the cosmos, a sacro-political machine designed to keep the Fifth Sun alive by fueling it with human hemoglobin. The dramatic New Fire ceremony, sparked in the thoracic cavity of a sacrificial victim every fifty-two years, ostensibly served to kindle every hearth in the realm and ignite a new age. Annual festivals of victimization simultaneously propelled the new age forward and cowed the populace. In portraying themselves as handpicked by the gods to organize gourmet protein banquets, the Mexica overlords were following very well-trodden Mesoamerican paths to legitimacy (González Torres 1985). I propose the term "surrogation anxiety" for the legacy of doubts about their worthiness that plagued each generation of rulers and fed their need for sacred shameless intoxication.

In one of the many narrative traditions studied by Mesoamericanists, the collapse of the Aztec elite was prophesied by a drunkard. This fine bit of irony is found in the twelfth book of the *Codex Florentino*, chapter 13 (Baudot and Todorov 1990, 90). Incense-burning Nahua priests, sent out from Tenochtitlán to reason with the Spaniards, are suddenly confronted by a drunken commoner from Chalco who informs them that they are too late; for too long Motecuhzoma ignored the plight of the common people, and now the Mexica world has come to an end. As *the truths of the drunkard* resonate in their ears and confound their minds, the priests realize that he is none other than Tezcatlipoca, the old moon-loving divinity responsible for the intoxication of Quetzalcóatl and the fall of Tula. Quetzalcóatl had been prophesied to return fifty-two years after his ruination (i.e., in 1519) to punish the regime of his usurpers. As explained by Davíd Carrasco, Quetzalcóatl was the perennial symbol of urban authority itself in Mesoamerica; the numerous myths and prophecies related to his return constituted an ironic and insidiously "subversive genealogy," a kind of Trojan horse that worked in the Spaniards' favor (2000, 9).

The incredible Quetzalcóatl coincidence was the last but not the only nail in the Tenochca coffin. Contrary to popular belief, the Aztec empire was not in the full vigor of its youth when encountered by Cortés. Approximately eight decades before the arrival of the Spaniards, the Mexica hierarchs stepped up the pace of their ritual killing machinery in order to maintain the status quo of compliance in the subject populations (Carrasco 2000:180–91). Such an increased investment in brutal legitimizing activities is symptomatic of a society in trouble. But why was the precontact Aztec empire already on the verge of collapse?

As the most crowded region of the hemisphere, its 25 million people had created a subsistence crisis similar to the one that had
strangled Europe before the Black Death. In 1505 famine prompted
several thousand Aztec peasants to sell themselves into slavery in
order to get enough food to eat. With too many trying to grow
maize on an eroded and degraded land, the people living in the
Valley of Mexico had walked to the edge of the precipice. (Nikifo-
ruk 1993, 73)

So even without the arrival of Cortés, how much time could have passed
before the Mexica met the same fate as earlier Mesoamerican hegemons
like the Toltecs? Empires collapse not from moral failure or mismanage-
ment but when their increasingly complex sociopolitical systems no longer
solve problems efficiently: "As the marginal return on complexity declines,
complexity as a strategy yields comparatively lower benefits at higher and
higher costs" (Tainter 1998, 122). "Ultimately, the society either disinte-
grates as localized entities break away, or is so weakened that it is toppled
militarily, often with very little resistance" (127). These two possibilites
were combined in the collapse of the Mexica-Tenochca empire: the Iberian
parvenus had no trouble finding allies among the ethnicities forced to supply victims for regular festivals or special temple dedications. Tainter cites
numerous polities for whom a lower, more sustainable level of complexity
was perceived as beneficial by groups weary of meeting the hierarchy's
goals. And again, the hierarchy in question had legitimated itself with the
aid of the very same Topiltzin Quetzalcóatl symbolic complex that called
for rapid, absolute downfalls. What also came to an end, thankfully, was
the final eighty-year compulsive killing spree overseen from Tenochtitlán's
Templo Mayor and motivated by what Carrasco terms "cosmic paranoia"
(2000, 186).

   Let us back up for a moment to pre-Hispanic days and attempt to gauge
the specifically alcoholic component of Aztec time reckoning. Enrique Florescano affirms that every great Mexica-Tenochca ritual was a matter "of
killing the time past, of canceling history constructed by the successive
accumulation of happenings, of reactualizing the original moment of creation, the time without wear in which the organizing principles of the universe were established" (1994, 24). Florescano omits to mention the
drunkenness that accompanied these cognitions, but if we adopt his line of
interpretation, derived from Mircea Eliade (1954), we might venture the
following: by imbibing vast quantities of fermented maguey juice, some of
the most cultivated minds of native America explored an alternative state
of consciousness in which they relived the founding myths of their privileged habitus. We would not find mourning here, presumably, nor nostalgia for those bygone days, but the actual alcohol-assisted restoration of
them in all their glory. The "eternal return" approach to Aztec rituals has
been challenged, however. In an incisive recent study, Kay Almere Read

strongly disputes the two Western-derived, mutually reinforcing dichotomies that underlie traditional approaches to Mexica time concepts. One is the sacred/profane binomial, the other the cyclical/linear differentiation. Neither captures the true spatial and temporal dynamics of Mexica calendrics, she argues. Unlike Eliadian ritual returns to an archetypal first time, "Mexica potent moments do not join the sacred and profane only temporarily. Instead, because the sacred equals the profane, multitudinous powers continually course through everything. A situation of profane sacralities is, therefore, always present" (1998, 193). Even more inauspicious for fans of Eliade is Read's radical rereading of calendar glyphs and their accompanying myths. "Much like the twisting motion of rope as it is being spun, new threads are constantly being twisted into Mexica-Tenochca time just as old ones are ending. Time spans partially overlap each other like fibers spinning together, creating an ever longer rope" (98). Aztec time-shaping is best understood in terms of spinning cosmic spirals, argues Read. The twisting, bending calendar was both cyclic and linear at the same time, but featured no *illud tempus* conceived as prior to all time, and no vanished ages came back in a pure or unchanged manner. Instead, there was discontinuity, risk, and genuine "developmental progression from one age to the next" (105).

What kept Mexica time moving forward, spinning and spiraling and creating, was biology itself: "The never-ending process of destructive transformation is a logical result of the Mexica spatio-temporal equation. . . . In the Mexica world, fertility simply does not happen without things decaying, rotting, and falling apart or being smashed, broken, and killed" (Read 1998, 84–85). Read disputes Davíd Carrasco's suggestion that pre-contact ceremonial landscapes were designed to produce ecstatic and dramatic experiences of godliness (Carrasco 1991), preferring to picture the *Templo Mayor* in rather prosaic terms, as "a center for managing how the age's beings changed places, how one order countered another, and how essentially organic and biological mutations would form" (Read 1998, 181). It may well be that there was no strict division between the sacred and the profane in the Mexica worldview; but if everything is routinely and profanely sacred all the time, why have rituals? Why get drunk? We know that the first Spaniards were astounded by the quantities of pulque consumed at the court of Moctezuma Xocoyotzin (1502–1520). Bouts of extended pulque-drinking were called for in the Tenochca calendar system, eagerly anticipated by every sector of the social pyramid, even the captives slated for sacrifice. There was nothing insubordinate or carnivalesque in this inebriation; to the contrary, it was entirely "pro-establishment." It served, among other things, to punctuate and legitimate the elite's supervisory role in the production and consumption of cosmic energy. Like López Austin (1980), Read continually emphasizes the biological or embodied nature of the Mexica spatio-temporal worldview; also like him, unfortunately, she does not explore how it might have actually gotten embodied by Mexica bodies. While certainly moving the argument in the right conceptual direction, they fail to integrate the most embodied transformational experience of them all: intoxication.

Suppose for a moment that binge-drinking occasions *mandated by the calendar* were nothing less than the official worldview's chemical truth anchors. Circumspect modern scholars may be drug-and-alcohol-free, but Aztec hegemons emphatically were not. However one may wish to picture the overarching shape of Aztec time — cyclical, linear, or spiral — alcohol must have served to vivify the time-shaping in the most credible, tactile, experientially valid ways possible. There can be no myths without rituals of truth production, as Lévi-Strauss managed to forget with every tome. Like blood pouring down the temple steps, alcohol pouring down royal *Pipiltin* throats and the occasional hallucinogenic enema were dependable triggers of sacred self-experiencing. In this I believe Davíd Carrasco's emphasis on miraculous, meaningful Mexica moments is more trustworthy. And surely Read would concede that some dates of the calendar were more "profanely sacred" than others.

Florescano paints the aftermath of Spanish conquest in bleak terms of temporal and cognitive dissonance: "Perhaps nothing marked for the defeated the sensation of abandonment and derangement of the world that followed collapse more than the proscription of the calendar system. . . . The Indians felt that they had simultaneously lost their relationship with the cosmic forces that sustained the world and their connection with a past that filled the present with meaning" (1994, 101–3). The literary laments of downfallen ruling classes form the basis of Florescano's analysis, and in this he follows the standard Mesoamericanist parameters established by Miguel León-Portilla (1959). But ought we conflate the resentment and confusion of displaced Nahua elites with the cosmovision or the preferences of the common people? Do today's university-educated specialists in ancient Nahua documents overidentify with the displaced hegemons? The peculiarly rapid collapse of Tenochtitlán shows, among other things, that "urban civilization" is not always perceived as desirable by the peripheral groups caught up in it. Regarding the experience of temporal dislocation: if the norm in the many regions of pre-Hispanic Mexico was "multicalendricality" (Hassig 2001, 129), then the demise of militarily enforced, pan-regional Aztec chronicity could only be perceived in catastrophic terms by (1) the cadre of highly trained urban priests whose livelihoods depended on the same, (2) the elite warrior classes who had utilized the religious calendar for their own empire-building political strategies, and (3) twentieth-century historians and archaeologists enamored of urban complexity whatever the cost.

The times had indeed changed, nevertheless, along with their modes of representation. Indigenous histories would continue to be written throughout the colonial period, but "they largely lost their linear temporal component, as one would predict, and focused on shorter, cyclical histories that bear only superficial similarities to the historical and temporal structures of the indigenous imperial past" (Hassig 2001, 152). Mesoamerican notions of cyclical time seem to infiltrate the earliest known play in an indigenous language, the 1591 Nahua-Catholic drama *Santo Miercoles*, "Holy Wednesday" (Burkhart 1996), but, in their obsession with distinguishing the Aztec ritual year from the Church one, the worried padres had inadvertently reinforced prior native notions of the cyclical kind.

Much of what we think we know about pre-Hispanic alcohol governance derives from the vanquished elites and their heirs; when writing under missionary supervision, they employed Classical Nahuatl — "the language modeled after the one used by those who controlled the ideological machinery of precontact central Mexico" (Klor de Alva 1997, 183). Their postconquest codices, of which Sahagun's *Florentine Codex* is the best known, would have us believe that precontact alcohol use was strictly controlled and regulated. Because the warriors perceived themselves as much closer to the gods than the groups they dominated, they were determined to protect their prerogative to *drink like the gods* — in unlimited quantities — during major rituals called for by the calendar system. Therefore they strove to halt "alcohol abuse" by the unworthy. Subjected to relentless propaganda and threats of execution, the cowed commoners of Tenochtitlán bowed to the elite's sacro-temporal script, dutifully performed their own ritual roles, wore their deferential masks, gratefully stretched out their hands for the occasional flask of pulque. As far as we know, only after the fall of the Aztec state would these urban *macehueales* or commoners be able to drink in aristocratic, quasi-divine quantities. But commoners living in areas not closely supervised by the state apparatus were continuously, guiltlessly drunk in their devotions. The sixteenth-century *Relación de Michoacán* portrays Purépecha warlords as contemptuous of the drunken dances organized by the commoners but unable to stay away from them! This document, two decades older than Sahagún's first writings, exudes an eroticized disgust for intoxicated women and the scent of urine wafting from the scandalous dance known as *Tzitiziqui Uaraqua*; the native priests themselves are characterized as given over to adultery and vice (LeClézio 1998, 230–32). The Aztecs did not attempt to police morals at the local level in far-off polities, and even in the heart of their dominions, Taylor concludes, "Evidence of pre-Hispanic abstinence is suspiciously thin and legalistic" (1979, 45). Rojas is even more sceptical, citing the large number of obligatory drinking rituals called for in both of the overlapping calendrical systems (1998, 241–49).

In the new Ibero-American world order, ironically, it was the surviving members of the Nahua aristocracy who were obliged to moderate their drinking and conform to the expectations of their bearded senior partners from Europe. "The perfect Indian drinker from a Spanish viewpoint was don Fernando Tapia, a rich cacique of Querétaro, who ate and drank in the

Spanish manner with his high table, chairs, and tablecloths" (Taylor 1979, 42). Don Fernando's best trait? — no one ever saw him intoxicated. Quite powerless now to threaten or execute drunken plebeians, the remaining Nahua nobles could only watch as the commoners communed with the sacred on a weekly or daily basis. "One important feature of early colonial drinking is the continuation of ritual celebrations as a form of worship in which devotion was measured by the degree of intoxication" (1979, 39). The indigenes were very devout in this regard, but we should recall that popular religious fiestas in old Spain itself were alcohol-friendly, to say the least (González Casarrubios 1985; Mitchell 1988, 117–18). In New Spain, numerous non-elite Spaniards were seen drunk and disorderly on feast-days. So we cannot assume that the invaders were models of sobriety, nor that Spanish drinking patterns made no difference in the cognitions that accompanied intoxication amidst the ruins of Tenochtitlán. And in any case let us avoid making what Cohen calls "gross assumptions about the relationship of action to belief" (1994, 20).

Is it quixotic to attempt a verisimilar reconstruction of what drinking really signified for the vanquished races of New Spain? In tilting at this particular windmill, it behooves us to understand that Mesoamerican drunkenness was not originally sacred anyway. It was originally *ecstatic*, which is not the same thing. The difference between ecstatic and sacred is the difference between molecular information processing in the brain and molar symbol making of the mind. It is the difference between energy pathways in the frontal- and temporal-lobe circuits, easily modified by toxins, and culturally sanctioned cognitions or interpretations. There are no core beliefs, from this perspective, only core algorithms and energy protocols that can underwrite many different beliefs. Sacred concepts come and go but the underlying brain chemistry remains. "If humans were not taught any religions, they would spontaneously create new ones out of ecstatic experience" (Goodman 1988, 171). For this reason, the great gods of an urban center are much more vulnerable to civilizational collapse than local spirits who linger on in good times and bad alike (Levy, Mageo, and Howard 1996). As Mesoamerican civilizations rose and fell over the ages, a versatile sacred being known as "Quetzalcóatl" was able to go with the flow and occupy many different niches on this god-spirit continuum (León-Portilla 1968; Piña Chan 1977; Carrasco 2000).

Fernando Benítez writes that drinking in the postconquest era was fundamentally different:

> The deserts of the central meseta, where the maguey was preferentially cultivated, were from the Colony's beginning the center of the most intense evangelization. When the Indians lost their warlike character, they stopped seeing pulque as the drink of the valiant and the wise, and converted it little by little into the liquor of the vanquished. In their bitterness, they all had access to de-sacralized

drunkenness and the young arrogated to themselves the rights of the old and of soldiers. . . . Mayahuel slowly departed, and her 400 breasts served to enrich the rogue who owned the huge maguey fields and transform him into an aristocrat. (Benítez 2000, 15)

With a little more empathy for the younger generation, we might surmise that youths colonized and victimized by the Spaniards felt entitled to the same quantities of liquor that Mexica priests had given defeated prisoners of war prior to dismemberment. But a second issue is more important and has to do with Benítez's characterization of said youthful drunkenness as "de-sacralized." If he means that it was no longer sponsored by the *previous* system of sacro-political aggression, we can agree. If he means that it had lost all sacred connections or associations, we cannot — especially if the binges took place within such an "intense zone of evangelization." It would be more reasonable to posit that drinking was not sacralized in quite the same way as before. The owner of the typical *hacienda pulquera* or pulque plantation may well have been a social-climbing rogue, but recent research indicates that both the efficient new operations of the hacienda and the workers' lifestyles were heavily Catholicized (Islas Escárcea 2000). This does not necessarily equate to orthodoxy; what the Spaniards had actually brought with them was a very eclectic religion, bulging at the seams with the repressed scripts of old vanquished rivals of the Mediterranean. Syncretism was both rapid and unusually coherent in New Spain — and keenly responsive to old class antagonisms: "One noteworthy feature of this synthesis was the identification of the supernatural patrons of the indigenous elite with the forces of evil, and the supernatural advocates of commoners with Adamic and holy figures in the Christian pantheon" (Ingham 1986, 9).

Octavio Paz maintained that Novohispanic Catholicism had denied creative participation to the Indians. With their manuscripts and temples destroyed, they were reduced by the Church "to the most elemental and passive of religious attitudes" (2000/1950, 246). Moreover, Paz reasoned, since the majority of newly Christianized natives had belonged to the lower classes, they were therefore "people of a poor cultural tradition" (247). We might want to repudiate this elitist equation of economic poverty with cultural poverty, and hypothesize instead that the slumbering divine rabbit tutelaries of oral tradition were startled awake when the sacrificial pyramids were toppled. The dawn of Spanish domination could very well have been a chance for *macehuales* to rediscover the more polyvocal, transgressive, or lunar/matriarchal modes of alcoholic consciousness that Huitzilopotchli's henchmen had little use for. A belletrist like Paz would lament the end of Nahuatl poetry-writing, naturally, but the demise of classes and deities that emerged with complexity does not spell the end of the sacred. "People living in poverty, marginality and contempt can claim sacredness for themselves in terms which are credible at least to them" (Cohen 1994, 41).

Historians agree that the arrival of the Spaniards brought about a drastic destructuration of state-dependent consciousness and a subsequent reduction of social solidarity to the local area. But perhaps Florescano goes too far in picturing this phase as "the pulverization of ethnic memory" (1994, 110). Ross Hassig recommends that we stop putting the cart before the horse in such matters:

> Rather than assuming that religion in cities was the full pattern while that in the countryside was simplified and scaled down, as the historical accounts lead us to believe, it may be more useful to see religion as practiced in villages and towns in central Mexico as the norm, and the practices in large cities, and especially Tenochtitlan, as hyperdeveloped and elaborated as a result of size and scale, such that the latter should be taken as the exception. (Hassig 2001, 124).

A recent study of Trinidadian culture finds that people already on the margins of a complicated chronopolitical regime will not be devastated when it collapses (Birth 1996). No longer an official god, for example, Quetzalcóatl resumed his elusive spirit existence in marsh and mountain and was later identified by imaginative Catholic clerics as — St. Thomas! (Lafaye 1983). Experts on physically and psychologically traumatized societies have observed that "The members of a culture will always, or most often, rebuild on a template or remnant of cultural customs and values" (Devries 1996, 408). But not just any fragment of a collapsed civilization can become a useful metonym of cultural continuity; it has to be something that was close to direct sensual experience (Levy, Mageo, and Howard 1996, 15). Drinking customs clearly fulfill this prescription. In ancient Mexico, Bruman notes, only two isolated tribes that knew nothing of fermented liquors were in "a cultural cul-de-sac" (2000, 10). Therefore, it is most plausible to propose that *pulque*, the ancient remedy for all ills *and* a tool of ecstatic self-experiencing, plus a natural lunar basis of time measurement, was a principal cultural template upon which the traumatized indigenes began immediately to rebuild their lifeworlds and reimagine their relationship to the sacred. Pulque was a transitional object and a meaning-machine, unwittingly made more available than ever before by Spanish agribusiness concerns.

Clearly there was something about the conquest and the devastation it wrought that caused the rabbit gods of drunkenness to breed as never before. Taylor identifies three significant changes in pre-Hispanic drinking patterns by the end of the sixteenth century: (1) a huge increase in the consumption of alcoholic beverages; (2) "the adjustment of peasant ritual drinking to the many feast days of the Catholic calendar"; and (3) the emergence of Mexico City as the hub of a thriving commerce in alcoholic beverages of all types, especially *pulque*, and site of New Spain's earliest *pulquerías* and taverns. Early in his study, Taylor clarifies that his main areas of concern — drinking, homicide, and rebellion — were chosen not for their supposed causal connection but for the abundant documentation available for each, more than sufficient to show the rapid growth of twin addictions: that of the population to *pulque* and that of the Spaniards to the tax revenues generated by its production and commerce. Pulque-producing Indian communities were protected by law. They represented an unexpected source of wealth for the Iberian colonizers, who rapidly revamped and rationalized the supply system. Many a viceregal palace or government building owed its existence to alcohol levies. Taylor says that "little solid evidence supports the view of peasants succumbing to a 'plague of mass alcoholism,' a view that pervades the literature on colonial America" (1979, 156). And yet he assembles abundant evidence to indicate that, in city or village, hacienda or mining zone, sierra and coast, a huge amount of drinking was going on in New Spain, cynically fomented by Spaniards in a position to do so. As Spain's churchmen and religious orders quickly introduced grape cultivation into New Spain for their own ritual purposes, commoners were confronted with an embarrassment of riches. Most local communities resisted the onslaught of foreign-tasting beverages, but, for reasons unclear to us, the Indians of Cholula and the coastal areas of Oaxaca quickly switched from *pulque* to Spanish wine and developed a capacity for its ingestion that astounded the friars.

The early history of Mexico City would seem to indicate that binge drinking in the context of a demographic die-off stokes a dizzying social freefall, a radical deterritorialization of consciousness, a whole new kind of dance with death: "The Plazuela del Volador was a favorite meeting place for Indian peasants, many of whom drank themselves into oblivion and spent the night passed out in the streets. Personal violence is strongly linked to Indian drinking in early Mexico City. Following the 1692 revolt, the parish priest of two Indian sectors of the city reported that during his long tenure he was accustomed to finding forty or more drunken, seriously wounded Indians in the emergency room of the Indian hospital every night" (Taylor 1979, 37). In *The Limits of Racial Domination* (1994), R. Douglas Cope argues that "Elite attempts to limit and regulate alcoholic intake among the poor represent an outstanding failure of Mexico City's legal system" (1994, 34). This "failure" of alcohol governance was in reality the successful interference of two other power systems at work in the capital: public sector finance via taxation and private sector commercial greed. There was simply too much wealth to be extracted from the production and sale of pulque; entrepreneurs "grew" the economy by planting agaves. As Viqueira points out, the typical "pulque aristocrat" began life poor but ambitious, amassed a fortune in mining or commerce, acquired agave estates, and purchased his title of nobility. "After all, if the Old World aristocracy owned large and reputable vineyards, why should the nobility of New Spain not acquire pulque estates?" (1999, 140). In the perennial disputes between abstemious moralists and taxpaying *pulque* aristocrats, the Crown routinely sided with the latter. Amassing a fearsome quantity of statistics, Viqueira substantiates that "the power of money nullified the ordinances designed to promote public order" (141). The corruption of the minor judges and officials charged with supervising the *pulquerías* can be placed under this same rubric.

Add to this the turbulence of what was quickly becoming the New World's first multiracial society: the new colonial elite was greatly troubled, writes Cope, by "the unexpected emergence of the *castas*, products of miscegenation, new kinds of people for whom names had to be invented: mestizos, castizos, zambos, and many others" (1994, 4). Cope recounts the life of a proletarian woman named Josefa who "fit the *casta* stereotype perfectly: she was insolent, unrooted, drunken, and possibly immoral" (40). Surely she had gotten in touch with her inner rabbit. Cope spells out the perennial threat to public order represented by the unruly progeny of racial mixing: "How could the heirs of the conquistadores sustain their rule over this multiracial melange without the benefit of a standing army?" (4). The reader might now be inclined to see plebeian alcoholization not as a failure of the laws but as a clever stratagem of colonial power, a kind of "libidinal bribery," whereby the servants steal "little crumbs of *jouissance*" from the Master but only perpetuate their own servitude in the process (cf. Zizek 1997, 34). It is remarkable to discover that, between 1521 and 1810, the hard-drinking denizens of Mexico City were able to mount but one major rebellion against their masters. The wild riot of Sunday, June 8, 1692, was apparently brought on by a shortage of corn and an excess of alcohol. For the plebeians, "the riot was a liminal, almost festive event, a moment of sudden and sharp role reversal but one that could not last" (Cope 1994, 160). "The riot began as a political message but degenerated as it proceeded, its political content seeping away, until it ended as an every-man-for-himself orgy of looting." The frightened viceroy banned the sale and consumption of *pulque* in Mexico City, but the king himself asserted that "the connection between the rebellion and the ingestion of pulque was tenuous" (Viqueira Albán 1999, 133). I am obliged to disagree with the king, who routinely put the interests of his Royal Treasury first, and side with those who blamed *pulque*. Intoxication is always a chaotic micropolitical particle accelerator; in 1692 it clearly picked up enough speed to push the subaltern hidden transcript across a critical social threshold and right onto the public stage itself (Scott 1990, 5). In any case, bootleg *pulque* and legal sales of "medicinal" *pulque* slaked the thirst of Indians and poor Creoles alike until the ban was rescinded in 1697 (Cope 1994, 39). If we flash forward one century, we find that "the city's spongy foundations were almost as saturated in spririts as they were in lake water. In 1784 the consumption of *pulque* reached 187 gallons for every adult resident of the city — plus perhaps 3 gallons of distilled alcohol" (Taylor 1979, 67). Great amounts of liquor were consumed during Christmas and

Easter festivities, which always got out of hand. A precarious balance had been struck between Apollo and Dionysus in Mexico, the inevitable by-product of schizogenetic colonial domination itself. At an institutional level, Mexicans bore the brunt of peninsular oppression, overseen first from El Escorial and later on from Madrid and Sevilla, mitigated by the Catholic Church and its consoling religious orders. Within the shadowy realm of unintended consequences, the epidemics that ravaged the populace had, as their charitable counterpart, the near-epidemic alcohol consumption fortuitously stoked by Catholic festivities.

Chapter 2
Anthropologists and Alcoholics

Can we take articles in the most respected journals of alcoholism at face value? Or should we ask which specific form of power-knowledge called them into existence, from which habitus they judge and categorize their Others? Most studies of drinking are written under the influence, says Joseph Gusfield, that of "the pathological frame" and the "malevolence assumption" (1996, 31–54). Following their review of thousands of such studies, three prominent experts conclude that research paradigms

> have historically focused almost exclusively on alcohol's possible effects as a moderator of *negative* affective states and reactions. . . . Unfortunately, experimental manipulations of positively valenced emotions are rare in alcohol research. . . . Still, considering the hypothesized major role of both negative *and* positive affect in drinking behavior and its consequences, it is puzzling that so few investigators have sought to study the full range of affect and to measure emotional valence specifically. (Lang, Patrick, and Stritzke 1999, 335–36, emphases in original)

The research bias becomes less puzzling when we stumble upon its sturdy cultural roots. In the course of U.S. history, notes Gusfield, "the alcoholic becomes one of the symbols of a fear of falling; of a threat in the personal drama of success and failure that is the key story of American careers" (1987, 87). For medical anthropologist Howard Stein, alcoholism is above all a "culturally styled syndrome," and alcoholics are "the chief players in the longest running morality play in American history" (1994, 209). The script for this play requires society and its lawmakers to set limits "spasmodically, punitively, self-righteously, and above all, temporarily."

Research priorities reinforced by hefty government grants are not unrelated to alcohol governance and national anxieties. All Americans, in truth, have been subjected to one form or another of "soul governing" when it comes to drinking and numerous other bad habits, with medicalization as the continuation of religion by other means. Mariana Valverde has called attention to the "thoroughly Protestant" origins of addiction, recovery, and abuse-survivor genres: "Despite the prevalence of genetic and familial determinism in contemporary explanations of behaviour, most of us do expect ourselves and others to flex the will and do battle against whatever inner slavery would otherwise be our destiny (Valverde 1998, 16). Sometimes a strong will is exactly the problem: American literary historians well know that William Faulkner was fond of flexing his iron will — it was the very quality that made him such a determined boozehound (Dardis 1989, 23–95).

When it comes to heavy drinking, one nation's slavery is another's freedom. Pertti Alasuutari discovered a striking contrast between the "alcoholism frame" favored by tenured scientists in the United States and the "every-day life frame" used by the hardy drinkers of Finland: "In general the state of drunkenness is a real realm of freedom for the Finnish man, a realm that offers bleak prospects but perhaps for this very reason is considered to possess an almost religious sanctity. The gates to the most sacrosanct places in this realm are open only to those blessed people who are prepared to sacrifice everything, including their self-discipline, for that freedom" (1982, 44). Paradoxical though it might seem from an American perspective, only through complete surrender to the natural determinism of a substance did these Finns find freedom. And there is more: inebriated Scandinavians "are involved in the cultural production of their identities in an ongoing attempt to impose order on disorder, to develop a meaningful account of the world, and to gain a measure of self-respect through the symbolic ordering of their environment" (50). Truly this is *self-constructive drinking*. Things have taken an even more radical turn in a large nation nearby:

> In Russia, vodka is thought of as a sacred and eternal substance, impervious to historical interpretation. . . . But the vodka drinking ritual also involves a harsh questioning of human conventions. It demands freedom from history, from responsibility, from health, even from life itself. This condition of free fall, of moral weightlessness and philosophical incorporeality, represents both an attack on the "rational" West and a haughty assertion of Russian truth. (Erofeyev 2002, 57, 61)

This raises the question of what makes drunken meanings and identities more "believable" than others? A preliminary answer is found in the somatic state in which they emerge. A drunkard's truth is as embodied as any truth can possibly be. We must not only assess the meaning of alcohol

in a particular society, but also *how alcohol means* in the bodies taking it
in. It is not a question of "anything goes." Long ago in India, cannabis was
the drug of choice for the priestly caste, "which they praised as a promoter
of contemplation, an aid to insight, a stimulant to thought, and a help in
attaining inner peace. The warrior caste, on the contrary, drank distilled
liquor, which they heralded as a reviver of sagging spirits, an invigorator of
sexual desire, a stimulant for the brave warrior, and the promoter of a
more zealous, active life. Marijuana they condemned for producing apathy
and lethargy" (Rorabaugh 1979, 179). The cultural meanings of a substance are not *determined* by the substance, but the meanings must be
minimally compatible with a specific substance's psychoactive properties.
What would Russian culture look like if for the past five hundred years
everyone had used pot instead of vodka? Would the typical Russian still
suffer from "the excruciating feeling of remorse and self-abasement that is
one of the essential elements of the ambivalent Russian personality?" (Erofeyev 2002, 61). Erofeyev would say no, and so would I.

Nordic alcohol researchers are often found at the forefront of an
enlightened, cultural-meaning approach to alcohol use (Sulkunen 1998).
They have allies in many nations, chiefly anthropologists who see drinking
in terms of its positive benefits for a given society. Dwight B. Heath boldly
claimed that "The association of drinking with any kind of specifically
associated problems — physical, economic, psychological, social rela-
tional, or other — is rare among cultures throughout both history and the
contemporary world" (1987, 46). Alcoholic beverages, as Mary Douglas
noted in her introduction to *Constructive Drinking* (1987), "make an intel-
ligible, bearable world which is much more how an ideal world should be
than the painful chaos threatening all the time. . . . They are not false
worlds, but fragile ones, momentarily upheld and easily overturned"
(11–12). As Dr. Elvin Jellinek himself observed, "Drunkenness can be a
kind of shortcut to the higher life" (quoted by Heath 1987, 33). Even when
an anthropologist is keenly conscious of the damage done by drink, she
may resist the imposition of the "alcoholic" label on the peoples under
study. Waddell makes the case in his volume on desert Indians:

> In the sense that drinking and drunkenness contribute to the via-
> bility of social group relations, no matter how narrowly defined, it
> is hard to label the resulting behavior as pathological. Meaningful
> relationships are confirmed by drinking; individuals define their
> self-worth by drinking; they communicate the desire for trust in
> each other by sharing drinks; and they even seem to enjoy being
> happily drunk with friends. (1980, 79)

Stein recounts the experience of one white counselor who found that his
client, a Ponca Indian of Oklahoma, identified the state of intoxication
with the very contours of his tribal identity. "The client certainly did not

deny his alcoholism, the behavioral dimension, that is; he only denied the pathological connotation — and the change implicit in accepting that label — of alcoholism" (1994, 213). The white counselor's paradigms finally prevailed in this particular case. Waddell details similar negotiations taking place on reservations throughout the Southwest, where Indians are "learning the languages of their benefactors — policemen, judges, ministers, AA groups, 'recovered' Indians, doctors, and other institutional personnel" (1980, 78–79).

Though certainly not as numerous as they are in the United States, Mexican alcohol counselors and researchers have reproduced the main paradigms under which alcoholism is understood and treated north of the border (Guerra Guerra 1977; Molina, Berruecos, and Sánchez 1983; Velasco Fernández 1991). This is justified in the narrow sense that alcohol in connection with modernization produces measurable similarities from one country to another. For example, a group of Mexican researchers got a grant to study a sixty-kilometer section of the highway between Mexico City and Cuernavaca. The road has many variations in altitude and numerous sharp curves, but seatbelt use by drivers and passengers is spotty at best. The investigators' main conclusion? "Alcohol intake is a major risk factor for severe injuries in highway traffic accidents" (Híjar, Flores, López, and Rosovsky 1998, 1551). The reader will immediately notice the cost-ineffective nature of this research. Beatriz Cortés indicts the psychiatrists of Mexico and Latin America in general for their lack of interest in developing fresh theoretical or culturally aware approaches to heavy drinking (1992, 108). Examples of this intellectual flaccidity are not hard to find. Ramón de la Fuente and his colleagues at the Instituto Mexicano de Psiquiatría simply translate American concepts and categories into Spanish (1997). As noted earlier, Dr. Ernesto Lammoglia prides himself on his total lack of originality: "This book does not attempt to modify, adulterate, or change anything that has been expressed, for almost 70 years, in the first publications of Alcoholics Anonymous" (2000, 17). Such culturally obtuse, autonomy-surrendering reverence for AA is exasperating but not surprising. "Whether or not it works to cure alcoholism," writes Valverde, "AA has certainly succeeded in developing a whole array of non-professionalized, low-cultural capital techniques for acting on oneself that have profoundly shaped our present" (1998, 19). One AA promoter whose zeal reaches missionary levels puts the number of groups in Mexico at twenty thousand (Aguilar Siller 1997, 82). The aforementioned Dr. Lammoglia provides a partial listing of AA groups in Mexico called *Grupos 24 Horas*, "24 Hour Groups" (2000, 265–83), this name the result of a nationwide organizational squabble that took place in 1975. In meetings of these groups one hears numerous references to the *Creador Omnipresente*, a tough-love paternal deity affirmed to be more helpful than vows to the Virgin of Guadalupe, a traditional Mexican way of coping with drinking-related difficulties.

Veteran anthropologist Stanley Brandes has recently published a study of men *Staying Sober in Mexico City* (2002). The trajectory of one small "Moral Support" group replicates the troubled deployment of twelve-step ideologies in Mexico as a whole: "In addition to uncertain meeting attendance, Alcoholics Anonymous groups in Mexico City sometimes seem to teeter on the brink of extinction. Mexican groups experience a constant process of fission and fusion" (132). It should be clarified that Brandes was not an "alcoholic" himself. He was warmly welcomed by the men of Moral Support but kept their group ethos at arm's length. "Although I occasionally felt guilty, I confess to harboring a mildly perverse sense of satisfaction from my stubborn refusal to abstain" (2002, 21). Brandes writes at length on the religious and spiritual aspects of Alcoholics Anonymous south of the border. Like earlier researchers, Brandes finds that "Protestantism and membership in A.A. are alternative routes to achieving sobriety," and indeed, "membership in A.A. might well prove redundant" for a Mexican Protestant (34). Nevertheless, Brandes affirms, it is AA's affinities with popular Mexican *Catholicism* that have proved crucial to its growth — elements like sponsorship, padrinos, saintly portraits of Bill W. and Dr. Bob, periodic fiestas of sobriety, even the spatial layout of the meeting room that "replicates the kind of sacred space that would be familiar to any Mexican Catholic" (42). "To join Alcoholics Anonymous in Mexico City does not mean abandoning one's religious tradition. It means adapting it to the circumstances at hand. This is one central reason why we should not be surprised that, despite thoroughly middle class, Protestant origins, Alcoholics Anonymous has been highly successful not only in Mexico but also throughout much of Latin America" (185). The problem with this thesis is that Mexican religious traditions are also deeply implicated in, *and often entirely complicit with*, binge drinking. If Mexicans drink because they are Catholic and refrain from drinking because they are Catholic, where does that leave us?

The men of Moral Support are largely at the end of their drinking careers, by their own admission the major use of their time on earth. At one meeting, "The men listened attentively to José and laughed loudly at his mention of pulquería, the kind of drinking establishment that most of them had frequented as active alcoholics" (2002, 181). Here Brandes does not elaborate — but here we must. A *cultural history* of Mexican alcoholism reveals that the megacity's *pulquerías* were sites of dense linguistic and folk poetic creation, that this creativity was rooted in the immense corpus of mythology surrounding the maguey plant itself, that *pulque*-producing haciendas were de facto Catholic missions in Indian territory. A cultural history would note that the evolution of Mexican identity through the centuries, including gender and racial identities, was inseparable from the nation's network of *pulquerías* (Lameiras 1995, 1998). Even a history of Mexican "culture" in the narrow elitist sense of the word would wind up in the same place, for the *pulquerías* of Mexico City attracted the attention of the educated and inspired the creative. Composers composed in them, writers wrote in them, artists sketched there. "La Rosita," a *pulquería* in the Coyoacán district, exemplified the high-low symbiosis. Inside there was a counter made of white cement, a wooden bench against the wall, two tables with four cheap chairs apiece, and a cement urinal barely concealed by a frayed curtain. Outside, on the wall facing Aguayo street, a visionary mural had been painted in 1943 by neighborhood resident Frida Kahlo and her adepts (Jiménez 2000, 36–41). Well into the 1990s, *pulque* production and consumption remained robust in neighborhoods undergoing rapid absorption by the megacity, and babies continued to receive their first tastes of *pulque* in feeding bottles. For many generations, alongside the explicitly Catholic elements, the world of Mexican binge drinking was one of daily carnivalesque revelry, street slang, and resistance to viceregal, Porfirian, or PRI despotism. The *borrachera* world was and is musical, romantic, salacious, death-accepting, and much given to the outer and inner staging of hilarious events.

With this brief cultural history in mind we can better understand why the disciplined men of AA often wax nostalgic for their lost paradise. They paid a stiff physical price to belong to it, granted, but now to live a healthier life they submit to what Zerubavel calls "mnemonic obliteration" (2003, 91). Past *borracheras* are to be recalled in one way only, or forever forgotten. The consequences of AA-enforced amnesia are many. For instance, men soon forget how drunkenness was their preferred means of recalling or communicating with those who had departed their bodies; they even forget their ancient comical or philosophical attitudes toward death. In men undergoing AA-sponsored cultural lobotomy, death anxieties resurface with a vengeance. The fear of being killed by alcohol in the long run is great among members, and the fear is hallowed in the very name *Grupos 24 Horas*. "To look too far into the future, which means for a period longer than 24 hours, is presumed to be an overwhelmingly burdensome goal, which can only backfire" (Brandes 2002, 116). Both north and south of the border, it seems, recovering alcoholics take things one day at a time. Interestingly, the active alcoholics studied by R. G. Smart also appeared to have "significantly shorter future time perspectives" (Smart 1968, 81). They did their *drinking* one day at a time. But Smart noted that, unlike teetotalers, his alcoholics suffered from a strange "insensitivity to future consequences" (83). Time is at the heart of the matter, it seems. As will be seen, Mexico's binge drinking communities are emphatically not 'in denial" about consequences and do not shy away from thinking about the future: in many cases, it is precisely eternity that is being sought, and found, in ecstatic timeless drunken moments. What we might call "equifinality," the eventual demise of drinkers and nondrinkers alike, is accepted as entirely natural, with stoicism and good humor. The contrast with the death-avoidance ideologies and rituals of Moral Support men is striking. What could have happened to tear them away from the folk philosophical matrix of the majority? Brandes affirms that AA is the last resort, the final social safety net for many migrants to Mexico City who never found stable employment or stable family lives. "What the meetings accomplish, as much as anything, is to structure the men's lives and fill otherwise danger-ously free moments with a small, tight-knit society of caring companions" (2002, 197).

Indeed, structure is everything. Brandes speaks of "the nearly relentless social control that is fundamental to the functioning of Alcoholics Anony-mous in Mexico City" (14). This single-minded control has chronopoliti-cal aspects, as could hardly be otherwise, including the inculcation of regularity, punctuality, and timekeeping. In personal speeches that "are supposed to last exactly fifteen minutes" (61) the men equate drinking not only with death but with dirt: "The words the men use most to describe their own prior physical condition are *meado, cagado, mugroso* — pissed on, shit on, filthy" (85). Still other narratives chronicle and simultaneously anathematize the men's splendid indifference to money during their drinking heydays. To abstain from drinking is to embrace cleanliness and frugality (87). The internal coherence of these themes can be found at a level of psychocultural analysis that makes the Protestant/Catholic distinc-tion seem superficial. When all else fails, when cultural and social support mechanisms are lacking and anxiety is great, the last safety net is the sphincter — understood as the set of psychic defense mechanisms that keep painful, murderous, or suicidal affect at bay (Shengold 1992, 51–78). We are dealing with a kind of psychic reduction that parallels the cultural one wrought by Alcoholics Anonymous dogma. By contrast, binge-drink-ing Mexico answers to a more fertile type of psychic destructuration, one that has long gloried in a Rabelaisian acceptance of corporeal imperfection or a Bataillean "performance of waste" (cf. Roach 1996, 123). This does not mean that alcoholized collectivities have no concept of stain or sinful-ness — quite the opposite; it simply means that *redemption is sought in drinking itself, not its refusal.* Michael Taussig makes much of Latin Ameri-can folk rituals where people are found "receiving spirit in glorious enact-ments of embodiedness, this body so long condemned to the taboo-world of the ambiguously unclean" (1997, 137). The anxious anality of AA men trying to stay sober in Mexico City finds cultural reinforcement wherever it can, that is, in the body-fearing legacy of Christianity available in both Protestant and Catholic versions. In a culture or in a mind, however, sphincteric defenses compete with other types of instinctual "drives" and psychic needs. Overcathexis can take place at any developmental level, but the levels cathected involve vast differences in modes of mapping time, seeking gratification, depleting or enhancing precious resources, releasing memories, imagining transcendence, and experiencing identities. In Mex-ico we find bodyminds seeking redemption with and without alcohol, in priapic indigenous drinking rituals and sphincteric nondrinking cults like AA. "Staying drunk in Mexico City" is an achievement in its own way, therefore, and ultimately more fascinating from any number of disciplinary perspectives.

The Mexican Catholic Church never came out in favor of binge drinking. Nevertheless, people whose identities are nominally and even recalcitrantly Catholic have enjoyed mostly guilt-free *borracheras* for centuries. The ramifications of this essential fact are explored in every chapter of my study. Here let us note that ordinary Mexicans literally have it both ways with their easily withdrawn *juramentos* or vows to the national matriarch — the Virgin of Guadalupe. That is why Mexico's AA missionary, Oscar Aguilar Siller, begs priests who are still condoning the vow-to-the-Virgin-of-Guadalupe method to send their parishioners to the nearest group of *Alcohólicos Anónimos* (1997, 82). But in Huixquilucan, a town being gobbled up by Mexico City, Rosa María Osorio found Guadalupan vows to be more effective than the unstable, here-today-and-gone-tomorrow AA group (1992, 32). In the opinion of Marina Martínez, a *curandera* who treats Mexico City's drunkards with herbal remedies, AA is "pure hypocrisy" (as cited by Campos Navarro 1992, 82). Doña Marina mocks the ease with which men temporarily slip the bonds of their vow to the Universal Mother by greasing the palm of the local priest. Priests find almost any excuse to be valid — deaths, births, baptisms, birthdays, saint's days, and so forth. Doña Marina distinguishes social classes by the liquors they imbibe, but says they are all the same in their enthusiasm for drink: "From what I have seen, only one fiesta in a hundred takes place without alcohol; the other 99% are pure binges, whether among the rich, the poor, or those in the middle" (80).

Both AA and folk medicine approaches contrast sharply with that of the Mexican anthropologist Julio Macuixtle García, who has nothing but praise for the religiously motivated binge drinking that goes on in a Nahua community located in the eastern ranges of the Sierra Madre (Veracruz). While members of the local middle class prefer beer, the workers and peasants stay with their *aguardiente* (distilled sugarcane alcohol, or rum) and their old Catholic drinking customs. In the late eighties, the binge drinkers banded together to expel the local adepts of Liberation Theology for attempting to put a halt to the traditional Catholic bacchanals (1992, 53–54). In true Durkheimian fashion, Macuixtle discovers that rum promotes spiritual cohesion and legitimates the social structure of the entire village. He vigorously denies a claim made by teetotaling Protestant missionaries that alcoholism has led to an impoverishment of the locals, and roundly affirms that any anti-*aguardiente* program put into effect would serve no good purpose whatsoever, but only weaken the continuity of local cultural identity.

It is not my intention to give Macuixtle the last word — at least not so soon. In a fascinating debate sponsored by *Current Anthropology* some years ago, public health sociologist Robin Room chided anthropologists for habitually downplaying or "deflating" alcohol problems in the cultures they studied (Room 1984). An official of the World Health Organization, Room had long been struck by the gap between alcohol studies conducted by epidemiologists and those done by ethnographers. Methodology was partly to blame: ethnographers studied villagers or rural groups while epidemiologists focused on urban working classes. More importantly, Room argued that the very development of American anthropology had been undertaken by "the Wet Generations" — liberal intellectual laymen who had come of age during the national backlash caused by Prohibition. It was the same cultural environment that led major American artists and writers "into drinking patterns that most Europeans found to be dangerous and unacceptable" (Dardis 1989, 11). Room notes that American anthropologists abroad had a strong desire to differentiate themselves from (a) missionaries, alcohol-and-tobacco-free as a badge of identity, and (b) colonial officials known for their racist tendency to exaggerate the alcoholism of the natives (1984, 175). Furthermore, the relatively brief amounts of time spent by ethnographers in distant lands robbed them of the long-term perspective of the epidemiologists. And finally the gender of the anthropologist himself, quite naturally drawn "towards the pleasures of the drinking group, usually male, and away from the private agonies the men's drinking may involve for women and children" (172). Room fully recognizes that high levels of drinking are seen as "normal" in numerous societies — but again faults anthropologists for their functionalist complicity with "the society's internal hegemonic structure in the setting of norms" (173), and their concomitant failure to gather dissenting or counterhegemonic views from individuals in the society under study.

These charges provoked illuminating responses from fifteen anthropologists who had done major drink-related fieldwork. Dwight Heath, criticized by Room for downplaying Latin American alcoholism in a career spanning three decades, was pithy in his reply: "Perhaps most ethnographers *do* differ in outlook from some more policy-centered sociologists. We don't feel obliged to teach people how miserable they ought to be feeling, and therefore, with respect to drinking problems (as with respect to anything else) we don't deflate what sometimes isn't there" (181). Michael Agar pointed out that "Problem inflation or deflation presupposes a privileged position from which the 'accurate' or 'true' problem is known. . . . Alcohol use is inevitably found to be a coherent social act, one that takes a variety of forms, usually not of the destructive sort" (178). But Jeremy Beckett intoned a mea culpa: having once argued that Australia's Aborigenes "had adopted the hard drinking of the frontier to reconstitute their shattered society and that in defying official prohibition they were conducting a pre-political resistance," he subsequently came to lament the destructive consequences that accompanied the positive ones (178–79). Juan Carlos Negrete removed some of the onus from American ethnographers by noting that, in Latin America, anthropologists of any nation idealize folk groups and minimize the existence of alcoholism in order to counter "the prejudiced and discriminatory perception of native peoples commonly held by modern urban and industrial society" (185). Both ethnographic and epidemiological approaches came under fire from Margaret Sanger, since they "generally employ a paradigm of normal versus deviant individuals rather than powerful versus powerless people. Epidemiologists work in a climate of 'expert' medical opinion that endorses dominant-group definitions. Their problem orientation contributes to the social control of subordinate groups" (186).

The participants in this spirited and still-instructive debate did share some common ground. No one defended the premise that alcoholism could be reduced to a simple disease that works its effects in a cultural vacuum. No one argued in favor of treating one drinking culture with concepts and methods devised by a different drinking culture. And naturally no one opposed sincere efforts to help addicts and substance abusers. Room's final point, valid in my view, was that the discredited "alcoholism frame" had ironically let ethnographers off the hook:

> The common procedure has been to hold the disease-concept stencil up against the data on the society observed, to note that the behavior in the society does not fit the stencil's pattern, and on that basis to offer as a conclusion that there is little or no alcoholism in the society studied. In a literal sense, such a conclusion may indeed be warranted, but it is a conclusion that slides right past the corollary question: if the alcoholism concept has a bad fit with the conflicts and problems involving drinking in the society, what is an appropriate and culturally sensitive way of characterizing these problems? (176)

In more recent writings, Room notes that the public-health perspective is quickly losing ground — not to anthropologists but to "global and regional free-trade agreements that increasingly treat alcoholic beverages as a commodity like any other" (1998, 798).

This itself suggests the most attractive and appropriate inital frame for cultural alcohol studies: the role played by drug-food commerce in the construction of civilizations. As William Jankowiak and Dan Bradburd reveal, "There is in fact a close relationship between the level of political complexity and the use of drug foods as trade or labor inducers" (1996, 719). Cacao, coffee, tea, tobacco, alcohol, sugar, sugarcane, sugar substitutes, opium, marijuana, honey, coca, cocaine, and cola drinks — they are all "pharmacologic agents that alter cortical stimulation, resulting in the modification of mental activity" (717).

> There is also a clear relationship between the type of subsistence and the chemical stimulants used to enhance a laborer's work performance. The more labor-intensive the subsistence system, the

greater the likelihood that a drug food will function as a labor enhancer. . . . Alcohol was commonly used as a labor enhancer on plantations and haciendas, in the mines, in the merchant marine, in the armed forces, and, during the earliest phase of industrial capitalism, in factories. . . . The agents of colonialism were faced with the recurrent problem of motivating and organizing a population in new or more sustained forms of labor when that population did not need or embrace the status symbols of the colonial social order. The response to this dilemma was to foster chemical dependency. (718)

The colonial and neocolonial fomenting of addiction is especially relevant to Mexico, formerly New Spain, where drug food production and commerce quickly became a different sort of gold for the Spaniards and their heirs. Any Mexican region could serve as an example of this process, but in this chapter let us focus on neocolonial chemical dependency in twentieth-century Chiapas, a genuine worst-case scenario that has greatly preoccupied Mexican scholars over the years. Benign, "no problem" anthropological approaches meet their most formidable challenge in Chiapas, since it is here that the medicalized alcoholism stencil or addiction frame would seem a very good fit indeed with the established cultural patterns of drinking.

In a 1987 study of "the alternative economy of alcohol in the Chiapas highlands," Thomas Crump finds that alcohol's oldest, most typically colonial use as a labor inducer was rediscovered in the year 1900. It was around then that the Ladino (non-Indian) oligarchy had cornered the market on *aguardiente*. At the top of the pyramid sat a family headed by one Moctezuma Pedrero:

> Pedrero owed his dominant position (which eventually gave him a near monopoly of the trade) to the fact that he was not only a distiller, but had set up also as an *enganchador*, that is as a labour contractor to the coffee plantations down towards the coast, once they had to recruit Indians from the highlands. . . . The system obviously worked best — at least for the *enganchador* and the plantation owners — when a high level of indebtedness was sustained among the Indian population, and what better means of achieving this result than to ensure that such little cash as the Indians disposed of was squandered on alcohol? (1987, 239)

The reform-minded government of Lázaro Cárdenas prohibited rum sales to the Indians in the late 1930s, but members of Chamula's religious hierarchy were exempt from the ban in the crucial area of fiesta sponsorship (241). This revised Cardenist order of things simply produced a new generation of rum monopolists — and a much-cited study of indigenous alcoholism that documented, among other things, the abject failure of prohibition in southern Mexico. In Ruth Bunzel's classic account (originally published in 1940), the Tzotzil people of Chamula in Chiapas quite simply lived to drink. "Everyone drinks, from the youngest child to the oldest woman; men as a group drink more than women, but all the women drink and some ingest truly enormous quantities" (Bunzel 1991, 219). Bunzel never failed to find the entire population inebriated on festive occasions. She once came across eighty people lying in a drunken stupor in the patio of the local church at two in the afternoon (220) — we can imagine her stepping over the bodies while counting. At a party she herself gave for the neighbors, eighteen people drank five gallons of aguardiente in a 24-hour period, then set out for more. Excepting babies, there was no one in the village she had not seen intoxicated many times. She calculated that the average daily consumption of *mula blanca* ("white mule," the cheap local rum) was about thirteen ounces per person. Climatological factors loomed large in local rationales for drinking: "Let's go warm up" was the usual invitation for a drink of *aguardiente*, a quick means to a pleasant corporeal sensation of warmth that mitigated the cold, penetrating humidity of the highland hinterlands (altitude 8000 feet).

As Crump's second phase blends into the third, a small number of families vie for control of the "alternative economy" of illegal stills "owned and operated by Chamulas in the remoter parts of the municipio" (1987, 239). In the end, it was a Mayan Big Man named López Castellanos who hit upon a way to utilize Ladino-owned truck transport along the newly built Pan-American Highway to distribute rum for credit all over Chiapas. Business was good. Crump concludes that "in the face of grinding poverty and unremitting exploitation, the Chamulas found in alcohol almost their only solace. They found in rum what Hogarth's London found in gin" (246). In summation, however, Crump found nothing of positive value in the drinking culture he studied, taking it for granted that money spent on rum was "squandered." His supply-side orientation did not seek to reconstruct the intentional states of the people; he did not ask what sacred or profane meanings inebriation might convey to the individual or collective Tzotzil consciousness. Therefore he could not explain the demand for rum in the Mayan Highlands in terms other than simple addiction and manipulation. Like Bunzel before him, he saw it all from the outside, and from the outside it looked horrible indeed. His observation that rum was the indigenes' only "solace" seems reasonable on the surface, and finds support in studies carried out by like-minded Mexican researchers (e.g., Bernal, Márquez, Navarro, Selser, and Berruecos 1985). Surely the Chamulas must have been drinking to "cope" with their unlucky circumstances — alcohol's ansiolytic or stress-reducing usefulness in this respect has been much explored by addiction scientists and psychologists (Sher et al. 1999, 84). Is this the end of the discussion?

Digging deeper, we find a study of drinking in the Chiapanecan highlands carried out by a team of nine anthropologists in 1964. Using a "cognitive systems" approach considered novel at the time, the group traveled between Chamula and the colonial city of San Cristóbal de Las Casas as they sought to explain the cognitive structure of the "drinking event," defined as "an instance of drinking at a single location by a single group of participants" (Wilson 1973, 125). A drinking event could be brief or extended and have any number of rounds. "The person who initiates the drinking event provides the liquor; the order of drinking reflects the rank of the participants relative to one another; the amount consumed often reflects the importance of the event; special service to the group or the initiator is paid or marked by liquor gifts" (121). When do people consider a drinking event to be appropriate? When they are sick, when there is a corpse, when they go to a fiesta, when they are petitioning a bride, when they marry, when they build houses, when they sell their land, when they baptize a child, when they visit one of the local Big Men (ibid.).

As in many other Indian and mestizo peasant communities in Mexico, the generous giving that accompanies religious fiestas is the responsibility of a cargo holder, variously called *mayordomo* or *alférez*. In Chamula it is a high visibility community service of great responsibility; no one volunteers until he dreams that "Our Father," in the guise of a man in a black coat and ribboned hat (cargo holder dress) comes to the dreamer's house to talk with him. The dreamer, well aware of the extra work and expense that community service entails, tries to get out of it, but Our Father won't hear of it: "But no, my nephew, you must do me this favor, therefore let us drink a little bit, for you must do me this favor, you will carry me, you will look for my flower, together we will go for three days [which the dreamer knows means three years]. Therefore embrace me to see if you can lift me," says the man in the black coat and the ribboned hat (145). This recurring, culturally expected dream will not surprise readers of "The Helpful Drunkard" (Steele, Critchlow, and Liu 1985). This study found that intoxication always increased the willingness of participants to assist with tasks they found burdensome or annoying when sober. Chiapanecan cargo holders know this instinctively: once they awaken, they go out and recruit their own ritual helpers with gifts of rum.

Dying automatically turns a person into the initiator of a Chiapanecan drinking event. At funerals, any funds left by the *ánima* himself or herself are used to purchase giant casks of *aguardiente* (Wilson 1973, 126). How much alcohol has to be bought? "Custom dictates that no less than two *limiton* be bought, and four or five is considered a possible upper limit. The *limiton* is equivalent to the Spanish *garrafón* and contains eighteen liters" (129). One Tzotzil told Wilson of a funeral he had recently attended, that of an old widower. The *ánima* was poor, there was little money for the funeral, only ten people showed up; but somehow a *limiton* of rum was purchased for the wake, and the guests were able to get together enough money for another *limiton* to be consumed outside the cemetery. "Consequently, in a period of a day and a half, ten people consumed about thirty-six liters of alcohol" (134). And this was a poor man's funeral.

To translate the word *ánima* as "dead person," as Wilson and his colleagues do, is not faithful to the spirit of the Spanish term nor its connotation of a liminal presence, so by all means let us retain the original in describing a typical wake. Following the arrival of the prayer sayer, the mourners drink liquor, dress the *ánima* in new pants and shirt, lay the *ánima* in the casket, drink more liquor, cook a rooster, drink more liquor, eat the rooster, drink more liquor, listen to more prayers, and drink more liquor. Each wake replicates the all-important, status-marking, gendered drinking order: grandfather of the *ánima*, father of the *ánima*, uncle of the *ánima*, drink pourer (usually a high ranking relative), prayer sayer, male neighbors of the *ánima*, elder brother of the *ánima*, senior musician, junior musician, male friends of the *ánima*, younger brother of the *ánima*, son of the *ánima*. Liquor is then dispensed to the women in the following order: grandmother of the *ánima*, mother of the *ánima*, wife of the *ánima*, aunt of the *ánima*, wife of the senior musician, wife of the junior musician, wife of the *ánima*'s neighbor, elder sister of the *ánima*, younger sister of the *ánima*, daughter of the *ánima* (131–32).

This sort of information is interesting, indeed colorful, but what does it explain? We see people passing the jug again and again, but what is the "cognitive systems" method concealing from our view? Focusing our attention on external roles and rituals, Anthony Cohen argues, "makes gross assumptions about the relationship of action to belief, as if the thoughts or mental states of ritual participants could be read off their ritual behavior. Why *do* we make these outrageous assumptions?" (1994, 20, emphasis in original). One answer to this rhetorical question might be our undying love of good old-fashioned functionalism, as seen in Alexander Joffe's study of alcohol use in ancient western Asia:

> During the Zhou period (1027–221 B.C.) in China, elaborate rituals of ancestor worship developed around sacrificial feasts and consumption of large amounts of millet beer. The individual who contacted the ancestor, the *shi* or the "personator" of the dead, was a family member whose social status was enhanced by performance of the role. The goal of the intoxicated state was to contact ancestors and demonstrate piety, thereby validating and strengthening the existing corporate family structure and social ideology of submission to parental authority. (Joffe 1998, 308)

Here we have roles, status, norms, piety, but not one word about what there might be in the heavy-drinking *experience* that could be conducive to people talking with the dead, or thinking they are. The experience, in other words, of an altered state of consciousness reached through rupture and rapture. Let us put the horse back before the cart: confirmation or reinforcement of hierarchical social identities — in China or in Chiapas — is built around a prior chemical conduit for reaching an ecstatic spatio-temporal zone (often identified with the sacred). Chemically resetting the brain to a desired frequency is the centerpiece; the rest could be regestalted as peripheral. In their rush to show how norm-governed everything is, too many researchers have ignored or sidelined that central transgressive frequency-resetting. In so doing they have not really come to grips with the phenomenology of drunkenness. Maya expert Christine Eber did tune in, to her credit, and at least attempted to explain alcoholized conciousness on its own terms: "Ritual drinking to intoxication, but not to the point of passing out, appeared to me as one way Pedranos try to connect an interior opening-up within themselves to an exterior flowering in the universe" (2000, 243).

Culturally stylized syndromes, Stein reminds us, are based in social consensus and are socialized intergenerationally; hence, heavy drinking in any kind of ritual context "serves as a vehicle to contain or express shared psychodynamics and likewise as a vessel in which to 'empty' one's idiosyncratic contents as well" (1994, 217). By no means should we avoid consideration of roles, status, and social identity construction; that is 50 percent of human subjectivity. But the other 50 percent, usually ignored, is self-construction via self-experiencing. We must not confuse one with the other, and we should not jump to conclusions about the "self" that is being experienced. "There is no universal transhistorical self, only local selves" (Fisher and Fisher 1993, 151). This local self, furthermore, does not need to be a phenomenologically unified self, or a complex self. It is intriguing to learn that Ruth Bunzel had no use for the "disinhibition" concept, since she believed that the drunkards of Chamula had remained at an extraordinarily low level of personality development — never reaching inhibition in the first place! The nurturing mother/thirsty infant dyad is powerful and pervasive enough to subsume all other cultural paradigms, she says, including marriage. Even two men drinking alone in a cantina must take turns playing nurturing mother to each other, pouring each other's drinks (238). In a word, booze as breast. The lucky Tzotzils experienced no headaches or dizziness, no vomiting, no visible hangovers or bouts of depression, no feelings of guilt or shame (225). Bunzel was suprised to confirm, again and again, that in a state of complete intoxication the men and women of Chamula were able to engage in most of the routines of everyday life "with full control of their faculties," and even to carry out "complicated commercial transactions of which they haven't the least idea later" (1991, 223). Christine Eber updates alcoholized self-construction in Chiapas:

> Traditional Pedranos have not developed the view that their selves are separate from unconscious processes nor that the need to drink daily is a distinct behavioral system. Since "alcoholism" and the opposition of mind to matter do not exist for Pedranos, they do not give "alcoholism" a life of its own and therefore do not see it as a force outside of their "selves" which they must resist. (2000, 148)

If either Bunzel or Eber is correct, we are compelled to ask which came first — the minimal self or the rum dependency? In his cross-cultural study of heavy drinking, Boris Segal conjectured that exposure to distilled liquors had a major effect on the phases of human growth and individuation (1986, 149). Should we view the self-less Indians of Chiapas as a case of arrested development caused by a sugarcane distillate?

Or would it be more accurate to see alcohol as a kind of mortar, useful for building a protective biocultural wall around what the people most wish to preserve from outside contamination? That such a wall exists seems likely. In the works of Rosario Castellanos, especially *Balún Canán* (1957) and *Oficio de tinieblas* (1962), well-meaning non-Indians from Mexico City are constantly confounded by Tzotziles who trust them no more than they do the local Ladino reactionaries. The daughter of a wealthy landowner, Castellanos grew up in Chiapas and was later employed there by the Instituto Nacional Indigenista. In her enthnographic fiction, Castellanos scrupulously avoids individualizing her indigenous characters; in her literary criticism, she assails writers who do not. Bunzel provides indirect evidence of the cultural wall's existence: utterly preoccupied with drinking, she tells us, the Indians of Chamula are nearly bereft of cultural creativity; they have no songs and never narrate myths or folktales (1991/1940, 219). They did not sing their songs or tell their tales to her, at any rate; other ethnographers have been more successful in this regard. A recent example is Gary Gossen's *Telling Maya Tales* (1999), a work that translates hundreds of Tzotzil folktales and songs collected in and around Chamula from a small group of informants — two of whom subsequently died from cirrhosis of the liver (32). Gossen does not explore the alcohol issue, but let us note that heavy drinking did not impede his informants' ability to remember and narrate the tales of the tribe. Anthropologist Ricardo Pozas criticized those who misinterpreted the heavy-drinking Highland Maya and, in particular, the alcoholized lifestyle of Juan Pérez Jolote, the cargo holder he had written about in a much-cited biography (Pozas 1952). Pozas argued that the people of Chamula did not drink "to forget" in the manner of tequila-swigging mestizos, but rather "accustomed themselves to drinking in the service of a social function, as a result of a perfect adjustment to the group, and in conformity with the role that alcohol plays in social relations" (as cited by Rodríguez Chicharro 1988, 128). Since we are back in functionalist mode, we can conjecture that the group-enforced intoxication of ritual office holders in Mexican indigenous areas might be a traditional way of keeping local prestige from mutating into community-exploiting, Ladino-style self-aggrandizement.

We will never know what would have happened if, in a world without greedy Ladinos, the people of Chamula had continued to drink their beloved *chicha* (fermented corn juice of lower alcoholic content). Obviously they were and are indebted, quite literally, to their neocolonialist labor exploiters and drink providers. But that emphatically does not mean that they depend on them for the *meaning* of that privileged drunken state of consciousness. Exteriority of supply does not govern interiority of experiencing. Even the "out of control" female drinkers Eber met were in control of the diagnosis (i.e., they identified their affliction with the soul-scorching coldness of the devil). Even Juan Pérez Jolote — chided by his fellow Tzotziles for being *aladinado* (having a "Ladino-ized" identity) — saves his Indian soul through a radical mode of desubjectification: he drinks himself to death. Although he had fought in the Mexican Revolution under several different caudillos, in the end Jolote undoes himself (his specifically "Mexican" self) in accordance with his sense of local desires and values. Whatever the degree or shape of the preferred self that emerged inside his drunkenness, it was clearly *intended* to ward off the prior residues or temptations of mestizoization.

A strong case could be made for seeing alcoholized states of mind and the time-maps they perpetuate as *everyday forms of state resistance*. Peasantry expert Tom Brass is weary of such talk, however, with its implied "unabashed celebration of a rural 'voice-from-below' engaged in quotidian/local/mostly individual resistance based on ethnic/gender/ecological peasant essentialisms" (Brass 2002, 2). He laments the "conceptual abandonment" of older paradigms — mass mobilization, revolution, systemic transcendence — and the neoliberal embrace of "a new and empowering form of identity/agency that occurs within capitalism" (ibid.). In a similar vein, Scott Cook asserts that for far too long "anthropological work in Mexican studies has been held hostage by the image of the indigenous other. Much anthropological discourse still debates the degree of market involvement of persisting Indian village utopias, while refusing to cope with the fact that Mexico is overwhelmingly mestizo and capitalist" (1993, 336). Cook calls for the de-ethnicization of anthropological paradigms, the better to bring them into line with what is now happening in the real world, "within the Mexican branch of the North American capitalization of labor." Note, first of all, that my exploration of alcohol use in context liberates me from any charge of peasant or ethnic essentialism. I maintain, for example, that if Juan Pérez Jolote's life had taken a different course, alcohol would have been *equally useful to him* in the construction of a fully "Mexican" identity, with Tzotzil cultural elements muted, eliminated, or reconfigured. His fellow Chamulas might have seen this as disgusting betrayal, but we would not be obliged to second them, thanks precisely to those new and empowering forms of identity and agency that occur within the Mexican branch of North American capitalism (to hijack the phrases of Brass and Cook). In this world, as it happens, we find many Indians at work constructing mestizo identities, as well as white urban Mexicans identifying with Cuauhtémoc, or migrating to Chiapas to become *subcomandantes*. We may lament the postmodern nature of these forms of agency, but they exist anyway. While waiting for systemic transcendence to break out, let us at least identify the identity network that has best allied itself with sacred power — the ancestral tribal community, the Church, the post-Revolutionary state, or postmodern would-be Che Guevaras.

Now come the teetotaling Zapatistas and their progressively more stringent, neo-Cardenist, anti-alcohol views — disseminated by now into every municipio in Highland Chiapas. Long-suffering women have been energized by *zapatismo* as never before, Eber observes: "Whereas in the past Pedranas did not speak out about their problems, today they are speaking out about alcohol. They state clearly that Ladinos and rum sellers have used and still use rum as a devastatingly effective tool to dominate them and their husbands" (2000, 246). I know not what course *zapatismo* may take, but I would conjecture that self-structures and time maps forged to keep sacred power close and ethnocidal forces at bay will be highly resistant to the encroachment of alien semiotics.

Meanwhile, back in the United States, a mass-circulation magazine unblushingly calls itself *Self*. Exaggerated and increasingly invasive ideas of what a true American self should be (and should *buy*) underwrite the unimaginative American view of alcohol as "escapist," as in Roy Baumeister's *Escaping the Self* (1991). But in view of Eber's study and many other recent Mayan ethnographies, it is hardly subversive to postulate that, despite its apparent lack of complexity, the alcoholized bodily self of Chiapas was and is very meaningful indeed. It was and is a creator of meanings, of patterns, and of possibilities undreamt of in Baumeister's philosophy. Fisher and Fisher are more reliable guides to such phenomena: "The particular conditions of a culture may forbid the perception of a self that even roughly parallels the self-structure Western culture takes for granted. . . . There is great latitude as to the kind of self-structure a culture can require its participants to fashion. A culture can demand a self of practically zero magnitude or one, at the other extreme, of the overblown dimensions common in the 20th-century West" (1993, 152). A "self" is not universal or transhistorical but local; it need not be complex; it need not be unified nor in a state of harmony with other self-states or quasi selves. For Christopher Bollas, "the true self is not an integrated phenomenon but only dynamic sets of idiomatic dispositions that come into being through problematic encounters with the object world" (1992, 30).

Apropos of the object world, however, we cannot fail to ask how social processes at the macro level might influence or enter into intimate modes of self-experiencing. In the view of James W. Fernández, colonial forms of self-awareness began in a highly unpleasant feeling of "peripheralization in respect to the economic and political structures of emerging Europe" (1995, 35). It is abundantly clear that such global galvanizers of local self-awareness have been mediated by the drug food commerce that played (and still plays) such a crucial role in colonial or neocolonial capitalist enterprises. We can also see, by the same token, how even the "simplest" local self-structures might encode a great deal of history. Perhaps the same script has been played out in many different areas: first, a power beverage like rum lubricates the encounter of the deterritorialized wealth of capital and a peripheralized laboring class. Then the newly abundant psychoactive substance becomes essential to native self-experiencing in funereal and festive contexts. Before long the indigenes become dependent on their own cultural appropriation. And in the end, rum-powered religious rituals reinforce modes of consciousness that are simultaneously at odds with and *enabled* by neocolonial capitalism.

Chapter 3
After Fifteen or Twenty Drinks

If you currently have a job in a late capitalist society and wish to keep it, you need to sharply distinguish your alcohol-off work hours from your alcohol-on leisure moments. Among the Tarahumara Indians of Chihuahua, however, drinking and working are not at all antagonistic. *Tesgüino*, their ancestral beer beverage made from fermented creamed corn, is always consumed collectively and in great quantities in rituals known as *tesgüinadas*, the vast majority of these being labor-intensive *tesgüinadas de trabajo* (Kennedy 1991/1963; Zúñiga 1986). Whenever there are major chores to be done — plowing, planting, harvesting, fence-building, fertilizing — a man prepares at least fifty gallons of tesgüino and invites people from all over his area to come, drink, work, and drink some more. "A man can choose to do the work alone or make tesgüino; the latter method is preferred because it saves time and because the euphoria of group participation is lacking in the relative solitude of daily life. Camaraderie is considerably reinforced by the effects of alcohol" observes John Kennedy (1991, 258).

Tesgüinadas have been around for centuries and were a constant source of frustration for missionaries. In 1681 a Jesuit priest riding along on his horse encountered a group of dead-drunk Tarahumaras and with the righteous ire of Christ targeting moneylenders he charged at a furious gallop, scattered the group, and smashed fourteen pots of freshly fermented *tesgüino*. For generations of less biased travelers, the drinking rituals have been a source of fascination. In 1902 Carl Lumholtz concluded that *tesgüino* was actually responsible for the perpetuation of the Tarahumara race, since "only when they are drunk do the shy Tarahumaras work up the nerve to make use of their marital rights" (cited by Kennedy 1991, 254). Extramarital escapades were also facilitated by corn beer intoxication under the dark skies of Chihuahua; in any kind of sexual encounter, sinful or not, it was the woman who took the initiative. Kennedy affirms that three hundred years of exposure to Christianity have not made a dent in the pride Tarahumaras take in their extreme states of inebriation (268). Whosoever organizes a *tesgüinada* without enough corn beer for everyone to reach the desired state will lose status in the community; not to drink as much as possible, conversely, is a breach of etiquette for women and men alike. Not to be invited to a *tesgüinada* in the first place is a sure sign of ostracism and an effective means of local social control. Kennedy notes that the most impressive thing about a work-related tesgüinada is the deafening noise of shouting, singing, and musical instruments "played by drunkards" — guitars, violins, harmonicas, acordeons — all in sharp contrast to "the usual tranquil silence of the rancho, interrupted only by the harsh barking of a dog" (267). Note the complete absence of peyote-munching mysticism that Antonin Artaud identified with the word "Tarahumara" (1992/1936).

During his time in the mountain communities of Chihuahua, Rogelio Zúñiga found nothing appealing in the smell or flavor of *tesgüino* — "it does not seem to justify the ten days of exhausting work that its preparation typically demands" (1986, 3). The most interesting thing in Kennedy's study is his calculation of the *tesgüinada* time-consumption factor: on the average, people attend between forty and sixty *tesgüinadas* per year, each lasting between fifteen and twenty hours, although thirty-six-hour bacchanals are not uncommon. Thus, the average Tarahumara devotes around 750 hours per year to drinking. But then, cautions Kennedy, you have to take into account the time spent in physically recovering from the rituals — a minimum of one day — as well as the considerable number of hours spent walking to and from them. And that's not even counting the considerable time and energy that the women spend in making the corn beer in the first place. A Tarahumara domestic unit organizing a *tesgüinada* will typically use about a hundred kilograms of its yearly corn harvest — enough to feed the family for a month. When all is said and done, Kennedy's conservative estimate of Tarahumara time-warping is "at least 100 days per year in activities directly connected with tesgüino and much of that time under its influence" (1991, 276).

One is tempted to keep on calculating. How many days are "lost" in inebriation per decade, or per century? The quantities become truly cosmic, more than enough to boggle our clock-ruled minds. Without a doubt, Tarahumaran time maps were very far away from those of the men who financed the railroads, answered telegrams, and lifted their glasses to don Porfirio. They are farther away still from the Mexican power elites of the twenty-first century.

In the community or individual *borrachera*, we confront a kind of time that cannot be measured with a clever device. How could we begin to understand the centuries that certain groups have spent inside Dionysian time coordinates? Do outside investigators even have the right conceptual tools to meet the challenge? Johannes Fabian made much of anthropology's subservience to colonialist-imperialist "chronopolitics," its shameful accomodation of "the schemes of a one-way history: progress, development, modernity, and their negative mirror images: stagnation, underdevelopment, tradition" (1983, 144). Unafraid to overstate his case, Fabian alleged that "thousands of aspiring and established practitioners of anthropology" had unwittingly helped to rationalize capitalist relations of domination through the repetitive exercise of "allochronic distancing" (151), by which he meant the theories, taxonomies, and literary conventions that enter into the writing-up phase of ethnography and inevitably betray the original fieldwork experience of close, personal, shared time. Structuralism made a positive scientific virtue out of this betrayal, Fabian asserted, by positing "a native society that would hold still like a *tableau vivant*" (67).

Never would I want to forget or disavow the time-collapsing drinking events I have enjoyed on both sides of the border, to the extent that I can remember them. Nor would I wish my (br)others' empirical presence to turn into their theoretical absence, paraphrasing Fabian (xi), who unfortunately offers little direction for avoiding such betrayals. Richard Shweder is more helpful, or at least more optimistic. He defines cultural psychology as the art of "thinking through others," which implies "the sense of getting the other straight, of providing a systematic account of the internal logic of the intentional world constructed by the other" (1991, 109). The intentional world constructed by a drunken other presents special difficulties, bizarre temporal coordinates not investigated by Shweder or his venerable colleagues. I believe it would be faithful to the spirit of his cultural psychology to postulate that, if you are attempting to reconstruct the intentional worlds of an alcoholized population, then "thinking through others" would require *drinking* with them a good deal of the time. And indeed, as we trek through the daunting farrago of alcohol studies, we find numerous examples of cultural psychologists *avant la lettre* who did not shy away from "drinking through others." In the 1960s Brian Stross carried out his fieldwork in a town in the state of Guadalajara that had thirty-four cantinas, all on the same block (Stross 1991/ 1967). Folk Catholicism scholar John Ingham writes: "The first year I found myself doing a good deal of serious drinking with the men of the village. Drinking was a social fact, and my personal inclination to abstain was usually deemed irrelevant. Nonetheless, the price paid in hangovers was repaid in friendships and better understanding of the male role" (1986, viii). Drinking played an important role in Matthew Gutmann's research in a working-class neighborhood of Mexico City (1996). Although by no means a boozer, Gutmann knew he had to remain on good terms with his *cuates* (drinking buddies), since they were his prime informants:

> We drank far more that day than we normally did. After we fin-
> ished off the first pint of *anís*, someone went to the nearby liquor
> store for another, and then another, until we had consumed a half
> dozen of these. Finally we switched to liter bottles, ultimately pol-
> ishing off two or three of the big containers. . . . During the rest of
> my fieldwork in Santo Domingo, several of my friends, and even a
> few men I hardly knew, would ask me, "Hey, Mateo, want some
> *anís*?" It became a running gag. (Gutmann 1996, 180–81)

These and many other scholars did not shy away from "the pleasures of the
male drinking group," to paraphrase Robin Room. Hence my appreciation
of anthropologist Christine Eber (2000), who did not eschew the pleasures
of the female drinking group. Eber spent part of the Chiapanecan "Crazy
February" in Tenejapa, not far from her main research location of Chenalhó in Highland Chiapas, north of Chamula. It is a breath of fresh air to
find passages like the following:

> I got drunker and drunker. I didn't have a flask to pour my pox
> into, so I just drank it down, afraid that I would offend someone if
> I didn't. I didn't like the burning feel of rum going down my throat.
> When it reached my stomach it made a nauseating mix with the
> churning pig entrails. (44)

Eber went on to dance and vomit the night away. I salute her, and all ethnographers who seek to think and drink through others in ways that do
not degrade local experiences and seek to reconstruct local states of consciousness in a verisimilar way. Both Gutmann and Eber got close to the
people they needed to get close to and carefully distanced themselves from
prefabricated academic or AA ideologies. They made progress in understanding mestizo proletarian or Tzotzil intoxication by using what
Anthony Cohen calls "the most potent investigative and interpretive weapons in the anthropologist"s armoury: his or her own experience and consciousness" (1994, 4).

All over Mexico, indigenous and peasant communities undertake
sacred mental journeys and dialogue with their dead with the aid of ine-
briants, euphoriants, and hallucinogens. If only we could walk a mile in
their *huaraches*, that is, reconstruct local intentional worlds. Anthony
Cohen formulates a rhetorical question: "How can marginal Indians, who
are shunned by the rest of society, think of themselves as having magical
power? If they do have it, why are they propping up the entire status hierarchy of modern Mexico?" (1994, 39). Cohen studies the Huichol *hikurita-
mete*, maize-farming pilgrims who transform themselves into gods with
peyote. This particular cultic complex has been studied by other brilliant
outsiders like Weston LaBarre (1989/1938) and Barbara Myerhoff (1974).
Cohen hypothesizes that when the Huichol flock once a year to Wirikuta,

their psychogeographical homeland, "it is not to search for their pasts or to do a kind of historical tourism, but to discover their essential selves, their selves uncorrupted by the taints placed on them by the contemporary Mexican nation-state" (1994, 39). This sounds somewhat romantic or essentialist, but I laud Cohen's attempt to "think through" the Huichol and their mescaline-munching shamans.

At the same time, I understand how tempting it would be to make light of foreigners who use the same substances as indigenes in order to discover "how they think." Davíd Carrasco wryly brings up the case of anthropologist Napoleon Chagnon, who spent seven years with the Yanomamo Indians of Brazil but never joined in their collective drug rituals. Provoked by a missionary one day, Chagnon broke down, had the shaman blow the magic powder up his nose, and went on to have his own ecstatic encounter with the *hekura* gods — one that was nevertheless filtered through all his European cultural baggage and associations (Carrasco 2000, 213). The shocking part of this story, for me, is not Chagnon's fanciful belief that he had finally penetrated the savage mind, but that he had managed to resist the shaman for seven years! Another Frenchman, Antonin Artaud, single-mindedly pursued a Tarahumara shaman to "turn him on" with peyote; local cooperation with the celebrated surrealist was ordered by the Cárdenas government as a favor to the French ambassador (Schneider 1992, 76–77). A similar desire to "break on through to the other side" has led numerous foreigners to Oaxaca to ingest Mazatec mushrooms; perhaps the most lucid was Gordon Wasson (1974). Schultes and Hofmann tabulated Mexico's psychotropic wealth in *Plants of the Gods*:

> Without any question the Peyote cactus is the most important sacred hallucinogen, although other cactus species are still used in northern Mexico as minor hallucinogens for special magico-religious purposes. Of almost equal religous importance in early Mexico and still surviving in religious rituals are mushrooms, known to the Aztecs as Teonanacatl. At least twenty-four species of these fungi are employed at the present time in southern Mexico. Ololiuqui, the seeds of Morning Glories, represents another hallucinogen of great importance in Aztec religion and is still employed in southern Mexico. There are many hallucinogens of secondary importance: Toloache and other species of the *Datura* group; the Mescal Bean or Frijolillo in the north; Pipiltzintzintli of the Aztecs; the mint now known as Hierba de la Pastora; Genista among the Yaqui Indians; Piule, sinicuichi, Zacatechichi, the puffballs known by the Mixtecs as Gi-i-wa; and others. (Schultes and Hofmann 1992/1979, 27)

Question: Could alcohol be "as good as" peyote, puffballs, and other Mexican plants for the invention or maintenance of visionary traditions? Support for this possibility can actually be found in an unlikely source:

American research studies of *alcohol myopia*. Psychologist M. A. Sayette calls the alcohol myopia paradigm "the most influential cognitive theory of alcohol's effects on social behavior to appear in recent years" (1999, 255). Alcohol myopia is defined as "a state of shortsightedness in which superficially understood, immediate aspects of experience have a disproportionate influence on behavior and emotion, a state in which we can see the tree, albeit more dimly, but miss the forest altogether" (Steele and Josephs 1990, 923). "By impairing cognitive processing capacity, alcohol consumption is purported to interfere with the ability to consider more remote inhibiting cues, leading one to attend only to those cues that are most salient" (Sayette 1999, 256). With enough liquor inside of us, for instance, the perceived benefits of promiscuous sex win out over worries about condoms and disease. Intoxicated people are more closely focused on "the immediate and the tangible" and tend to be oblivious to "the nuances and implications of events" (Lang, Patrick, and Stritzke 1999, 360).

If these researchers are correct, "alcohol myopia" could easily bring about the *focusing* required for trance induction — one of many substances or procedures with this capability, another means to the same end. Julian Jaynes famously hypothesized that human consciousness rests upon the vestigial substrate of an ancient, terribly authoritarian type of cerebral organization that he called "the bicameral mind" (1990/1976). It was his way of accounting for the four stages of a psychocultural paradigm still operative in phenomena of diminished mentation all over the world: (1) a strong and collective "cognitive imperative" (i.e., a cohesive group's cultural expectancies and general will-to-believe); (2) formally ritualized induction procedures "whose function is the narrowing of consciousness by focusing attention on a small range of preoccupations"; (3) the trance state itself, an apparatus for tuning in to the all-important (4) "archaic authorization" — successful and truthful communication with some sort of supernatural or charismatic presence (Jaynes 1990, 324). From a psychocultural point of view, it is a question of trading one kind of "higher" consciousness for another.

In global ethnographic perspective, the affect-charged *experience* of authorization underwrites all manner of sacred concepts. "The unifying entities of ecstatic states can be anything: dream time ancestors of which each person is an incarnation, clan totems, various deities, a chosen people, Nirvana, individual gurus, political movements, Nature, or social movements" (Hayden 1987, 85). The new scholarly field that some call "neurotheology" is based on the premise that neurons firing in brain circuits precede and indeed *enable* myths and beliefs. Unless we are determined to fetishize indigenous belief systems, we have to recognize that even local insiders, when in trance, reinvent and recreate and occasionally "distort" mythological traditions. Recall the four hundred rabbit numens of pre-Hispanic folklore. They represented a *collective* expectation that heavy drinking leads to a near infinite variety of idiosyncratic outcomes, each as "true" as any other. In this sense, therefore, the natives and the visiting French surrealists are on the very same psychological footing.

Somewhere in the mountains of Chihuahua, Antonin Artaud came across a young, friendly indigenous couple who knew many of peyote's secrets: "From [the husband] I received marvelous explanations and very precise clarifications regarding the way in which peyote, in its trajectory through the nervous system, resuscitates the memory of sovereign truths, through which human consciousness, according to him, recovers the perception of the Infinite, instead of losing it" (Artaud 1992/1937, 79, my translation). During his long periods of confinement in French lunatic assylums, Artaud returned many times to those magical moments in the Sierra Madre (in his mind), writing that "Peyote returns the self to its true origins. Having emerged from such a visionary state, one can never again confuse falsehood with truth" (1992/1944, 323). In more recent times, University of Paris professor Dominique Dufétel has traveled among the Otomí and used their ancestral drink *pulque* to trigger surrealistic but culturally informed visions in her own bodymind:

> Inebriation with pulque — that small death of initiation — is sweet and sacred, and always accompanied by some ritual. . . . At the end of my intoxicated night I have dreamed a dream of whiteness, in this moment of inner silence I have seen the Plumed Serpent. Upon waking, I discover your sleeping presence. Dark moon, lace of obscurities, a crescent of fragile silk between my thorns, you awaken and taste my intoxicating sap, black eye of sweet lips, you will be your executioner and I, my victim. (Dufétel 2000, 86)

Reading this, who could possibly doubt that this Frenchwoman "became her own rabbit?" (as the Otomí would say). Anthropologist of consciousness Andrew Strathern reminds us that "Embodiment is what makes the knowledge experientially real" (1995, 123). The supernatural is always experienced through the body; a preferred version of the self is always experienced through the body; a sufficiently alcoholized body can be an organ of legitimacy.

It would be silly to ignore that genuine hallucinogens dislocate human brains more fundamentally than alcohol. But in view of Dufétel's night of the drunken moon, not to mention a vast oral tradition of analogous indigenous experiences, it would be just as silly to deny that alcohol has psychotropic properties or uses, and simply perverse to say that alcohol cannot lead to what Jaynes called "archaic authorization." Chemically induced credibility is not the only kind, but it is powerful and often addictive because it saturates perception with affect-laden schemata and blocks interference from "higher" brain centers — possibly because the time frames they depend upon have been blocked at a molecular level of the brain by the toxin (Anderson and Mandell 1996, 88). It goes without saying that Artaud did not really "think like a Tarahumara" nor did Mme. Dufétel drink like an Otomí, but unquestionably they experienced the same time-warping saturation of perception that indigenous groups found desirable, and the same massive enhancement in the meaningfulness of the surrounding environment and objects, images, and people therein. In other words, both natives and foreigners were rewarded with a huge net increase in "semioticity" (Lotman 1990; Zamora 1998).

Under the influence of one inebriant or another, the low and the powerless were the original true believers. Alcohol's role as truth serum is a commonplace in Mexican folklore, and in many areas *la verdad del borracho* ("the truth of the drunkard") was a socially sanctioned protest vehicle. When Nahua nobles engaged in sacrally legitimated drunkenness in pre-Hispanic times, they had no doubt about the reality of their experiences or prerogatives. And when their demise was prophesied by a god on a bender, there was no room for argument. With apologies to aging hippies or enthusiasts of Carlos Castaneda, we find no mass peyote use in colonial and postcolonial Mexico, just *pulque* drinking before and after Mass, at levels verging on the miraculous. When Indians are asked to explain their rituals, Bonfil says, "the participants cannot verbally formulate their reasons for doing things" (1996, 133). This suggests that (1) they are put off by the anthropologist making the request, or (2) the things they are doing in the rituals derive from a different semiotic, a different time frame, a different psychic space of self-experiencing, and perhaps a radically different way of representing history. Sacred intoxicated time and the selves instantiated therein do not somehow lie outside of social or historical time — just the opposite, argues Strathern: "We have seen a consistent pattern in societies with complex histories for aspects of these histories to be encoded in possession-trance behavior. It is as though the state-dependent theory of learning and memory had there been written large on the canvas of social history" (1995, 129). The ecstatic Huichol communion with the deer god, for example, is state dependent in that it takes place inside cruel capitalist Mexico, and state dependent in being impossible to reconstruct without peyote. Remembered only vaguely back in the *colonias* of San Luis Potosí, "it is a moment clearly set apart in social time which is not assimilable to ordinary experience, and may not be recapturable in memory other than by repeating the act of pilgrimage" (Cohen 1994, 40).

Becoming-rabbit, becoming-deer: both varieties of psychic metamorphosis are highly resistant to representation by centralizing semiotics, therefore relevant to our quest to gauge the extent of post-Conquest stress disorders in New Spain. As seen earlier, *borracheras* were promoted by get-rich-quick colonial elites for their own purposes and pursued by the indigenes for *their* own purposes. Among the latter, hypothetically but perhaps indemonstrably, we would find the containment of traumatic memories and the instantiation of a desired quasi-dissociative mental balm, or perhaps a pleasing pseudo-dissociative stupor, a trance that may also have been a healing space-time, a way of "working through" underlying traumatic gestalts that merits more attention from PTSD therapists. Unfortunately, the more one proves that alcohol can be a trance-inducing substance, the less we are able to decide if the massive increase of drinking in New Spain was post-traumatic or not. How can we accurately gauge the extent of post-Conquest stress disorders when their most direct signs, dissociation or unusually high susceptibility to dissociation, are exactly what the massive alcoholization of a population would mask? We are actually talking about two different categories of psychocultural sequelae of the Spanish invasion, our view of the one blocked by the documented immensity of the other.

The priests and bishops of New Spain understood the numinous within a stationary, molar realm of representations; the marginalized peoples they sought to control preferred a much more direct contact inside the molecular realm of alcoholic becomings — and the Church was obliged to deal with it, century after century. The very notion that alcohol could be used to induce a therapeutic trance state beggars our paradigms. "Unlike American Indians," notes Howard Stein, "for whom alcohol use is in large part a successor to the incorporation of the supernatural in vision quests and shamanistic trance, in American culture any loss of control and dissociation *must* be accompanied by and rationalized by denial" (1994, 213). But the history of the Chiapanecan rum economy suggests that there was something in colonial and neocolonial exploitation that intensified local desires to overturn consciousness itself. Let us not be in denial, therefore, but open to the possibility that the indigenes either treated or prevented the worst psychological effects of death and conquest through voluntary, quasi-dissociative states of trance or possession trance. Such a line of thought would tend to decenter the Eurocentric concept of the self that currently underwrites treatment modes for trauma survivors. The therapeutic mandate to consciously reintegrate all dissociated memories, for example, rests on a belief that the healthy self is a unified, complex, autobiographical self. An unassimilated id shall give way to an ego that is, among other things, punctual: "Since dissociation involves the loss of a continuous sense of time, schedules, regular appointments, and routines are essential" (van der Kolk, van der Hart, and Marmar 1996, 321). Despite her good intentions, a PTSD expert can be as caught up in Fabian's "denial of coevalness" as the next researcher, as impatient with other modes of temporal processing, as eager to recapture resistant memory modes and bring all the associative pathways under centralized semiotic control. We ought to consider alternative ways of "working through" trauma that are more sensitive to local cultures and local self-clusters, perhaps better able to engage the temporal disruptions wrought by the trauma itself. In existential psychology, "Distortions of the feeling of time necessarily result in distortions of the meaning of life" (Ellenberger 1958,

106). We should replace "distortions" with "changes" but retain the basic idea in what follows.

In hundreds of Mexican towns and villages, and in the megacity itself, a fiesta is still an authorized opportunity to distort time, that is, to get as intoxicated as possible. People never have to wait long — "communities celebrate 5,083 civil and religious occasions throughout the year in which no more than nine days go by without a fiesta somewhere in Mexico" (Beezley, Martin, and French 1994, xiv). That's not including life cycle fiestas — weddings, baptisms, funerals, first communions, *quinceañeras* — all the occasions for binge drinking cited by the *curandera* doña Marina. All over Mexico, then, we find that temporal experience is indeed cyclical — not in the manner of a cosmic calendar stone, but in the regular nonlinear alteration of sober and drunken interactional states. Which came first, the sobriety-intoxication cycle or the work/fiesta dialectic? Which maintains which? What are the competing chronopolitical forces in motion? Stein suggests a simple rule of thumb for investigating cultural differences in the use of alcohol: first determine the state *from* which escape is sought, then analyze the state *to* which escape is sought (1994, 212). As is clear from the immense body of ethnographic writing about Mexican drinking, the "from" and the "to" escape modes may differ not just at a national level but from one ethnic group to the next, one village to the next, one cantina to the next.

Let us exemplify this via Michael Kearney's classic study of the binge-drinking *mestizos* (formerly Zapotecs) of Ixtepeji, Oaxaca, based on research carried out in the mid-1960s (Kearney 1991/1970). The condition from which escape was sought: a poor, sad, boring village where people mistrusted or feared each other and homophobia abounded. The state escaped to: a glorious artificial world of fireworks, band music, loud voices, abundant food, and close encounters with other men while listening to speeches praising their brotherhood, virtue, and honor (340–41). The chemical catalyst for this magical transformation of lack into excess was the local mezcal, consumed with a mock grimace in ritual rounds whose pace was set by the group rather than the individual. The local ritual of serving and drinking did not resemble Tzotzil-style maternal suckling in the least but something far more "macho." Although the final result was usually collective stupor, Kearney stressed that numbing was not the goal but just the opposite: sensory and sensuous *intensification*. The desired state of quasi-Dionysian frenzy was meant to maximize every moment, if one can imagine Dionysos dancing to the fast-paced, tuba-dominated music of village bands. The men of Ixtepeji had found a way to exploit the only source of inalienable wealth they possessed — emotion — within a time frame totally oriented to the present moment. Deriving neither joy nor hope from the idea of the future, Kearney's people much preferred the positive electric charge derived from collective drunkenness, so radically different from the endless monotony of their daily lives. They were doing exactly what was possible within the constraints of their unlucky habitus, and most accepted the deleterious effects of heavy alcohol use with stoicism and good humor.

To his credit, Kearney did not turn a blind eye to the "dramatic and extreme personality transformations" that sometimes appeared as the *Ixtepejanos* grew older (1991, 349). He also found that it was extraordinarily difficult for a man to escape the village's collective escape mechanism. "It's as if an alcoholic tried to abstain while living with 500 other alcoholics" (Ibid.). So when the state to be escaped finally became gamma alcoholism, with its "vile and violent" impulses, a man of Ixtepeji had but one escape route: a *sabatista* identity, i.e., conversion to Seventh Day Adventism. Kearney surmised that the growing size of this sect in Oaxaca could be traced directly to the negative side effects of the heavily alcoholized local variety of Catholicism. For many men who attempted to become abstemious Protestants, however, it was only a matter of time before their old friends found a way to convince them to relax, relent, and have a drink. Ixtepeji peer pressure had brought plenty of would-be teetotalers back into the fold of the traditional Catholic escape vehicle, whose chief fuels were alcohol, testosterone, fireworks, fiery words, and — underwriting it all — the conviction that an intense life is preferable to a long one.

In sensing that time maximization was of the essence, Kearney anticipated the basic thrust of Alfred Gell's *Anthropology of Time* (1992). Unlike Fabian, who only complained about allochronic distancing, Gell actually devised a way to model the internal time maps of different cultures, subcultures, and individuals. For Gell, the crucial theoretical concepts to be grasped lay in what he called "the economics of temporal opportunity costs" (213).

> Our evaluations of both objects and events in the actual world depend crucially on our notion of what constitute the alternatives to these objects and events, in the penumbra of non-actual worlds surrounding this one. The alternativeness relation where activities are concerned is their temporal opportunity cost: activities which have high opportunity costs are ones which have highly advantageous, highly feasible alternatives in terms of the map *of the field of possible worlds* imposed by a given culturally standardized construction of reality. (217)

What Fabian called the problematic simultaneity of the other's time with that of ethnographic writing becomes, with Gell, the problematic coexistence of very different notions of opportunity costs, of "navigation in time" strategies, of "temporal maps" guiding not only the use of resources but the very perception of resources to begin with. What Stein calls "the state to be escaped from" would translate, in Gell's vocabulary, to "origin-worlds," while the more desirable state of consciousness would be called the "goal-world." Normally the idea is to get from one to the other in the most economical way, which in Gell's scheme means the one with the least opportunity costs. As a rule, "we hope to realize these aims in such a way that the attainment of any one aim does not rule out the attainment of too many of the other ones" (260). Gell observes that we all live out our lives in the shadow of good or bad choices made years before; sooner or later the chickens come home to roost and "the dark web of causality stands revealed" (219). For example, the Texas native George W. Bush decided at age forty that the time he spent drinking was literally robbing him of good opportunities for career advancement. So he stopped, and the rest is presidential history. This shows how crucial one's habitus is to one's perceived resources and time-mapping strategies; the "alternative world" of a run for the White House is simply not applicable to most members of a society.

If we reconsider the village of Ixtepeji as it was in the 1960s and inquire about "possible worlds" available there, it is clear that for most men collective *borracheras* could not possibly have involved high opportunity costs, and indeed made perfect sense to them in a world of objectively limited opportunities. Going "on-the-wagon" in Ixtepeji would not have facilitated a campaign for the presidency; it would only have alienated important lifelong friends. Gell offers a formula that will be useful to us in the future: "RESOURCE + TIME = PRODUCTION OF AN EVENT TO BE CONSUMED" (213). For better or for worse, a radically dissimilar countertemporal goal-world was in very close proximity to the drab Ixtepeji origin-world, and getting there seemed to entail very small resource costs. Collective drunkenness was very much a realistic strategy in other words; the drinkers really reached a subjective goal-world that was deeply important and meaningful for them. The transition was and still is rapid, to say the least, but entirely understandable in terms of indigenous knowledge and praxis. We can easily see how a present-oriented time-mapping would leap at the chance to go to an orgiastic, heavy-drinking fiesta in which all manner of human bonds and desired self-states are experientially validated. Only after hundreds of such fiestas over a twenty-five or thirty year period could the accrued costs make themselves apparent in the form of serious health problems. Gell is no cultural relativist: "It is merely patronizing to leave exotic ethnographic models of the world uncriticized, as if their possessors were children who could be left to play forever in an enchanted garden of their own devising" (324). This brings us right back to the classic contrast between the biomedical and the anthropological perspectives — the former very attuned to the health costs of drinking, the latter to the benefits: communitas, peer respect, redistribution of wealth, male-bonding, procreation, stress-relief, ecstasy. And note: We are the ones living in an "enchanted garden" if we think it will be easy to persuade certain groups to adopt different time-mapping strategies. It is quite easy, by contrast, to see how scandalous a guiltlessly hedonistic or death-welcoming culture might be for a culture as medicalized and death-fearing as our own, character-ized by the compulsive search for longevity and *more time*.

In Latin American drinking cultures, the taste for dizzying transitions between boring origin-worlds and counterfactual but ecstatic goal-worlds must be related in some way to the brusque temporal discontinuities brought about by colonial capitalism. My own rhetorical question: What if the invading colonial power inculcates modes of time-mapping that are just as enchanted or fantastic as those of the indigenes? Bullfighting, for instance, is based on the belief that it dignifies a man to wager a huge amount of time (i.e., the rest of his life) on the outcome of a few seconds. When compared with this particular Spanish export, binge drinking in Ixtepeji seems more rational than ever.

The analysis of temporal opportunity costs leads inevitably to issues in the anthropology of altered states of consciousness (ASCs). Venerable psy-chological anthropologist Philip Bock prefers to speak in terms of "alter-native" states of consciousness, thereby avoiding "the presumption that our everyday way of experiencing the world is 'unaltered' or normal in any absolute sense" (1999, 213). In his classic study of future time perspectives in alcoholics and social drinkers, R. G. Smart proved that the heaviest drinkers in any society have significantly shorter time horizons and a marked "insensitivity to future consequences" (1968, 83). We are not going out on a limb, therefore, to hypothesize that alcohol radically changes or influences our perceptions of opportunity costs and our tem-poral mapping, or that alcoholized time-mapping interacts in untold ways with a cultural belief system. In drinking cultures of the enchanted-garden type, people *waste no time* in using the alcohol ASC to produce verities or allow them to emerge. The heavy use of spirits is often connected to the perceived proximity of the spirit world, moreover, and here we find yet another link to the brusque disruptions caused by capitalist Christian drug-food commerce. Early on, colonized peoples learned to expect the unexpected, and surely Gell, were he alive, would not restrict us to easy-to-calculate quantities of economic capital that are simply "squandered" or "misallocated" by Talcott Parsons's goal-lacking deviants. We have to con-sider the possibility that apparently disadvantaged people might be in pos-session of unknown volumes of cultural or emotional capital that are revived, renewed, maximized, and perhaps *increased* by drinking, counter-intuitive though it might seem. One common way to increase resources via drinking was noted years ago by David C. McClelland: "Men drink pri-marily to feel stronger. Those for whom personalized power is a particular concern drink more heavily" (as qutd. by Heath 1987, 45). Women find power in drink as well — especially sacred power (Eber 2000, 149). Even when the organ damage or shortened life spans have been cognized, the drinking goes on. Yes, you died young, but yes, you reached ecstasy innu-merable times and you built fragile dream worlds better than this one. As it turns out, the most accessible and immediate machine of cosmic truth production is also quite habit-forming, so at some point it becomes impossible to distinguish ethnophilosophy from addiction rationale.

The archetypal exploitative labor contractor/liquor distributor of Yucatán surely had a practical understanding of the time maps of his clients; at least he knew that the average Indian was willing to sell himself into virtual slavery just to keep some kind of magic alive and flowing. In a document from 1748, the Zoque people of northwestern Chiapas referred to their favorite drug food as *aguardiente hechizo* — "hexing rum," since it cast a spell and made them sell their farm goods at ruinous prices; it is still comparable to an *hechizo*, affirms ethnologist Laureano Reyes Gómez (1992, 70). Crump notes that the rum-for-labor system worked best when the Indians were kept in a state of permanent indebtedness; coffee plantation *enganchadores* like Moctezuma Pedrero had first claim on workers' wages, and Ladino shopkeepers were next in line (1987, 241). In a poem penned in Mérida in 1937, the high point of Pedrero's liquor monopoly, Octavio Paz portrayed not alcohol but money as the mortal enemy of Yucatán's illiterate peasants and their "*subterráneo sistema fluvial del espíritu*" ("subterranean river system of the spirit") (Paz 1989, 41). On second thought, let us say that the coffee or hemp economy, the alcohol monopoly, and the spiritual economy flowed interdependently, mutually reinforcing each other in neocolonial capitalist circulation. The spirit world had become alcohol-dependent; it was not autonomous, but it was real and durable (cf. Lambek 1996).

More than economic rationality enters into time mapping, and capitalism itself must adapt. Eduardo Menéndez documents an amazingly tolerant work environment throughout Mexico, especially in industries with strong unions that "tend to overprotect the worker who abuses alcohol; they grant him 'union permits' or 'licenses' so that he may continue his binge or cure the hangover" (1992, 156). Some syndicates are quite effective at keeping workers from losing their jobs due to alcohol-related problems, but in other industries an inebriated worker can be fired on the spot. Sometimes a business owner tolerates a man's "irresponsible attitude" in order to pay him less (156). During the mid-1980s, Menéndez relates, 12 percent of the labor force of the state-owned oil monopoly PEMEX was always missing on Mondays (147). This statistic seems astounding when we recall that PEMEX workers earned some of the best wages of the entire Mexican working class.

From time to time one finds a Mexican ethnography in which drinking really is the rational thing to do, from a purely practical, financial, future-oriented viewpoint. In a recent study of ceremonial drinking events in Santa María Atzompa (Oaxaca), Ramona Pérez stresses that

> up-and-coming families and female heads of households will not risk losing the opportunity to show publicly the extensions of their relationships and will ignore health issues, personal problems

associated with drinking and employment constraints in order to participate. The fiesta and the concurrent ability to drink have become such strong social and political forces within the community that health risks ranging from recurrent dysentery to diabetic shock to physical abuse are considered normal repercussions of participation. (2000, 368)

The women of Santa María Atzompa play ever more important roles in the local crafts industry, but to maintain their hard-won status they must hold their own at hard-drinking Catholic fiestas. Despite serious physical problems, the woman president of the glaze cooperative knew that missing the community *borrachera* was not an option: "I have earned my place here, my presence is in demand at the fiesta. But if I do not go, if I am not strong, then I will lose. The others who wait to take my position will use this time to talk about me, to convince people that I cannot do my job because I am a weak woman" (as cited by Pérez 2000, 368). We could be dealing with a clever addiction rationale, but I think not. In Santa María Aztompa, among women who clearly have their eyes on the long term, and for whom drinking's accrued costs are already quite apparent, the Dionysian show must go on.

The temporal contradictions that vexed Fabian are still relevant for researchers who share close personal drinking experiences with "the other." How can we wake up the next morning and provide a systematic account of the internal logic of inebriated intentional states without unduly warping the original time-warping experience? Sometimes, through a fog, we recall that the very meaning of life emerged the night before in a special ritual or quasi-ritual time-out-of-time. Such moments are highly resistant to representation within the sober formats of nonfiction writing, reading, and tenure-clock-watching. One scholar who studied the introduction of standardized measures of time and space into the isolated lifeworlds of Iceland pointed out that the new "absolute" measures never eradicated the earlier, more local, more idiosyncratic pace of life (Hastrup 1985, 56). "Indeed," writes G. J. Whitrow, "man's unwillingness to abandon natural bases of measurement was for long a hindrance to the development of a scientific system of timekeeping" (1988, 17). Earlier modes of temporal processing cannot be associated solely with chemically induced trance states, of course, but it is from inside such states that they best *resist* the encroachments of alien semiotics, that is, nonecstatic ethnographic soberwriting. On the other side of campus, biomedical or epidemiological frames of analysis manage to avoid the problem altogether — a drinker's subjectivity is simply not one of their variables. Alcoholics Anonymous narratives are sometimes quite good at reproducing the so-called drunkalog, but only to persuade people to renounce their original time-travel experiences (but nostalgia for them creeps in subversively). Poetic or musical modes of representation are clearly more in keeping with the affects and perceptions of an alcoholized consciousness. Although constrained to use prose in this book, I constantly fall back on analogies and metaphors, like the one derived from legendary Mayahuel, the goddess whose four hundred breasts suckled four hundred divine rabbits (*centzon totochtin*). With this seemingly exact number the indigenes meant to indicate that behavioral outcomes of *borracheras* are too numerous to count. The need to keep this multiplicity in mind, this massive alterity, has led me to adopt certain rhetorical devices in this book. I quote songs, skip from one end of Mexico to the other, attempt witticisms, constantly cede the podium to other voices, and occasionally digress in pseudo-barroom or *tertulia* style, somewhat in the manner of distinguished writer/drinker Armando Jiménez (2000). The reader's patience is much appreciated.

Promising tropes of comparison begin to blossom as soon as we realize how pointless it is to define binge drinking in strictly quantitative terms, for example, exactly how many drinks were consumed in two hours at the fraternity party? The universal physiology of drinking tells us little about its local, culture-bound phenomenology. The binge drinking experience has to be approached humanistically, in rigorously inexact qualitative terms, on a case by case basis. Contrary to AA dogma, alcohol is not the great equalizer; it will not turn a fraternity pledge into Peter O'Toole. It is true that in every bender we are dealing with psychic deterritorialization and subsequent reterritorialization, a place escaped from and one escaped to, but the places can be supplied by a local culture as shallow as that of Sigma Chi Delta or as deeply rooted (metaphorically) as that of Santa María Aztompa. Exurban prosperity is no indicator of psychic depth, nor does poverty imply an impoverished symbolic network, pace Paz. Suppose, for instance, that one is the fortuitous beneficiary of a centuries-old cultural legacy that never broke with the Catholic taste for figuration, that never reterritorialized on "the atheism of the concept" (Deleuze and Guattari 1994, 92, 102–3). Inside such an intentional world, the magical mental shift of a *borrachera* necessarily begins in a thoroughly antimodern relationship with the figure — that is, a given transcendent icon, emblem, representation, symbol, synthesis, myth, drama, or song — and the effects, as well as the affects, would be cathartic, aesthetic, ecstatic, pseudo-mystical, or quasireligious. If this sounds Baroque, it should. At a sufficiently epiphanic stage of mental destructuration, paradigmatic figures tend to manifest themselves as events. When extensively ramified cultural figures are liquified in alcoholic *aggiornamento*, their primordial *kairos* status is restored in moments that seize and fascinate the consciousness with great veracity.

In both reality and fiction, the binge drinking cultures of Mexico arrange for the hereafter to be installed right here, right now — somewhat in the manner of a *tableau vivant*! This is the prodigal root metaphor that Fabian spurned and I embrace. The actual number of drinks required to reach this apparitional zone depends on the person. Malcolm Lowry, for example, could still write poetry after "Thirty-five mescals in Cuautla" (Lowry 2000/1962, 56) — but a refrigeratior throbbing in the cantina triggered all manner of lugubrious visions. Mexican composer José Alfredo Jiménez was a light drinker by comparison:

Qué bonito y qué bonito	How nice, I say how nice,
es brindar por una ingrata,	to toast the standoffish one,
y a los 15 o 20 tragos	and after fifteen or twenty drinks
llevarle una serenata.	go and give her a serenata.

The whole point of the counting is to *lose count*, of course, to reach a mental terrain where one drink more or one drink less could not possibly make a difference. In chapter 6 we will see how writers in intimate contact with one drinking culture or another represent Mexico in figurative, apparitional, time-collapsing terms, *appropriately*, and are very attuned to questions of fate and luck. Mexico's most proficient drinkers seek to extract more beauty and pleasure from beauty and pleasure, or transcendent meaning from life's ugliness and pain. They are incurably romantic to the point of necrophilia. At their worst, they are ruthless buffoons; at their best, enchanted gardeners.

The American "alcoholic frame" has propagated an image of the drinker as essentially deceitful, expert in all manner of tricks and subterfuges to keep on guzzling. Caroline Knapp's 1996 account of her "love affair" with drinking is typical in this regard: she had bottles hidden in the most ingenious household nooks. There is no autochthonous Mexican equivalent of such books. South of the border, in labyrinths yet to be penetrated by AA ideology, heavy drinking is commonly associated with truth production, not clever deception. Hence the coherence of alcoholized wakes featuring *la Muerte* playing her old Baroque role as the stripper away of illusions, vanities, and lies. The Iberian Peninsula was and is a visionary-friendly place (Christian Jr. 1996). In Mexico and throughout Latin America, missionaries cultivated the allegiance of the people by indulging their penchant for the apparitional, the visionary, and the miraculous — so many unquestionable types of truth whose rebirth, in superficially secular contexts, is assisted by demon rum midwifery. Friars of many orders coincided in seeing *pulque* as the devil's brew (Viqueira 1999, 153ff), which it was, in the sense that it helped people spice up and personalize the doctrines fed them by the Church. An entirely different sort of "liberation theology" underlies the ecstatic sacralization of a drunkard's specific spatiotemporal coordinates, no matter how pathetic they seem to outsiders. Any definition of "identity" should include whatever spatiotemporal moves people make to protect or facilitate such revelatory moments, and naturally whatever arrangements are already available in the culture. The latter could range from a national system of cantinas to the festivals of the religious or secular calendars. In Mexico, such spatiotemporal arrangements articulate with apparitional modes of consciousness as well as traumatic personal histories of one kind or another. The initial rebuffering of a traumatic temporal rift does not take place in an "unaltered" state of consciousness, that much we know (van der Kolk 1996, 287–89). Taken as a whole, these psychocultural resources promote an ecstatic kind of sense making: preconceptual, emotive, reconnective even if paranoid, unusually fixative, sometimes selfish to the point of sociopathy. The identity-affirming experience need not be, indeed cannot be, identical to itself with every appearance.

Once identity is understood in experiential terms, it is clear that poverty, illiteracy, and despotism cannot stand in the way of its actualization, although they will guarantee its stigmatization. Like Fabian's clock-watching capitalists, Porfirian intellectuals sought to subjugate Time itself to accomodate one-way schemes of progress and development (Fabian 1983, 144); with little interest in the subtleties of proletarian consciousness, they were quick to identify national stagnation with images of the alcoholized Indian, "apathetic" peasant, or recalcitrant urban worker. The lower-class Mexican mestizo, in their view, was too indolent, dreamy, wasteful, anarchic, and irreflexive to be trusted with the nation's resources; only a strong, scientifically minded government could protect Mexico from the typical Mexican, *que mandar no sabe y obedecer no quiere* — ("who doesn't know how to command and doesn't wish to obey") (García Cantú 1963, 102). Such resistance to "progress" implies resilient alternative time-mapping modes. From the earliest years of New Spain we spy spirited forms of temporal mutiny (i.e., drunkenness) emerging from urban ethnic chaos; alcoholized Indians and *castas* found four hundred ways to subvert Spanish semiotic domination, even as they dutifully helped the invaders erect churches and *cabildos*. Alongside the excessive drinking we find other unauthorized gateways to the sacred. Fray Bernardino de Sahagún was convinced that Indians secretly mocked reasonable performance standards set by the Church; in the miraculous apparitions of the Virgin of Guadalupe, he saw nothing but "idolatrous dissembling" (Sahagún 1956/1576, 3:352). Fray Maturino Gilberti admonished the so-called Tarascan Indians to worship Christ, not the crucifix that he and his fellow friars had made so ubiquitous; fray Francisco de Bustamante attacked Archbishop Montúfar for supporting the Guadalupana cult, and so on (Ricard 1947, 40–71). All over Spanish America, "the theater of ritual reversal" still counters the forces of state persecution with confusion or counter-confusion (Taussig 1997, 125). José María Infante documents many complicated and confusing Mexican rituals that distort Catholic norms, including Christmas in Zinacantán (Chiapas). There the traditional *posadas* portray the Virgin Mary as "a woman in the habit of sleeping with so many different men that nobody wanted to assist her in the birth of her son, except for her older brother Joseph" (Infante 1998, 143). The fact that half the locals do not speak Spanish surely works in the devil's favor.

In somatic semiotic resistance, there is active, ongoing generation of meaning in the heads of the people involved. Formerly hidden transcripts emerge in all their queerness, and incoherence becomes a coherent strategy of resistance. During the viceroyalty, many religious movements and uprisings in Indian towns were born in an unexpected folding in the fabric of local time, often induced by alcohol, that turned the town into a sacred radiating point, a beacon for heterodox folk religiosity. One can study the words of deranged local prophets (Gruzinski 1989), but one should also study the nature of the popular demand for them. Consider the street versions of Christ's Passion that were and are common throughout Mexico. Already apocryphal when brought to New Spain by the missionaries, processional liturgy went on from there to incorporate so many bizarre motifs that one strongly suspects the proximity of secret agendas. In what we might call "the Passion according to Mexico," one type of semiotic resistance — the popular misconstrual of Christ's sacrifice — is redoubled by the somatic heresy of drunkenness. A good dose of obscenity never hurts either, as in the *Semana Santa* fiestas of Nayarit's Cora Indians. Come Holy Wednesday, Christ-torturing ceremonies presided over by white-clad "Jews" give way to the traditional Dance of the Turtle. "The dance begins with a soloist who imitates an orgasm, and then the other dancers unfasten their pants and dance touching their buttocks and imitating ritual coitus" (Infante 1998, 145). Come Good Friday, the "Jews," now armed with toy pistols, pursue a Christ-Child all around the plaza. Captured and taken to the church, the boy is tied with cords to an adult Christ; then both are paraded through the streets and returned to the church. This is actually the part of the fiesta *with which the priests cooperate*. Once outside the church again, however, the people carry out "a farce of the previous procession, in which evil spirits go around reading texts in the manner of priests, pronouncing meaningless phrases" (146). Following a series of outlandish routines with a Centurion and a donkey, the "Jews" recommence their turtle dancing, "clutching their penises and pointing them towards the church" (Ibid.) The turtle is considered an erotic symbol by the indigenes of Nayarit, but maybe we are dealing with something more than the survival of a fertility cult. Why not derive their highly developed taste for farce from colonial and postcolonial cruelty? As it happens, "some persons embrace absurdity as an act of revolt, as a means of mirroring back to others that they feel they are being treated absurdly" (Fisher and Fisher 1993, 193). Who could deny that the Cora Indians have been treated absurdly for nearly five centuries by "forward-looking" governments of every type and ideology?

In colonial contexts all over earth, we find obscene or parodic appropriation of the personas of "colonially privileged characters" (Strathern 1995,

127). "Carnivalesque practices thus attempt to invert consciousness, to render ridiculous what has become normative, to show turbulence and negation beneath conformity, to emerge as spirits of protest against the perceived sickness of society." The occasions for such standardized deviations were supplied by the church calendar once or twice a year, but diverse forms of linguistic subversion were used all day and every day by society's losers — known in Mexico as *léperos* during the colonial period and *pelados* since the nineteenth century. As studied by Jeffrey Pilcher, these heavy-drinking friends in low places specialized in "linguistic camouflage," "malevolent humor," "verbal misdirection," and "double-entendres with obscene allusions" (*albures*). The phallic nature of this verbal humor would later be psychoanalyzed by humorless intellectuals. Both *léperos* and *pelados* possessed a general readiness to engage in farcical, eccentric, or crazy acts known as *vaciladas* (Pilcher 2001, 8–13), sometimes called *chingaderas* in our day. Drinking was the typical inspiration or trigger, and Mexicans also use the term *vacilada* as a synonym for "binge." Although originally associated with drunken fools and layabouts, the *vacilada* proved to be perversely empowering; in the years after 1910, says Pilcher, it became a vehicle of political critique and was crucial to "the development of the archetypal character that culminated in Cantinflas" (29).

The Revolution did make a difference in the sorts of identities that could be enlisted for purposes of state legitimation. Even the prodigal "mestizo drunkard" identity was rehabilitated and given a place at the table — much to the horror of Roger Bartra (1987, 107–12). In Bartra's Mexico, a corrupt and despicable one-party rule dominated the people by paternalistically equating them with rum-soaked *pelados*. Bartra refused to identify with this identity, of course, but everywhere he turned he found more evidence that the all-powerful "*cultura dominante*" wanted just that. Mexican elites successfully maintained their power through stigmatizing identity-imputations, in his view, and he replicates the practice by tacitly taking ordinary Mexicans for fools. Other writers assume the same, and indeed we find a genuine continuity of misunderstanding uniting the Porfirian intellectuals of the 1880s with the Gramscian intellectuals of the 1980s. Both writerly generations accepted the dominant chronopolitics as normative and never fathomed rebellious modes of time-mapping kept afloat by alcohol. As if Foucault or Deleuze or Certeau had never been born, Bartra and others remained beholden to juridico-political notions of power, theoretically blind to micropolitical forms of resistance, disdainful and dismissive of mass-mediated parodic subversion in Mexico.

Most people assume that Cantinflas was the invention of Mexican comic actor Mario Moreno Reyes (1911–1993). Without casting doubt on Moreno's comic genius, Pilcher sets the record straight:

> There was nothing particularly original about Cantinflas, nor could there have been to succeed in a popular theater based primarily on

improvised interactions with the audience. He shared mannerisms, jokes, and costumes with countless contemporary performers. . . . Even his supposed innovation of *cantinfleando*, talking a lot without saying anything, had been the gimmick of Vale Coyote from the nineteenth century puppet theater. . . . A theater critic later asserted that nobody interpreted the vulgar drunk better than Cantinflas, not even Roberto Soto in the role of Luis Morones during an orgy at his Tlalpan ranch. Soto presented the alcoholic at the edge of a coma, worn out from drink, while Cantinflas presented him in all of his euphoria and grandiloquence. (31–32, 57)

Note the alcoholized hypomanic continuum. The role of heavy drinking in the evolution of Mexican linguistic subversion is encoded into the very name "Cantinflas," by all accounts the garbled conflation of "cantina" and "*te inflas*" ("you get loaded"). Ilan Stavans reproduces one variant of this story in *The Riddle of Cantinflas* (1998, 39), but overlooks any connection between Moreno's verbal pyrotechnics and the binge-drinking cultural background. Stavans devotes much ink to the classic *Ahí está el detalle* (dir. Juan Bustillo Oro, 1940), but somehow omits to mention that Cantinflas is drinking to excess in almost every scene in which he appears. The "riddle of Cantinflas" certainly cannot be solved by ignoring the drunkenness clue. Intoxication is unquestionably relevant, moreover, to the playful homosexual *albures* that permeate every classic Cantinflas movie. As noted by Pilcher, "Another cinematic convention for reassuring audiences about gender-crossing scenes, in Mexico at least, was the consumption of alcohol, which allowed the macho to drop his guard and express his emotions" (2001, 63).

Unamused, Roger Bartra targets Cantinflas as the ultimate embodiment of the drunken *pelado* character who only *seems* to be transgressive and power-defying but really possesses an uncanny potential for dictatorship legitimation. He concedes that social injustice is often criticized in Cantinflas movies, "but it is a conformist critique that proposes flight instead of fight, sneaking away instead of struggling" (1987, 147). Even Cantinflesque incoherence is malevolently coherent: "Cantinflas is not only the stereotype of the poor urban Mexican: he is a painful simulacrum of the profound and structural link that must exist between the despotism of the State and the corruption of the people. . . . The confused verbalism of Cantinflas is not a critique of the demagoguery of the politicians: it is its legitimation" (1987, 150, my translation). Due to such corrupt role models of PRI-orchestrated interpellation, Bartra's Mexico was in horrible shape; indeed there was nothing in its popular culture that did not legitimate one-party dictatorship in some way. Forms of wordplay and speech that others found to be subversive were in fact the surest sign of the opposite. This logic, for want of a better word, can also be found in cultural journalist Carlos Monsiváis (1999). With truly appalling condescension,

Monsiváis affirms that every Mexican comedian, Cantinflas included, is obligated "to serve as a vehicle for childish language that, through inversion, sanctions a culture of submission (the reproduction of Indian, peasant, and, most often, popular urban speech as the expressions of the adult child)" (Monsiváis 1999, 67).

What we find in such essays is not dispassionate cultural analysis but dogmatic views held by elitist writers in full modernist flight from what their intellectual father called "the amorphous mass element" (Gramsci 1971, 340). In the world according to Gramsci, the "intellectually qualified strata" are the ones who count, the ones invulnerable to brainwashing, the only ones capable of active creativity (341). In Gramscian thought, ordinary people "are condemned to an essentially passive role, and thus to acting merely as the depository of heterogeneous and chaotic ideological influences which originate 'above their heads,' so to speak" (Mészáros 1989, 403). Not Bartra and Monsiváis alone, of course, but many other Mexican authors found Gramscian notions flattering to their self-concept at one time (Krotz 1991, 185). The result is a large body of published cultural commentary that denies agency, sees popular creativity as a contradiction in terms, and portrays mass-mediated comedy as a childish "culture of submission." At least Stavans avoided such sovereign contempt in his essay on Cantinflas.

If we step back and contemplate the past five hundred years of Mexican history, we can see that a finite number of sign-producing systems emerged to cooperate or compete with the Laws of the Spanish Fathers. Following a suggestion by Deleuze and Guattari (1987, 135–36), we might delineate a Mexican indigenous assemblage, its drinking patterns included, that was much abused by history but fortunate enough to retain the remnants of a "presignifying" semiotic — collective, multiple, polyvocal. We could then identify the Spanish colonial viceroys and bishops, as well as the creole elite and their heirs, with a despotic "signifying" semiotic — discursive uniformity, control, replication, circularity, hyper-vigilance unto paranoia. In the clash and mixing of two civilizations, vast numbers of mestizos, peasants, urban workers, artisans, and shifty *pelados* came to possess a "passional" semiotic that fueled legitimate class struggles and domestic squabbles alike. In this social assemblage, the one Eric Wolf called Mexico's "social shadow-world" (1959, 242), we find psychologies of sexual pessimism, sadomasochism, machismo *sensu strictu*, and what Erich Fromm termed "matriarchal alcoholism" (1996/1970, 178). Lastly, we can identify a rebellious, seminomadic, "countersignifying" semiotic, sustained through the turbulence of Mexican history by men on horseback, rancheros large and small, bandits, brigands, upstart *cristeros*, and opportunistic tequila barons from Jalisco. In presenting their brand of semiotic analysis, Deleuze and Guattari add that "Things are even more complicated than we have let on" (1987, 133) — but we require no further complications at this time. Three of the above metasemiotics were characterized by a strong alcoholic component in their general social composition; therefore suffice it to say that any regime of signs that in some way served to counter despotic signification found tactical support in the diffuse, polyvocal, heterogeneous, extremely ambivalent "logic" of the intoxicated body itself. The body is the eternal source of Certeau's "surreptitious creativities" (1988, 96). Both Charles Baudelaire and Julia Kristeva, to accumulate Europeans, would be delighted to discover that Mexican drinking cultures are privileged sites of madness, holiness, poetry, and pleasurable breaches of symbolic coherence (cf. Kristeva 1986, 93–101). In homage to one more authority, Mikhail Bakhtin (1984), a good number of alcohol-friendly semiotics can be grouped under the rubric of the "carnivalesque." This is precisely the framework chosen by folklorist José Limón to interpret the fajita-grilling, cerveza-swigging, crotch-grabbing workmen of Mexican-American South Texas (Limón 1994, 123–40), denizens of Mexico's "social shadow-world" in broad daylight.

One would think that alcoholic thinking is either a natural ally of the carnivalesque metasemiotic or its functional equivalent. But how exactly does an "alcoholic" think in the midst of a mind-bending bender? Sociologist Norman K. Denzin was one man who made the intellectual journey and lived to tell about it:

> The ability to reason, to think coherently, logically, and with any kind of temporal order has vanished. The alcoholic's language continues to turn and twist metaphor and metonymy into patterns of speech that appear to reflect deep, inner, primary processes of self and consciousness. There primary speech patterns of self ordinarily are inhibited in common discourse. But they are the primary discursive structures of thought that order the alcoholic's self-dialogues. Partially released by alcohol, partially ingrained in his or her consciousness, they become familiar patterns of thought for the alcoholic. The twisted, poetic, metaphorical, metonymic patterns of speech thus serve to place him or her outside the realms of ordinary speech and interaction. (Denzin 1987, 109)

Denzin was no poet and no postmodernist, I hasten to say; he was utterly opposed to the unsettling mental mode he describes so well. But let us note the extraordinary similarities shared by the alcoholic semiotic as described by Denzin, the resistant sign regimes uncovered by Deleuze and Guattari, the carnivalesque logic explored by Bakhtin, and the pomposity-puncturing mode of speech that came to be identified with Cantinflas. Given the destabilizing power of comic nonsense in human societies (Davis 1993), it would seem unwise to consign its Mexican variants to a "culture of submission." Viqueira, who has studied colonial Mexican carnivals in depth, does not rob the populace of agency; he calls attention to an edict issued in 1722 by an archbishop obsessed with the "dishonest

womanly transformations" that accompanied the drinking and the dancing of *Carnestolendas* (Viqueira 1999, 104). It took more than a decade for
colonial authorities to bust up the biggest street party of the year, but colonial power could not stop daily carnivalesque sociolinguistics and multicultural imbibing: "The *pulquerías* that jutted out into the street were
often simply small booths nestled against some wall and protected from
the weather by a roof of shingles. There, a multitude of Indians, *castas*, and
poor Creoles got drunk in the midst of the flow of people coming and
going" (99).

The larger lesson is that alcoholized or alcohol-friendly semiotics cannot be so easily captured by a state identity apparatus. They can be hailed,
cajoled, and subsequently abused by such an apparatus, but we must never
omit to ask "who needs whom?" Sometimes power is forced to compromise with its own mockery in order to function at all. If and when that
happens, is the resulting state apparatus stronger or weaker in consequence? In his visionary overview of Latin American political psychology,
Michael Taussig was pleased to discover "that wonderful phenomenon
wherein what is opposed to the rigor of Law partakes of its language and
power, the *tarifa extraoficial*, for instance, belonging both to the world of
officialdom and to a burlesque of that world in its meaning as an illegal
bribe that is so routinized that it is essential to governing" (1997, 23).
Taussig sees the glass half full; Bartra finds it half empty and affirms that
the archetypal *pelado*'s obscene word plays and ambivalent speech patterns
are nothing less than "a subtle invitation to bribery." Moreover, "the
intrinsic corruption of the pelado is present in the entire political system"
(1987, 150). It seems strange to talk about how corrupt and slippery the
political system is, how deeply compromised it is by an abjectly irresponsible *pelado* mindset, and yet simultaneously exalt the system's power. If
anything, the pathetic weakness of the Mexican state apparatus is what
comes shining through here. Instead of seeing Cantinflas and the semiotic
family he represents as the legitimation of power and the emblem of a submissive culture, why not give them credit for keeping power eternally off
balance in Mexico? Why not give them the respect they deserve as "local
authorities?" (cf. Certeau 1988, 106). Always ready to hold Mexican popular culture to a Che Guevara standard of probity (without renouncing
their own privileges), intellectuals miss the power of the pleasure principle
and the strength of resistive semiotics that twist discursive forms provided
by the "dominant culture" to their own purposes, leaving power structures
no choice but to cooperate. Again, who needs whom?

The transformations of sense into nonsense and then back into sense
are not so hard to follow. First we have the discourse of power, then we
have invisible but massive proletarian appropriations of said discourse,
then we have appropriations of the proletarian appropriations by clever
entrepreneurs from one class or another in ways that sustain their own
habitus or confirm elite prejudices. Is that the end of the cycle? Clearly not.

Recycled modes of proletarian speech are then re-reappropriated by the people themselves for their own deviously creative and satirical purposes, without the guidance of "the intellectually qualified strata."

Binge-drinking cultures really exist, they are human-all-too-human and they continue to present major challenges to our ethics and our powers of translation. Mexico's well-intentioned elites view the masses through a lens darkly, searching for signs of alienation or metaphysical solitude. A doctor's incompetent analysis of a symptom does not mean that all is well, however. Indeed there are other, more imperious logics that live alongside the strategies of cross-dressing Cantinflesque confusion discussed above. In the mental universe of binge drinking, deadly serious confrontations with causality, fate, or evil can take precedence over the comic. In time a drunkard may lose the ability to laugh at himself, thereby rendering himself vulnerable to a whole new category of demons. There are manic Mexican identities, moreover, that function according to a logic of "*No me digas que no*" ("Don't say no to me"). Elitist writer Martín Luis Guzmán understood this logic well enough not to say "no" to the soldier forcing him to drink to excess in the dark streets of Culiacán (as will be seen). Drunken intolerance of negation can also lead to big problems on the domestic front when a spouse neglects to accomodate the grandiosity of her man's quasi sacred but touchy self-concept. Unpleasant as it might be, spousal abuse is morally justified in the minds of many men whose thought patterns have been adjusted by alcohol, and these issues must be explored in due time. Let us just say here that an *enhanced* consciousness is not necessarily a more complex, enlarged, or enlightened consciousness. It simply means a more intensified one, one considered more immediately valuable by its possessor, one with the power to invest the object world with more meaningfulness than it might otherwise have for the sober. In the final analysis, there are no core beliefs in the brain, only core algorithms, procedures, and protocols that process cultural resources and invisible personal historicities in at least four hundred different ways. In the enchanted gardens of Mexico after fifteen or twenty drinks we find flowers and weeds in equal abundance.

Chapter 4
Bodies and Memories

Conquerors and colonists awarded grants of land-with-workers were known as *encomenderos*. Eager to extract as much labor as possible from their indigenes, these Iberian overlords were willing and able to relocate entire populations to hard-work zones, further shortening local life expectancies. Spanish missionaries outraged by Spanish excesses dreamed of segregating *their* Indians in a vast monastery far from the exploiters. Meanwhile, viruses and bacterial infections that arrived like stowaways in Spanish bodies brought about one of the most notorious demographic catastrophes in memory. We can scarcely imagine the psychological wounds that accompanied the deaths of so many — 60 to 80 percent of the population in some areas (Cook 1998). For centuries epidemics continued to travel along the same commercial routes set up by the Spaniards for the liquor trade and for all other goods and services. Typhus, to take one example, came and went at least thirty-two times over three hundred years, claiming victims from all races and classes.

One powerful stress-relief medication was made available to all, and, by the middle of the eighteenth century in *Bourbon México*, alcoholic consolation was woven into the fabric of everyday life: "The drinking house functioned as a reassuring institution in a society subject to the anxieties of accelerating corn prices, periodic epidemics, and job insecurity" (Scardaville 1980, 647). Numerous Spaniards and Creoles of Spanish descent took comfort in drinking: one colonial observer declared that the difference between white and Amerindian drunkards lay only "in the liquors each employed to get intoxicated" (as cited by Corcuera 2000, 60). The end result was often the same: scandalous public disorder. As the eighteenth century drew to a close, the sector of the governing elite whose wealth was not alcohol-dependent grew ever more vigilant and oppressive, increasingly intolerant of plebeian *borracheras* and raucous festivals. High-ranking representatives of the Church feared that festive inebriation was a holdover from devilish pre-Columbian days — and they were not far off the scent. Juan Viqueira sides with the subaltern targets of viceregal and ecclesiastical intolerance: "It was not enough that they had to work more every day, to live one on top another in the city's *vecindades* (tenements) and *arrabales* (marginal neighbor-hoods), to suffer increased racial discrimination, but they even had to endure all this abuse cold sober and take part in religious processions with a serious and even severe manner" (1999, 121). Rather less empathic is historian Sonia Corcuera de Mancera, who has chronicled colonial alcohol conflicts in a number of publications (1994, 1997, 2000) using much the same ideology, and quite often the same tone, as the moralistic diatribes she exhumes. She lauds the Aztec overlords who supposedly sought to protect "the family unit" from the effects of alcohol (2000, 56). In discussing the drunken riot of 1692, she refers to the "mental blindness of the Indians," their "perturbed intelligence," the "irrational joy" they felt in rebelling against the authorities (1994, 198). For her the nineteenth-century custom of *San Lúnes* (Saint Monday), so beloved of the artisan class, was just a "sad institution." Mexico's drunkards of today are simply "ridiculous" (2000, 63). Since we are not seventeenth-century prelates, let's not feel threatened by the spectacle of classes dissolving into masses, subjects dissolving into ecstatic self-experiencing, and hidden scripts emerging despite all efforts at intimidation. To accept the institutions of family, religion, and state as normative and the elite view of *pulque* consumption as the last word is like trying to explain communism using only anti-communist sources. Viquiera is more thoughtful, pointing out that extant moralistic harangues tell us next to nothing about the Mexican underclass reality. "This culture came from daily resistance to exploitation and survival strategies within situations of extreme poverty. It also originated from the effort to find small pleasures within a miserable and oppressive life" (1999, 215).

Discussing the urban riot of 1692, Cope observes that "the structures of Hispanic domination could not be dismantled in a day" (1994, 160). One could argue, conversely, that said structures were dismantled *every* day that a plebeian could dismantle his own brain with *pulque*. Yet another might observe that the Ibero-Mexican colonial edifice was split from within. No amount of sermonizing could prevail against the lawful, protected *pulque* trade and the taxes it produced; mass drunkenness was, among other things, the joyful obscene underside of alcohol governance. It is also true that the unsubtle mode of consciousness destructuration favored by plebeians took place within a time frame legally determined by the Masters. Viqueira believes that

> during the seventeenth and eighteenth centuries, the regulations imposed by Spanish officials on pulquerías implanted a compulsive manner of drinking. These regulations prohibited pulquerías in

enclosed locales to have any sort of distractions there, such as musicians or dances, to have food stands nearby, or to have any seats. Thus, patrons were forced to remain standing in the expectation that they would not remain very long. The predictable result was that customers drank their pulque as quickly as possible. (1999, 156)

Naturally the guileful consumers found ways to circumvent the regulations, that is, by bribing *alguaciles* and *corregidores* to turn a blind eye to dancing and a deaf ear to music. But Viqueira's point about compulsive drinking should be addressed: millions of liters of *pulque* were indeed swallowed within dominant spatio-temporal coordinates. This does not mean, however, that the resulting states of consciousness or the self-experiencing thereby instantiated were *determined* by said dominant coordinates. The doorway to molecular time may be subject to surveillance, but the time itself cannot be; it is always available for uses not sanctioned by or even visible to the hierarchy.

Tactics of resistance varied with one's place on the social map, then as now. Although they had been wholly complicit in Tenochtitlán's cosmic terror, members of the surviving Nahua intelligentsia perfected "magical and linguistic maneuvers aimed at distancing the effects of the Europeans and thwarting their intentions" (J. J. Klor de Alva 1997, 188); an indigenous "counternarrative of continuity" was the result. Working within the interstices of the official colonial discourse, "Nahuas accomodated and affirmed themselves in dangerous but functional ways. Had there been no plague followed by widespread depopulation, these tactics might have permitted them to survive into the twentieth century as a dominant bilingual and bicultural community" (189). With resistance taking place at all levels of indigenous–Spanish interaction, the degree of cultural disintegration suffered by the native peoples of New Spain may not have been as severe as once thought. James Lockhart affirms that "indigenous structures and patterns survived the conquest on a much more massive scale and for a longer period of time than had seemed the case when we had to judge by the reports of Spaniards alone. The indigenous world retained much social and cultural autonomy, maintaining its center of balance to a surprising extent, concerned above all with its own affairs" (1991, 20). Miguel León-Portilla famously defended the underlying continuity of Mesoamerican culture (1992); Guillermo Bonfil Batalla went further and labeled mestizo Mexico as "imaginary" in *México profundo* (1996). Poor and illiterate Indians worked against the system too, with the means at their disposal: collective drinking rituals. Every historian of colonial alcoholism documents the civil disorders it caused; in so doing they reveal that some sort of energy always flowed or fled, that fissures and cracks always undermined the molar macrosegmentarity of colonial institutions (in Deleuzo-speak). Even under the Bourbons, the jurisdiction of the Royal Audiencia failed to

inspire sufficient fear in the unlettered: "For instance, in the religious procession to celebrate the Ascension of Our Lady in the parish of Santa
María, some drunken Indians, without guidance from any priests, carried
out the image of the Virgin amid colossal disorder and stopped in front of
balconies to show it to the residents" (Viqueira 1999, 115). This ecstatic
approach to the mother goddess may seem like small potatoes, but the
dividing line between a fiesta and a rebellion is porous.

Outside of Mexico City, reconfigured local identities were consolidated
and celebrated in fiestas of excess scheduled by the Christian calendar
itself, putting many a priest in a tight spot. Alberto Carrillo discovered a
long letter written by a puritanical curate who spent the year 1680 observing patronal festivals in the mountains of Michoacán. In every town or village the people were eager to spend everything on costumes for the mock-
combat dances of "*moros y cristianos*," as well as food, musicians, bullfights, gifts, and huge quantities of liquor — much of it consumed just
before entering church to hear Mass. The priest discovers the devil's work
in this, an infernal stratagem for seizing something holy and turning it
into sin. Those able to stagger from the church to the bullring for the collective baiting rituals are often wounded and ocasionally killed by the
bulls, reports the priest. He regrets that his numerous efforts to reason
with "the principal Indians" of each town and persuade them to do without the fiestas have failed (Carrillo 1993, 335–45). As John Ingham points
out, Indians participating in ritual dramas and drunkenness "did not cease
to regard themselves as moral persons" and they continued "to suspect
that the Spaniard was the one who had closer ties with the Devil" (1986,
156).

Historian William Taylor was at pains to distinguish unstructured
urban-style drinking in *pulquerías* and cantinas from the norm-governed
forms of ritual drinking that prevailed in Indian and campesino communities. "Community rules about drinking and drunken behavior varied
from place to place, and many communities could no longer enforce the
old rules of behavior, but clearly there *were* rules that allowed for periodic
heavy drinking, especially by adult males, and condemned solitary, unso-
ciable tippling" (1979, 59). For Taylor, these rules and meanings were
inseparable from the strong sense of local identity that had filled the vacuum left by the epidemics, the forced transfers, and the breakdown of
regional pre-Hispanic ethnopolitical units. "In a word, villages seem to
have drawn in upon themselves to survive in the colonial period" (158).
Having divided and conquered, Spaniards furthered their aims through
control of clocks, calendars, and church bells. As Ross Hassig notes, "The
only coordinated time was Spanish, and even if most towns retained indigenous calendars, they were rapidly falling out of sync with each other in
the absence of an indigenous centralizing force" (2001, 152).

Why not consider binge drinking in the context of other social mechanisms that Indians and campesinos used, first to survive and later on to

thrive? "The three primary processes that have made possible the persistence of Indian cultures are resistance, innovation, and appropriation," states Bonfil (1996, 132). Under the category of nonviolent "daily strategies" of resistance, Bonfil mentions the strong attachment to traditional practices — the cargo system and the cargo holders known as *mayordomos*, the fiestas, the ceremonial expenditures — they were all "periodic affirmations of the existence of the group" (136). Curiously, Bonfil does not mention the huge amounts of alcohol processed by such ritual systems; we find no references to the fermented or distilled beverages that Indians considered indispensable for periodic affirmations of group identity. Unlike the plow, domestic animals, crops of non-American origin, and numerous artisan techniques, distilled alcohols do not appear in Bonfil's discussion of "cultural elements that were originally foreign but that subordinate groups have made their own" (1996, 137). One would never guess that for many decades ethnographers have portrayed Mexico's indigenous communities as thoroughly alcoholized. Bonfil almost seems in denial about possible unhealthy or dysfunctional behaviors present in *Deep Mexico* (i.e. his idealized nurturant collectivities). Why? The answer may lie in his desire to silence anything reminiscent of racist stereotypes. "Drunken Indian" was the chief stereotype, the perennial identity-attribution, found again and again in colonial and Porfirian diatribes alike.

Bonfil wanted to believe, above all, that at some level the indigenous world had remained essentially untouched, with a stable identity core true to the ancestors and only superficially affected by the arrival of the hated foreigners. For this line of thought, identity is something eternal that can be rescued when threatened, reclaimed when the time is ripe; similar notions of identity were behind numerous messianic revolts and rebellions in rural Mexico. This kind of nativist or tribalist thinking is a survival strategy, no doubt, but not a legitimate research method. How people convince themselves that they have recovered their true selves is the issue to explore, not their actual recovery, quite impossible outside the realm of fantasy or essentialist rhetoric. Recall how the Tzotzil leader Juan Pérez Jolote drank himself to death in order to save his Tzotzil soul; inebriation helped him piece together a self without apparent use of the mestizo elements he had been exposed to all his life. Had he desired just the opposite, liquor would have been his ally just the same. The orgasm is another bodily or somatic route to the experience of identity, it turns out; when *Carnaval* comes to Rio de Janeiro, anonymous group sex in trains, bars, and bathrooms makes some people feel "extremely Brazilian" (Parker 2003, 218–27). So we need to focus not on the recovery of unspoiled identities but on hedonic or ecstatic reinventions of identity that stifle interference from alternatives.

Bonfil deploys a black-and-white distinction between the real, authentic, deep indigenous Mexico and the imaginary or fallacious mestizo identity foisted upon the people by Mexico's Westernizing governing classes.

The problem lies not in Bonfil's slighting of huge population groups that are indeed of mixed racial ancestry and explicitly identify themselves as mestizos. In this he follows other Mexican historians who have chosen to avert their gaze from the feverish sexual activities of the Spaniards, their acquisition of whole harems of more-or-less willing indigenous women, their documented ability to sire dozens of multicultural children (Herren 1991). The problem, rather, is that two of the primary paths of indigenous survival that Bonfil proclaims — innovation and appropriation — are de facto mestizo solutions. They are nothing less than the essence of Mexican mestizoization, in the view of Bolívar Echeverría (1994, 36), who proposes the term *codigofagia* for a subjugated culture's ability to swallow a dominant semiotic but then transform it by forcing it to digest the still smoldering ruins of the conquered code. The result is something entirely new: in the case of colonial Mexico, a "baroque ethos" not to be thought of as syncretic or combinatorial but as emergent. For Serge Gruzinski, the mestizo element of the Mexican baroque imaginary was not so much a racial category as a strategy, one repeatedly applied to both art and life (2001, 96–160). In New Spain, he affirms, the first signs of serious nomadic identity-switching are to be found among the Indians who resisted the sacrament of matrimony. They were situational polygamists who flaunted the Inquisition and used urban multiracial chaos for their own purposes. Here today and gone tomorrow, they hid out in northern deserts or on the tropical coast, a different woman and a fresh identity in each locale (Gruzinski 1994, 17).

More original still, not to say fanciful, is the great importance Gruzinski attributes to the use of hallucinogenic compounds in the emergence of Mexican baroque art and beliefs. He portrays New Spain as "a hallucinated society" (19) in which Indians, mestizos, *negros*, *mulatos*, and marginalized Europeans consumed miraculous mushrooms on a regular basis. Their "voluntary excursions into hyperreality" stimulated the development of spectacular perceptual skills that were immediately put to use in the decoration of churches, thereby making Mexico the first postmodern nation (ibid.). Far be it from me to discount the importance of any mind-altering substance in the elaboration of culture, and Gruzinski has an initially plausible case when we consider Mexico's amazing pharmacological bounty (see chapter 3). Nevertheless, priests and friars from the land of the famous witch/procuress Celestina (Spain) were not caught off guard. The magic mushroom supply was impeded from the earliest days of the Conquest; the Church and the missionary orders enforced a "zero tolerance" policy with regard to peyotl, ololiuqui, teonanacatl, and the other plants and fungi that were so obviously reminiscent of European witchcraft and herbal devil worship. Although numerous clerics referred to the fermented juice of the maguey as "the devil's brew," it was never to be suppressed as the plants were. I gladly concede that there were a few *pulquerías* in colonial Mexico City where one could purchase "pulque mixed with herbs and roots and even peyote, which gave the drink a much greater kick" (Viqueira 1999, 130).

Whatever the available supply, Gruzinski overstates the demand. Psychotropic substances were used not by masons, artisans, and church employees but by ostracized divinatory and healing specialists: sorcerors, shamans, *curanderos*. Even those indigenes we identify with peyote, the Huichol of the Sierra Madre Occidental, believe it dangerous to "linger" in Wirikuta, their spatio-temporal zone of archaic authorization. The Huichol enjoy a less rigorous form of self-experiencing when they smoke *Tagetes lucida* (a strongly scented perennial herb) while drinking corn beer (Schultes and Hofmann 1992, 57). "Ecstasy is not fun," in the words of pioneering mushroom expert Gordon Wasson (in Devereux 1997, 112), by which he meant that the Mazatecs of Oaxaca did not visit the underworld for hippie-style recreational purposes. Schultes and Hofmann repeatedly found hallucinogens inspiring as much fear as respect in different regions of Mexico. The Tarahumarans' word for the pachycereus cactus, *wichowaka*, is also their word for "insanity"; they avoid cultivating certain frightening plants; there are mushrooms in Oaxaca that not even the shamans will use, and so on (1992, 51–57). So would it be accurate to picture late-colonial Mexico as one vast Woodstock?

Another big weakness in Gruzinski's hallucinated-society hypothesis: In their cross-cultural study of drug foods, Jankowiak and Bradburd state that "Of the 94 societies in our survey, not a single one relies on hallucinogenic drug foods to alleviate hunger or enhance a labor activity" (1996, 720). Alcohol, by contrast, is useful in labor-intensive economies all over the world. In Mexico, it was with alcohol and no other substance that the crucial compromise was reached between the colonial labor system and collective binge drinking. The Otomís and other groups studied by Fernando Benítez could begin every workday with several glasses of *pulque*; to start out the day with one little mescal bean would have been far too "deterritorializing," making work of any kind impossible — especially the exacting, highly skilled sort of work that goes into Churrigueresque decoration. Moreover, there is a vast difference between the artistic styles of Huichol yarn paintings and the interior ornamentation of colonial churches. The former manifestly seek to replicate visions obtained during peyote pilgrimages; the latter is more of a *naïf* reproduction of southern Spanish polychrome sculpture, with no evidence of the "entoptic" imagery or hallucinatory form constants clearly on display in Huichol yarn paintings (Sayer 1990, 137–38). The virtuosity of indigenous stone carvers was extraordinary, but guided by friars every step of the way. This is not to say that indigenous modes of *seeing* the finished product did not intersect in unique ways with those of Europe. As Lois Zamora argues,

> Today, colonial churches in many parts of Latin America display a density of images equal to that of the folded pages of the Nahua

and Maya codices. The baroque style that characterized Latin American colonial art and architecture from the late sixteenth century through the mid eighteenth is analogous to pre-contact modes of visual expression in its profusion of forms, its refusal of a single unifying perspective, and its structural and compositional uses of natural motifs. (Zamora 1998, 337)

Zamora goes on to laud Gruzinski's work on Mexican icons, but she does not derive them from drug use, and please note her use of the word "analogous." Other art historians look at the same baroque Novohispanic treasures and emphasize their continuity with Iberian traditions (Wroth 1997; Rubial García 2002). Gruzinski's "war of images" (2001) can be seen as one more chapter in Christianity's eternal struggle with premodern pantheism. You do not have to go to Latin America to locate a perfectly idolatrous relationship with baroque icons: for that you can stay in Spain (Mitchell 1990). And the *Semana Santa* celebrants of Córdoba, Jaén, and Sevilla were not taking peyote in their patios.

Gruzinski's strange stress on hallucinogens has an even stranger counterpart: an utterly negative view of indigenous drinking rituals. In his first study on the subject (1979), alcohol is envisioned as a disease, a scourge, a devouring mother. In *Man-Gods in the Mexican Highlands* (1989), Gruzinski portrays initiation into the drug-taking *curandero* lifestyle as one good way to escape "the dreary apathy of alcoholism" (81). Colonial historian Taylor had taken note of the mountain of ethnographies that portrayed the sociocultural utility of collective drinking; he criticized scholars who saw only pathology and epidemic. Though aware of Taylor's work, Gruzinski cannot concede any possible utility for the binge drinking that characterized the period of his expertise.

> Alcoholism . . . constituted one of the scourges of indigenous culture and probably had since the period before Cortez. With the Spanish conquest, alcoholism became as well one of the spectacular manifestations of deculturation, the schizoid system of a state of social and cultural disorientation, the stigmata of an infantilization undertaken more or less deliberately by the colonial system. . . . The thing is that, unlike pulque (the fermented juice of the agave) and other alcoholic drinks of more recent origin, the drug [*pipiltzintzintli*] never became a fermenting agent of deculturation and degradation. (1989, 109, 120)

Flying high above the degraded indigenous hordes, in Gruzinski's view, were the anti-alcohol/pro-drug *curanderos* who initiated a number of short-lived apocalyptic cults. Antonio Pérez regularly consumed hallucinogenic substances, "letting himself be carried away in the whirlpools of a millenarianism that was reinvented in Indian country and that rediscovered for itself the mad hopes of the European movements" (165). Pérez also discovered that he had a God-given right to sleep with other men's wives (167), very much in the manner of modern cult leaders. The Mexican messiah was arrested in 1761 and his Virgin of the Volcano cult dismantled: "It had, however, ensnared almost one Indian in ten in an area that runs from the south of the valley of Mexico to the north of the valley of Las Amilpas, and extends west to Tepoztlan, making a corridor 60 kilometers wide" (170). In other words, 90 percent of the Indians in the area were *not* ensnared. Gruzinski finds that in the cases of two other would-be messiahs, "it was the Indians who rejected and denounced the vision of the man-gods, whom they accused of nonsense and stupidity!" (178). He turns such failures into a new kind of success, delighting in the fact that each of his man-gods "was an exceptional formulation, at the opposite extreme from apathy, withdrawal, and deep deculturation — the fate of those marginal souls who still make up the bulk of the Mexican population" (180). Gruzinski's earlier approach needed those masses to be degraded, their psychology and popular practices dismissed; it required the infantilized bulk of the population to be incapable of creation or innovation. Hence the dilemma: if you abandon such a biased withdrawal of agency from the people, you also have to abandon the romantic, Castaneda-like exaltation of *pipiltzintzintli*-popping curanderos, in which case you condemn your prior research to quaint irrelevance. So instead, in subsequent publications (1994, 2001), Gruzinski discovers that colonial drug use was quite widespread, that Mexico was a "hallucinated society," that indeed the obscure paranoid guru Pérez "revolutionized the terms of the debate" (2001, 202).

In writing this book I took a less tortuous path. Instead of making rare forms of dissociation normative for Mexican cultural creativity, I simply recognize that the altered state of consciousness known as the *borrachera* was an active, inventive, and subversive mode of cultural creativity that was "as good as" any hallucinogen, and infinitely more popular. I did not have to go out on a limb. Examining the evidence without bias, as did Taylor, it becomes quite clear that for almost five post-Conquest centuries the psychoactive drug of choice, consumed massively in every religious celebration in every locality, was fermented agave juice. The alcoholization of the populace might have been strategic on the part of the Spanish "aristocrats of pulque," but it was tactical on the part of the colonized; it truly was adaptive resistance. Michel de Certeau forever removed the mental blinders that made us see consumption as essentially passive:

> Submissive, and even consenting to their subjection, the Indians nevertheless often made of the rituals, representations, and laws imposed upon them something quite different from what their conquerors had in mind; they subverted them not by rejecting or altering them, but by using them with respect to ends and references foreign to the system they had no choice but to accept. . . .

> The strength of their difference lay in procedures of "consumption." (1988, xiii)

Certeau was not specifically referring to beverage consumption, but to consumption as a different variety of popular *production*, a mobile form of intelligence immersed in practice, one capable of subverting the social order through "a clever utilization of time" (39). Dismissive references to "the dreary apathy of alcoholism" cannot survive this insight. Time was the Indians' great invisible resource, and the temporal trickery that alcohol facilitates was quite obviously the tool to be used in the struggle with vice-regal chronopolitics. When the oppressed residents of Mexico City revolted in 1692, booze was blamed, not *pipiltzintzintli*. Time-warping drunkenness was destined to become the truly *popular* and *collective* realm of wondrous events in New Spain, the psychotropic sacrament of the despised majority, the sponsor of dizzying journeys into the afterlife via a mediating vortex, of hurried sexual encounters in back streets, of ritual spousal abuse. One cannot ignore such massive daily forms of alterity and still claim to be an authority on the popular. Certeau's consumption-as-production paradigm goes double for the more mestizoized distillates of the agave, the prized mezcals of Oaxaca or Jalisco. Tequila, like any other toxin worth its salt, restores presence to representation, saturates contemplated objects with meaning, disinters buried scripts, and speaks through the wounds of trauma. Both tequila masters and tequila slaves would agree with this point (Orozco 2003).

Casting aside the elitism and the "apathy" rap, we begin to see that the motivations and dynamics of binge drinking are easily connected to those of the rebellions that flared up and died away *by the hundreds* in colonial and postcolonial Mexico. Elements of deterritorialization, temporal opportunism, thaumaturgy, primary process, truth emergence, and credulity can be found in both psychologies. Alcoholism and Catholic-derived messianism were compatible, and in any number of villages they were mutually reinforcing. The binge-drinking cultures of Yucatán clearly retained a revolutionary potential:

> On November 19, 1761, the Indians of the town of Quisteil, located six leagues from Sotuta, were gathered in a *conjunta*, or meeting, dedicated to planning the celebration of the upcoming feast in honor of the patron saint of the town, Our Lady of the Conception. As was common in the *conjunta*, a lot of liquor had been consumed and many of the participants were drunk. When the meeting was about to end, an Indian named Jacinto Canek proposed that the funds gathered for the next festivity be used to prolong the *conjunta* for another three days. The proposal was enthusiastically received and approved by the townspeople. In the drunken brawl that followed, a ladino merchant named Diego Pacheco was killed

because he refused to sell the Indians the liquor they demanded. (Florescano 1994, 158)

Canek went on to orchestrate his own coronation as Little Moctezuma, King of Mexico. He may have had the same mental problems as Gruzinski's Indian messiahs, but note the favorite psychotropic substance of his followers. We reencounter the same logic of "Don't say no to me" in many other ethnic drinking cultures. Canek's delusions were probably rooted in passages of the Chilam Balam books that "refer not to a Second Coming in the millenarian sense but to a third, fourth, or fifth coming — more accurately, to one in a theoretically infinite series of recreations of the same event" (Farriss 1995, 129). Indeed, time was of the essence. Paranoid messiahs drew their power from the eternal, their tippling followers lived in the present, and powerful clock owners were always one step ahead. In Quisteil the colonial authorities stepped in, stamped out, and violently reimposed chronopolitical order. Taylor recounts other eighteenth-century uprisings that began as collective binges, including one in the town of Tenango (State of Mexico) in 1762. It was sparked by "the district lieutenant's search for contraband liquor on the evening of the patron saint's fiesta. In one house he found many men and women getting drunk around a large pot of tepache [*pulque*]. As he tried to make arrests, the church bells were rung and a multitude of people descended on the house. The lieutenant and his militiamen barely escaped with their lives" (1979, 125). Either the addiction was strong or the locals were very protective of their identity, that is, their calendrical system of gateways to ecstatic self-experiencing.

In the context of post-Conquest adaptive strategies, we should simply expect the state of drunkenness to serve as the matrix for the construction or preservation of very anti-*gachupín* attitudes. Oneiric-confusional *borracheras* that once served as a final line of defense against ethnocidal forces would remain hostile to competing temporal paradigms. In the second half of the eighteenth century, the viceregal government and the Church hierarchy colluded in an effort to "de-Indianize" New Spain via the seizure and sale of property belonging to local lay religious organizations known as *cofradías* — "with the justification that this would avoid the natives' squandering their property on drunken binges, idolatrous feasts, and other excessive expenditures" (Florescano 1994, 182). Clock-watching Bourbon modernization in Mexico involved the deliberate disruption of traditional ritual drinking patterns, but the targeted drinking cultures would have their revenge. I propose the following debate topic: colonial alcohol *dependence* was a major chemical and cultural catalyst for Mexico's eventual *independence* from Spain.

To argue the affirmative, the links in the chain of logic might be as follows. Alcoholization and Catholicization had gone hand-in-glove during the initial viceregal period, however unwittingly. The rapturous, time-collapsing, and apocalyptic aspects of Catholicism were the first to win favor among the indigenes and the strongest and deepest in subsequent centuries. These doctrines were underwritten — made truthful — by *pulque* intoxication during religious festivities. From the earliest days of New Spain, moreover, marginalized native time concepts had found an ally in those of the Franciscans; these in turn derived from breakaway Cisterican abbot Joachim de Fiore (1145–1202): "While meditating in his Calabrian retreat on the mystery of the Trinity and how it related to the time-process he had moments of intense spiritual illumination that led him to formulate a new millenarian philosophy of history" (Whitrow 1988, 81). In New Spain, Fray Jerónimo de Mendieta vehemently criticized the greed and corruption of incipient mercantile capitalism; some of the missionaries seemed as addicted to their eschatological fantasies as the Indians were to *tepache* (Phelan 1972). Both kinds of practices allowed hatred and anger to accumulate around traumatized psychic zones, from a psychoanalytic viewpoint. Marginalized class and ethnic identities were also revitalized through the alcoholized merriment of street songs. Carnivalesque incoherence articulated with other deterritorializing flows, in Deleuzo-speak, and by the dawn of the nineteenth century a subversive cultural cocktail had found numerous fans among the friars, as shown by Inquisition records (Rivera Ayala 1994, 43). Dominican Fray Servando Teresa de Mier undercut every rationale of Spanish rule with his "upside-down gaze" and radical Guadalupan sermons (Rotker 1998, lvi). Exile to Spain was his reward. Meanwhile, in several Mexican monasteries, alcohol, cards, and women had become an alternative Holy Trinity.

Eager to modernize, Bourbon authorities tried to crush the indigenous and mestizo *cofradía* networks in which time-warping was the end and heavy drinking the means. In other words, the proletarians were already in possession of Certeau's counterhegemonic "tactics," which oppose hegemonic strategies through "a clever *utilization of time*, of the opportunities it presents and also of the play that it introduces into the foundations of power" (Certeau 1988, 39, emphasis in original). If knowledge is power, embodied knowledge is even more powerful, analogous to the "materially effective practical negation of the dominant reproductive structures" recommended by Marxists (Mészáros 1989, 408). Is there a more practical material/bodily negation of dominant temporal or spatial strategies than tactical drunkenness? Attempts to sober up local groups by force had proved disastrous, and the endemic corruption of local officials made alcohol governance a farce. How, then, could we not see Mexican sacrofestive binge drinking, along with the grievances and the rebellious/mythic fantasies it nurtured, as an essential impetus for the chaotic, *trancelike* independence movement begun by the messianic priest Miguel Hidalgo on September 16, 1810?

If the logic chain I have forged is strong enough, we are now in a position to reconfigure and upgrade Victor Turner's interpretation of Hidalgo as "social drama" (1974, 98–155).

It is possible that the religious, even prophetic side of Hidalgo's nature responded only too vigorously, if somnambulistically, to the ardor of his Indians and their violence in shaking off three centuries of Spanish oppression. Certainly the unconscious and irrational components of the insurrection rapidly came to flood out those of conscious calculation. But in this, perhaps, lies the secret of its compelling power over subsequent Mexican history and its potent influence on Mexican art and literature. (Turner 1974, 110)

Several pages later, horrified by the slaughter of Spaniards that accompanied Hidalgo's putsch, Turner reserves liminality to the "criollo middle position" and denies it to the indigenes (118–19). This is a strange, unnecessary evisceration of his own concept. The trail of mutilated white bodies from Guanajuato to Guadalajara (Krauze 1997, 97–99) strongly suggests that the insurgent priest and his Indians were immersed in fanatical sacred time and acting in accordance. There is nothing more anti-structural than a bloodbath. And many a Mexican has killed or been killed in states verging on psychological automatism, without achieving communitas. Turner did not use PTSD concepts, but he did speak of "the cumulative experience of whole peoples whose deepest material and spiritual needs have for long been denied by power-holding elites" (1974, 110). Had the indigenous communities "worked through" their traumas in a clinical setting, Hidalgo might have had a hard time recruiting followers, or perhaps their submerged personalities would not have been so murderous.

Binge drinking in peasant and indigenous communities did not come to an end with independence from Spain, nor did rebellious grievance nurturing and occasional messianic outbursts. During the period 1819 to 1906, serious uprisings took place in Chiapas, the State of Mexico, Chihuahua, Guerrero, Hidalgo, Jalisco, Morelos, Michoacán, Nayarit, Oaxaca, Puebla, San Luis Potosí, Veracruz, and Zacatecas (Reina 1980). In *The Power of God against the Guns of Government* (1998), Paul Vanderwood grapples with the role played by mestizo messianism in the rebellion of Tomóchic (Chihuahua), violently crushed by Porfirian forces in 1892. Vanderwood's study triggered a number of high-profile forums and debates that cannot be gone into here, but it is clear that the *tomochitecos* — genuine victims of Porfirian modernization — sought relief in social trance and charismatic leadership. Many preferred to seek an apocalyptic death right here, right now, in contrast with the slower alliance with the death instinct that characterized a nearby binge drinking culture, the Tarahumaras. In both groups, however, we find a structurally similar, apparitional mode of thought and the same legacy of time-warping, intergenerational grievance nurturing seen above. As Gilbert Joseph notes, "Making sense of the consciousness of participants in rather fleeting moments of rural collective action — episodes that rarely leave a cultural trace — is no easy task" (1999, 365). This holds double for rural collective binge drinking episodes, obviously, but I think we can at least discern some of the traces, especially the one whereby the authorization of eternity itself is acceded to in the fleeting moments.

"Group-fantasy is not 'like' a dissociated trance-state," Stein insists,"it is a trance in origin, structure, and function" (1987, 385). Other experts speak of "social trances" and link the success of charismatic leaders to their ability to activate unconscious schemas in people who survived childhood by conforming to arbitrary authority (Berghold 1991). Was Mexican peasant psychology already quasi hypnotic? Norman Cohn's exploration of messianic conduct throughout history might support such a notion (1961, 1975), Weston LaBarre's ghost dance phenomena might be relevant (1972), René Girard's "magico-persecutory thought" would be germane (1982), and equally apropos would be William Runyan's study of stress-induced cognitive distorsions at the group level (1993). A social trance is hedonistic (at least in the short run), internally adaptive, and brings pleasure to the people entranced. Guilt is extinguished, anxieties relieved, feelings of helplessness appeased. To introject "higher" demands is to lessen the amount of psychic energy invested in defense (Berghold 1991, 237). One need no longer deny aggressive impulses if they are perceived as desires of a superior will. Bloody deeds that once occurred in the name of religion thereby reappear in the name of revolution. "The revolutionary pole of group fantasy becomes visible in the power to experience insitutions themselves as mortal, to destroy them or change them according to the articulations of desire and the social field, by making the death instinct into a veritable institutional creativity" (Deleuze and Guattari 1983, 63). Pick a Mexican village — Quisteil, Tenango, Dolores, Tomóchic — in my view, the predisposition to social trance was always there, held in place by shame-inducing racism, autonomy-crushing business practices, mock-violent folk customs, grievance nurturing, and generations of binge drinking, with the stressful epochs of Mexican history as a backdrop. A *borrachera* was (and is) do-it-yourself messianism: no waiting required. I challenge students of "peasant consciousness" to prove me wrong.

In laboring people of flesh and blood, trauma-evolved constellations are characterized by certain symptoms. These symptoms are noticed by the elite but are liable to be interpreted within frameworks of prejudice. Alan Knight analyzes thirty years of Mexican thought (1910–1940) and finds a troubling development among *indigenistas* who impute to the Indians "a collective psychology, distinctively Indian, the product of centuries of oppression, transmitted through generations. In its more extreme forms, this theory makes Indians the carriers of a kind of Jungian collective unconscious no less determinant of their being than the old biological imperatives. And, given that racism involves the imputation of such ascribed and immutable characteristics, such psychological determinism seems to me to be racist, as was its biological predecessor" (1997/1990, 94). Knight is certainly right to assail Samuel Ramos and his ilk, but he then extends his psychological-determinism-is-racism parameter to all who have written of trauma, collective memory, or collective psychological legacies (94–95). In so doing he throws the baby out with the bathwater. Of course there is no such thing as a national psyche that can suffer or be healed, but there is such a thing as the cross-generational or intergenerational transmission of trauma that can affect large networks or cohorts of people inside of a nation. Today this phenomenon is being investigated throughout the world (Robben and Suárez-Orozco 2000; Brewin 2003; Cairns and Roe 2003; Zerubavel 2003). A groups' reactions to historical misfortune vary in terms of the culture and the trauma, but the reactions are never limited to one generation. Israeli psychiatrist Rena Moses-Hrushovski (1996) describes the fixative transhistorical patterns in terms of "deployment" — the psychological tendency for individuals and entire generations to "remain in the bunker long after the war is over," stubbornly preserving their dignity by allowing no past wrong to be forgotten. Grievance nurturing characterizes both religious and secular realms of culture in Mexico, according to historian Luis González y González:

> The official martyrology of Mexico is, perhaps, the most populated one on earth. Where else do we find a more copious recollection of deaths and catastrophes? People and government alike find recreation in recalling the macabre manner in which some of the nation's heroes became cadavers. Like the Jews, we Mexicans take pleasure in remembering calamities and persecutions. (1998, 77)

Now how in the world could such mulling over and exaggeration of past humiliations and defeats be pleasurable? One possible reason has been supplied by David Shapiro in his study of psychological rigidity (1981). The actual goal of the chronically aggrieved, he writes, is the compensatory attainment of a "moral victory," whereby a passively experienced shame or inferiority is transformed into an active stance, a "principled act of will" or a "martyr's pride" (1981, 119). The relevance of this to Mexico can scarcely be exaggerated. González y González affirms that the "masochistic" way of remembering collective events is one of the chief modalities of Mexican cultural expression as a whole (1998, 73).

The peculiar pleasure of the process results from a mastery of shame. The shame itself gets collected over time and preserved in traumatic neural networks, mental hells where the past is neither forgiven nor forgotten. People are good at repressing threatening ideas and emotions, observes Christopher Bollas, but the result is a growing "colony of banished ideas — a group that paradoxically gains in strength as it is oppressed" (1992, 73). In Mexico, as glimpsed by Malcolm Lowry, "remorse haunts the whirlpool where the past's not washed up dead and black and dry but whirls in its gulf forever, to no relief" (Lowry 2000, 128). The processes of traumatic nucleation and "masochistic" grievance nurturing are surely relevant to the particular character of cultural memory in Mexico. Drinking binges do not dispel these processes, quite obviously; they preserve and exacerbate them. A single individual's *borrachera* can serve as a private echo chamber for local or regional traumatic networking.

Emerging national leaders of the 1920s sought to monopolize cultural recreations of the bloody years of civil chaos, offering monuments, tombs, and icons of Zapata to unify the nation, but no monopoly on memories was achieved. There were simply too many competing mnemonic traditions in circulation — "each with their own heroes and villains, sacred and bitter anniversaries, myths and symbols" (Benjamin 2000, 21). Let us add that memories are in bodies as well as in minds, that group *borracheras* remained important means of access to their body-minds as heritage sites, with every mental or physical scar meaningful. Men that would themselves become icons embodied this process while still alive. "Zapata was the living memory of Anenecuilco," writes Krauze (1997, 279), a village in the heart of Morelos that had never forgotten its land grievances throughout the colonial period, independence, and the Porfiriato. "Midway through 1910, Zapata carried out his tiny local revolution and took back the land lost in 1607" (281). Jesús Sotelo Inclán (1970/1943) saw Zapata as the culmination of a long chain of precursors who passed the memory-torch forward in time. If this does not qualify as the intergenerational transmission of trauma, what does? Octavio Paz was correct to emphasize the profoundly restorationist impulse of Zapata and his followers, their yearning for a past golden age never quite grasped by eager futurists of the Left (2000/1950, 289). Thus it can come as no surprise to learn that Mexico's charismatic icon of agrarian reform was also an able practitioner of alcoholized rural recalcitrance, as described by Alan Knight:

> Zapata quit Mexico City and sloped off to his headquarters in the small provincial town of Tlatizapán, where he drank, smoked, socialized, fathered children, and attended cockfights. . . . In this, as in so much, Zapata was typical rather than exceptional. Other popular leaders swilled pulque or aguardiente, danced through the night, and played the torero in improvised bullfights. Their educated advisors, would-be civilian gray eminences, were shocked and confounded. (1990, 239–40).

Let us note that Zapata did not use alcohol "to forget" what needed to be remembered, and indeed his macho carousing enhanced his charisma and status among aggrieved common men. We should also remember that it was the treacherous Guajardo's repeated offer of free beer that finally persuaded Zapata to ride into Chinameca one April afternoon in 1919 (Martínez 1996, 98).

The social-memory role of the individual drunkard has been documented by ethnographers. In the village of Amilpa (Oaxaca), Philip Dennis found intoxicated men enjoying much greater verbal latitude than their sober fellows, all to the benefit of local society. Thanks to one inebriated *amilpeño*, an injustice never digested by the village was finally served up at a banquet given in honor of the district school superintendent:

> When [the superintendent] had made his own pompous after-dinner speech, full of flowery promises, a drunk who had been listening on the periphery of the crowd lurched forward and stood at the foot of the banquet table. He called the superintendent a liar, asked why none of the previous promises had been fulfilled, and shouted that he wouldn't believe any of the new promises being made. There was embarrassment among the crowd, but also delight. The drunk had forcefully stated the village's real position, which differed considerably from the polite front being presented by the village authorities at the banquet table. (1975, 857)

Dennis demonstrates that the drunkards of Oaxaca played a useful, even institutionalized "anti-role" that temporarily subverted the many hypocrisies of everyday life (860). Of particular interest was a skilled social commentator and public gossip named Demetrio, much in demand around Amilpa: "Once drunk, he speaks in rhyming couplets, stringing couplets together into barbed and witty speeches" (858). The popular song corpus makes antiheroes out of town drunks; one *corrido* portrays "Pancho Rivera" stumbling along the street in his dirty hat and ragged pants, drinking tequila even in church. "The whole town gives him a wide berth/he's very dangerous owing to his loose tongue."

Famous works of twentieth-century Mexican fiction reenact such popular expectations and definitions. Mariano Azuela's documentary novel of revolutionary upheaval features a vagabond poet named Valderrama whose role is quite similar to that of Demetrio in Amilpa: both articulate their alcoholic insights in pithy epigrams. Grievance-nursing and alcohol go together in Azuela's account; his revolutionary binge drinkers are scarred, touchy, and in no way forgetful of decades-old debts demanding reimbursement in blood. In many novels obsessed with the betrayal of the revolution, the cultural injustice collecting is further fed by all manner of conspiracy theories (e.g., Francisco Martín Moreno's bestseller *México negro*, 2000/1986). Imbibing and recalling go together in Mexico: in *The Death of Artemio Cruz* (1964), Carlos Fuentes shows familiarity with the cultural pattern: "In the dark he felt for the bottle of mezcal. But it would not serve forgetfulness but to quicken memory. He would return to the beach and the rocks while the white alcohol burned inside him. . . . Liquor was good for the exploding of lies, pretty lies" (1964, 75–76). In this particular case, the undead Artemio Cruz goes on to remember how he really met his beloved — not on a beach, as previously confabulated, but during a rape he perpetrated while his troops ravaged Sonora.

Eventually the truth will come out, in fiction and in reality, thanks to mezcal's magical truth-effects. All over Mexico, binge-drinking cultures and individuals found their own way of exploding the "inauthenticity" that supposedly characterized Mexican life, in the view of disaffected dramatists like Rodolfo Usigli. Gramscian, top-down, body-less accounts of identity construction can spot a few high-cultural traces of trauma, but they miss the mother lode of cultural intimacy altogether (Herzfeld 1997). Roger Bartra ably compiles national character myths, but ignores their ritual embodiment — surely a mortal sin in an anthropologist. Whatever serves to master shame will *necessarily* figure more prominently in discourses of identity formation, from one end of the color-class spectrum to the other. The alcoholic liquefaction of trauma-induced shame is a major sociomnemonic technique in Mexico, as useful as any other and probably more popular.

Chapter 5
Allá en el Rancho Grande

The Aztec temples were toppled, the Valley of Mexico subjugated, socio-mnemonic reprogramming well underway. Bulls and horses proved crucial to the Conquest as a day-to-day phenomenon, an endless series of gritty micro-conquests not contemplated by the Spanish crown's idealistic *Leyes de Burgos*. "From the moment of its introduction, the bull posed a menace to the Indian community. Throughout central and southern Mexico bulls invaded Indian cornfields and destroyed crops; indeed, Spaniards repeatedly ran their herds into Indian lands with the aim of driving the Indians away. Villages and entire regions were depopulated in this manner. . . . As elsewhere in Mexico and Guatemala, beef butchers were Spaniards as well" (Ingham 1986, 146). Much of the colonialist "dirty work" would be undertaken by an emerging meat-loving class of poor whites and *castas* who steadily opened up new avenues of economic activity, fair and foul, under the auspices of well-connected Spaniards. The job usually called for the occupation of indigenous lands previously depopulated by bulls or epidemics; in many cases enough Indians had survived to put up a fight. The basic model for future economic development was already in place by 1580, the year that marks consolidation of the Zacatecas area as a vast new source of mineral wealth. Men were needed to occupy and cultivate rural zones on the periphery of Zacatecas and other mining centers. As Esteban Barragán points out, only men who had not found something better, men with little to lose and everything to gain — like the first *conquistadores* themselves — accepted the risks and hardships of these peripheral areas (1999, 72). More or less nomadic, more or less successful, what they had in common was the appellative *ranchero* and the eternal readiness to pick up and go elsewhere, to some other sierra or borderland or *frente de colonización*. Small but ambitious ranchero groups emerged as a kind of firewall against the fierce warriors of the so-called Gran Chichimeca, the mountains and desert plateaus farther north. *Ranchero* gender identity was inseparable from rough and risky outdoor labor, and their gun-toting physical mobility came to be synonymous with relentless social mobility. *Rancheros* who had settled as tenants on the corner of some vast hacienda sometimes waited a century before receiving title to the lands on which they worked and raised their families and livestock — hence the rationality of long-term memory and grievance-nurturing techniques. Many haciendas were big enough at the time of original creation to evolve into as many as two hundred sizeable, independent *ranchos*, also called *rancherías* (Barragán 1997, 90). The new owners referred to themselves as "Spanish," but for the most part they were mestizos or *criollos amestizados* (mestizoized Creoles), even blacks and mulattoes. They shared "the same passion for horses and bulls, firearms and private ownership of the land" (70). They were not peons, in other words, but proto-bourgeois groups who underwent an intense process of social differentiation but retained a consistently patriarchal system of values, honor codes, and drinking customs that remain influential to this day and quite relevant to areas of Mexican culture in the United States.

Ranchero communities were peripheral to the dominant economic order, and in general they had tenuous and conflict-ridden dealings with the powers-that-were. To this day most *rancheros* hold that the best government is no government at all. But they spoke Spanish, they accepted Spanish values, and in short order they developed a racial consciousness quite different from that of the indigenous communities they encroached upon. *Rancheros* were "obsessed" with the symbolic opposition between whites and Indians and the qualities presumed to belong to each stock (Barragán 1997, 98). *Rancheros* had no patience with Indian communal structures, and certainly no respect for the sort of work they did (e.g., handicrafts were considered "old woman's work"). *Rancheros* did keep their distance, however, from indigenous sorcerors and shamans (229). Alcoholic beverages constituted a major category of symbolic opposition. Originally, *mezcal* was the Nahuatl word for "baked agave." This particular foodstuff predated not only corn and frijoles but New World agriculture itself. Knowledge of pottery was not necessary for its preparation or consumption; baked agave was so widespread and important in ancient Mexico that Bruman calls it "the universal understory upon which the later food resources were superimposed" (2000/1938, 12). Mezcal in the sense of distilled liquor, however, was unknown to both Indians and Spaniards until a few unknown men in the shadows created it, certainly within the lifetime of Hernán Cortés (1485–1547). As a substance that emerged when Indian modes of maguey processing met Hispano-Arabic distillation techniques, mezcal is an apt and traditional emblem of Mexico's racial evolution. Another symbol of *mestizaje*, the Virgin of Guadalupe, appeared to Juan Diego during the same time period and left her portrait on a cloak made from maguey fibers. In what follows I retain the Spanish spelling for mezcal to avoid any confusion with mescal beans, mescal buttons, or mescaline.

The small- or large-scale production of mezcal, as well as the ideology that emerged over time to encourage its consumption, are inseparable from the "*ranchificación*" process described above. Scholars surmise that New Spain's first mezcal distilleries were located at the bottom of *barrancas*, or ravines, where water was abundant and species of wild agave grew nearby. Stills called *alambiques* employed a rudimentary apparatus of clay pots to heat the fermenting maguey juice and condense the sweet alcoholic vapors. Ethnohistorian Manuel Durazo recently found the people of Iturbide (Nuevo León) elaborating mezcal with the very same equipment (1998, 334). It was and is a "low-tech" operation, a labor-intensive but also low-risk endeavor. Even now clandestine stills located in remote areas permit small mezcal and tequila manufacturers to elude taxation. In colonial times, men who set up stills in ravines were non-Indian scofflaws who lived close to the land with makeshift technical knowledge and eager apprentices. These men, *rancheros* or ex-*rancheros*, knew how to get into the remote ravines and then out again with cumbersome jugs of liquor. The microregional "test markets" for the initial product included themselves, other white and mestizo invaders of the hinterlands, and the occasional indigene persuaded to sample a much more potent derivative of the ancient maguey. Mexico's first moonshiners could not have failed to notice that consumption of their product had dramatic social consequences, clearly observable within a few decades of the Iberian takeover.

Although *pulque* and mezcal were sons of the same divine plant, they encoded different ethnohistorical trajectories and connoted disparate lifestyles — rooted the first, relatively rootless the second. The emerging *ranchero*/mezcal ethnicity endured and thrived by adapting itself to New Spain's main model of economic development, the one linked with power elites, urbanism, mineral wealth, and exportation (Luna 1999, 69). This model set the overall pace and rhythm of growth in conjunction with incipient transnational capitalism, generating certain domestic demands that less sophisticated models were in a position to supply. For this reason, the *ranchero* modus vivendi and its products were almost always integrated into a regional supply network. Military garrisons, mining operations, towns, and fledgling provincial capitals had to be supplied with food and drink, by necessity. Certain zones were thereby poised to prosper for basic geographical reasons, for example, the Guadalajara area with its numerous *rancherías* and a mezcal-producing hamlet named Santiago de Tequila. Situated on the road that connected Mexico City to the Pacific port of San Blas, the town was perfect for supplying colonias and even missions in northwestern Mexico. The special-tasting mezcal of Santiago de Tequila helped white men, including white men of the cloth like Jesuits and Franciscans, to bear the solitary burdens of their ongoing civilizing efforts (Muriá 1994, 20). Routes for smuggling tax-free mezcal to mining centers in nothern Mexico remained active until well into the twentieth century; by the time the gringos learned their lesson and prohibited Prohibition, large quantities of high-quality mezcal had been smuggled across the border. During the 1920s the Texas Rangers were authorized to shoot Mexican smugglers on sight, and frequently did (Durazo 1998, 328). In New Spain, in sum, the evolving demand for mezcal and other types of alcohol signified robust but perhaps parasitical economic growth. "In 1778, in the mining areas alone, it was estimated that 80,000 barrels of *chinguirito* (cheap domestic cane alcohol), 20,000 barrels of Spanish brandy, 10,000 barrels of domestic anise liqueur, and 1,000 barrels of Spanish liqueur were consumed. . . . Officials of the Juzgado de Bebidas Prohibidas claimed in the mid-eighteenth century that cane alcohol was virtually impossible to control because the distilling equipment was simple and easy to conceal" (Taylor 1979, 55). Naturally these numbers pale in comparison to the quantities of *pulque* that were being produced and consumed, quite legally, in the same areas; *pulque* would continue to be Mexico's most common alcoholic beverage well into the twentieth century. A nineteenth-century Mexican geographer claimed it was easy to distinguish *pulque* drinkers from enthusiasts of *chinguirito*. "Those in the first category were dull, slow, and belligerent, whereas those in the second were joyful, resolute, and content" (García Cubas 2000/1904, 73). An aficionado of distilled liquor products, García Cubas was nauseated by the lack of hygiene in Mexico City's *pulque* transportation system, that is, swollen smelly pigskins carried on dusty mules by unkempt drovers. "It seems incredible that so much filth produces so much wealth!" (73).

Protectionist Spanish kings repeatedly reminded their New World subjects that liquor distillation was a peninsular prerogative, but to no avail. The booming supply of domestic distillates therefore provides a good example of the tactical dissembling that characterized the Creole class in their dealings with the peninsular Spaniards who ran Mexico. González y González prefers the term *discreción* for the complex of traits that, in his view, constitute one of the great "modalities" of Mexican culture (1998, 58–64). The components of *discreción* included smoldering hatred of Spaniards, a readiness to hide one's true intentions, and a talent for hypocritical courtesy rituals. González y González asserts that upper-class whites born in Mexico quickly adopted lying as one of their essential survival mechanisms (64). Here we find a striking difference between the value systems of the *ranchero* groups that distilled mezcal and the Creole notables who set up illegal supply networks during the viceregal period. Like the hardnosed Spaniards themselves, *rancheros* were known for calling bread bread and wine wine; their *palabra de hombre* or word-of-man honor traditions provided a certain degree of stability in areas where viceregal authority was weak or nonexistent. Creoles were "discreet," but truth-telling was and is the hallmark of *ranchero* culture. There are literally hundreds of *ranchera* and *norteño* songs that elaborate on the words "*Te juro*" ("I vow to you"), including "I vow to you that I'll stop drinking, gambling, and whoring."

Many varieties of bootleg mezcal were as good as any distillate imported from Spain (Durazo 1998, 333). In colonial and modern times alike, wealthy *rancheros* financed *ranchos de vino* — itinerant cooperatives that went from one agave-growing area to another with their mules and stills. Experienced *ranchero* distillers were in great demand, since they knew how to make the most of the agaves available in a given locale, expertly tinkering with the *alambiques* to infuse more proof into the final product. There were clients everywhere. With strong roots in the world of *rancherías*, the social class that eventually specialized in agave distillates had traits that set them apart from "business-as-usual" in colonial Mexico. These qualities would one day loom large in the formation of the nationalistic imaginary. The original *ranchero* personality configuration was by no means imaginary, however, but eminently material-historical, and mezcal played an essential role in the maintenance of kinship and social ties. What clinical experts call "alcohol expectancies" were forged in *ranchero* rites of passage — baptisms, weddings, funerals, and *matanzas* (seasonal pig-slaughtering fiestas). Locally distilled mezcal was their drink of choice, prized for its euphoriant and medicinal qualities: *Para todo mal, mezcal, y para todo bien, también* (For everything bad, mezcal, and also for everything good). In his cross-cultural survey of drunkenness, Peter Field equated an increase in family or group hierarchization with a decrease in drunkenness (1991/1962, 103). This was decidedly not the case in *ranchero* culture, where intact patriarchal structures were celebrated and *renewed* with periodic, no-holds-barred drinking.

The throats that were really thirsty for the so-called wine of the mezcal belonged to the mixed-race populations of larger towns and mining areas like Zacatecas or San Luis Potosí. It is especially ironic that *ranchificación*, an eminently rural phenomenon, was crucial to the emergence of an urban *alcoholización* that was simultaneously ally of and obstacle to progress. Powerful elites sought to control the pace and rhythm of modernization in Mexico, but at every turn they had to contend with workers still entranced by a special, preindustrial temporal consciousness derived from festive inebriation. Fiesta cycles were dear to the men and women drawn into the silver-mining machine; in the new frontier towns, their time-mapping modes immediately clashed with those of the town fathers (usually peninsular Spaniards). As had been the case since the beginning of New Spain, the streets themselves were the space of this tug-of-war, this emerging "resistant adaptation" (Beezley, Martin, and French 1994). Despised groups who dominated the streets but nothing else — Indians from Sonora or Oaxaca, mestizos, Afro-Mexicans, refugees, renegades, *pícaros,* and drifters — were all exiled from "the intricate web of traditional relationships that had sustained customary rituals in their home communities," notes Cheryl Martin (1994, 109). Two important festival ingredients were readily available, however — alcohol and bulls — both supplied by *rancheros*. Bullfighting enthusiasm was so great among the populace that employers were afraid to curtail the events lest the workers "revolt or migrate elsewhere" (102). Martin does credit the Spanish founders of the Chihuahua cabildo with tight control over popular culture; they limited the proliferation of many fiestas and kept unruly Carnival celebrations out of town altogether (99). But the elites of New Spain, small and beset with infighting, could not monopolize the organization of urban space. Carnival or no carnival, daily dancing, gambling, and womanizing were common in Chihuahua and such activities were invariably accompanied by alcohol. So-called *mezcal minero* was the strongest part of the underground economy; it was resistant adaptation in a baked clay container (there were no bottles at the time). It renewed sacred rural memory links; it promoted alternative uses of city spaces, e.g., public defecation (Viqueira 1999:98). Mezcal epitomizes the outflanking of Foucault wrought by Certeau: "The language of power is in itself 'urbanizing,' but the city is left prey to contradictory movements that counterbalance and combine themselves outside the reach of panoptic power" (Certeau 1988, 95). Such weapons of the weak played a significant role in the final downfall of Spanish town fathers, as seen in chapter 4, and remain crucial to today's thirsty urban nomads discussed in chapter 9.

Mexican independence from Spain accelerated the *ranchificación* process in ways good and bad. The breakup of huge haciendas was accompanied by an even more aggressive annexation of lands once occupied by indigenous groups. In 1810 there were six thousand *ranchos*; a century later, fifty thousand. There were more *rancheros* than ever, and most preferred to reside in newly created towns at least several months out of the year (Barragán 1997, 39). These were Spanish-speaking towns, whiter in outlook if not in color, free in a folk liberal way, suspicious of the central government, possessed of an entrepreneurial mindset quite unlike that of the old *hacendado* class. At the same time, interestingly, *ranchero*-style Catholicism was more orthodox than that of the indigenes and campesinos combined. Numerous members of the Mexican clergy hailed from *ranchero* communities that would never share the anticlerical views of Mexican liberals or priest-baiting ideologues of the Mexican Revolution. From a strictly economic vantage point, however, Mexican liberals "coincided in seeing the rancheros — the small independent producers — as the most dynamic element in society" (39). The *ranchero* value system was destined to emerge intact from jarring decades of uncontrolled social and economic change. *Ranchero* drinking customs were inseparable from a phallocentric Ibero-Mexican honor code and an ethos of horse-mounted individualism that seemed spectacular to unlucky hacienda peons.

By the middle of the nineteenth century, most of the maguey fields near Santiago de Tequila were controlled by *rancheros* specializing in the production of *vino mezcal*. Less than half of what they produced went beyond the borders of Jalisco; mezcal was made in many other parts of Mexico and competition was fierce. The patronal festivals and marketing fairs of other localities were key to achieving initial brand-name recognition for "Tequila." Jalisco had the good fortune to be the native region of a superior species of bluish-tinted agave (now known as *Agave tequilana Weber*). And, the biggest anomaly of all, these special agaves were not being used for *pulque*. *Pulque*, we must stress, was still the psychoactive beverage of choice, both in "Deep Mexico" and in Mexico City, where it was served in literally hundreds of pulquerías and enjoyed by all ethnicities. Indigenous communities and huge *haciendas pulqueras* located in the states of Hidalgo, Tlaxcala, and Mexico specialized in the elaboration and delivery of *pulque* to the future megacity. In Jalisco, however, *ranchero*-led assaults on the indigenous population had led to an abandonment of *pulque*-production techniques, along with the other uses once made of the agaves. The plants still covered communal lands in great abundance, nonetheless (Luna Zamora 1999, 37). Jalisco was home to numerous closely knit *ranchero* families ready and willing to upgrade into dynasties; they now competed to appropriate those tribal lands, turn the remaining Indians into peons and maguey-harvesters, and set up distilleries.

The career of one Cenobio Sauza sums up the evolution of the tequila industry in the latter part of the nineteenth century. Born landless in Tecolotlán (Jalisco), he moved to Tequila in 1858 to work in the distillery of José Antonio Gómez Cuervo. Sauza rose to the rank of director, scrimping until he had enough capital to buy five mule-driven wagons and set himself up as a regional distributor of mezcal. In the meantime, the aforementioned Gómez Cuervo had become Jalisco's governor and an outspoken supporter of agroindustrial alcoholization. Cenobio Sauza — still a nobody, a *don Nadie* — finally bought his first distillery in 1873 and thereafter devoted himself to the relentless acquisition of maguey fields (Agráz 1963, 20). By the decade of the 1880s Sauza was one of three tequila entrepreneurs in a position to import high-tech distilling equipment from abroad, in preparation for the boom they knew was coming with the construction of Mexico's railroad system. The Guadalajara to Mexico City line was completed in 1888; one year later, the tequila tycoons of Jalisco had already shipped 238,458 liters of their precious mezcal to the nation's capital. By then everyone was calling Sauza "don Cenobio," an honorific befitting a man who owned five million maguey plants. That was a million more than the governor. The new equipment Sauza installed in "La Antigua Cruz" allowed him to produce ten thousand barrels of tequila per year (Agráz 1963, 32–37). His greatest coup was yet to come: in 1896, making full use of the loopholes permitted to elite Mexicans by don Porfirio, don Cenobio obtained the last agave lands of Jalisco still in tribal hands (Luna 1999, 107). Sauza had finally bested his powerful competitors, the Cuervos.

It was the culmination of a process begun centuries earlier: de-Indian-ization, colonization, fragmentation, privatization, more de-Indianiza-tion, and commercialization. The period known as *el Porfiriato* (1876–1911) was characterized by a flawed but functional articulation of Mexico's two macroeconomic models — one accelerating the pace of life, the other helping society adjust to it via temporary time-outs that often involved the "squandering" of workers' energies. The tequila barons of Jalisco were part of the regime's business expansion but, at this point in Mexican cultural history, their product was not an identity sign of the elite. Let us crash a party attended by Porfirian Mexico's most affluent people, recreated for us by genial historian William Beezley:

> Honoring Díaz's birthday in 1891, a committee composed of the nation's most important government and business leaders arranged a remarkable formal dinner, concert, and dance for some five hun-dred guests, including municipal presidents from across the coun-try, in the National Theater. Only honored males had seats at the tables arranged on the theater floor, although their wives and daughters enjoyed the event from theater boxes. The elaborate menu, presented in French, featured Spanish sherry followed by seven French wines and concluded with Cognac Martell. The con-cert, on the other hand, featured Italian composers, especially Gio-acchino Rossini. (1994, 180)

Alcohol facilitates the instantiation of preferred versions of the self, fictive but not necessarily false; this instantiation is especially effective in the con-text of an identity-corroborating social event. Add to this the urgent mood of *simulación* (dissembling or role-playing) that characterized the Euro-phile monied classes under don Porfirio. Octavio Paz claimed that Mexi-can elites shared nothing of importance with their progressive foreign counterparts, only an unrequited "unilateral imitation of France" in mat-ters of taste (2000/1950, 276). Let us recognize what a convincing imita-tion it must have been, however, after one glass of Sauterne, another of Chateau Laffitte, another of Chambertin, then a bottle of Champagne. The Porfirian elite's fictional self-construction was enhanced by drinking pricy liquors in luxurious settings on prestigious occasions — one of the innu-merable banquets, balls, or concerts that regime-courting groups orga-nized to pay homage to Díaz. A newspaper artist depicted a sumptuous feast at the Escuela de Minas in Mexico City: forty elegantly-dressed gen-tlemen lifting their glasses to don Porfirio, uniformed waiters rushing to refill them (Krauze and Zerón-Medina 1993, 39). Perhaps French wine served the same function as Franco-Mexican positivism — to keep people from noticing that their President had no clothes, that is, no real legiti-macy or popular mandate. Perhaps fine cognac narcotized the *mauvaise conscience* that Paz says they suffered from (2000/1950, 276). Many future intellectuals of the Revolution did start out as the spoiled bohemian scions of families living the francophonic Porfirian good life (Blanco 1977, 30).

To recall Gell's equation: RESOURCES + TIME = EVENT TO BE CONSUMED. The resources available to the "Porfirian smart set," as Beezley calls them, were considerable, many of them confiscated from the Catholic Church or indigenous communities over the decades. With the exception of the bullfight, the kind of events useful to upper-class identity construction had veered away from those of traditional Catholicism: "Ostentation through consumption replaced community ceremonial sponsorship as the measure of social status. Private celebration of holidays reflected the individual character of economic activities as opportunities for personal profits increased dramatically during the dictatorship" (Beezley 1994, 179). In conjunction with the magic of group consensus and the right date on the calendar, the substances consumed would have produced all the somatic self-verification one could wish for. A guest at the Porfirian party mentioned above, or one of the next nineteen birthdays celebrated in a similar manner, would have felt himself very *belle époque*, not backwards or gauche. Perhaps he would have raised his glass to don Porfirio's young wife, doña Carmelita, credited with the "bleaching" of her mestizo husband (181).

Meanwhile, back at some vast hacienda, the unbleached peons would be reaching paradise with *pulque* or *aguardiente*. The regime's well-wrought facade of scientific progress and European manners had a back story: regressive neofeudal social stratification. When Maximilian died, so did his plan to reestablish the juridic personality of indigenous communities and force *hacendados* to return lands they had usurped. Under Díaz the usurpation would not only be condoned but accelerated, until a sizeable country lay mostly in the hands of 830 landowners. The *gachupines* were back, with the blessings of don Porfirio; in Morelos, Indian towns a thousand years old were devoured by the modern machinery of Spanish-owned sugar plantations. Elsewhere, haciendas as large as one hundred thousand hectares "were entities that consumed their own products, closed up within themselves in time and space, more aristocratic luxuries than business ventures" (Krauze 1997, 219). This rural combination of autonomy and time-freezing, much pondered by urban writers, was facilitated by the fact that most haciendas produced their own supplies of rum and bulls.

One historic irony of bullfighting was its enthusiastic support among poor masses who never would have chosen it as a way to escape poverty. Resigned to their lot and "to the slow battle with the paltriness of life," peasants and workers were nonetheless willing to deify those few who were not resigned nor inclined to hard work (Hoyos y Vinent 1914, 223). Bullfighters were men with nothing to lose and something to prove, and their suicidal valor, rarely watched in a state of sobriety, bipolarized rural proletarian psychology throughout the nineteenth century. Mazzantini, a matador who had become a political boss in Spain, was the first Spanish bullfighter of stature to travel to Mexico. In the bullring of Puebla, he dedicated his first bull to the top Mexican matador of the moment, Ponciano Díaz Salinas. The two matadors embraced diplomatically in an 1887 corrida attended by General Porfirio Díaz and the cream of Mexican society. Fistfights broke out among fans, however, owing to the radically different images of each bullfighter: Mazzantini, posh and well-educated; Ponciano, already a folk hero and hard-drinking hedonist. Ponciano and his crew went to Spain in 1889, attracted much attention for their giant mustaches, and triumphed everywhere. By 1897 the tequila-loving Mexican had developed liver disease; symptoms included yellow skin and fainting in front of bulls. Dead two years later, his name survived in *corridos* and the occasional cantina cry of "*¡Ora, Ponciano!*" Another Mexican bullfighter of great renown, Rodolfo Gaona, visited Madrid in 1913 and dedicated a bull to the exiled, severely alcoholized General Victoriano Huerta (Claramunt 1989, 2:32). Horse shows, bullriding, and Mexican *jaripeos* provided additional theaters of masculine display, then as now. When Carnival comes to Tlayacapan in the much anthropologized state of Morelos, a corral is set up in the central plaza and local versions of a very nonbourgeois masculine identity begin:

> It is considered manly to mount bulls. Riders ridicule men who refuse to ride by questioning their manliness: "Why don't you mount one? Come on! Are you afraid? Aren't you a man?" . . . When asked about the risk of injury and death, bull riders may say that riding a bull is a *gusto* (pleasure) even if it ends in death. (Ingham 1986, 147)

Even people who cannot read or write have their version of "death-wish aesthetics." Drinking oneself into an early grave would be another, equally romantic version, a valiantly manic negation of societal negation.

The hacienda system had exacerbated color-class prejudices and male gender anxieties, and thereby reinforced the masculine love of ritual rupture, decade after decade. The middle classes were not amused. In turn of the century Chihuahua, "residents of San Antonio del Tule, Huejotitan, and Rosario, where legal and illegal alcohol sales were rife, petitioned for relief from the disorders, obscene shouts, and even pistol shots that accompanied drinking sprees" (French 1994, 195). Some twenty-five years later, "middle-class politicians in Michoacán declared a war on alcoholism among the lower classes" (Boyer 2003, 206), with federal schoolteachers as the shock troops. Some people were in favor, some were not.

> Whereas anticlericalism and the ideal of campesino militancy alienated womenfolk in many agrarista communities, the message of temperance in drink and gaming appealed to women who had to keep their families in order. . . . The temperance drive sometimes

provoked a backlash, as well. People who hawked alcohol ranged from politicians whose family members had cornered the market in some villages to women who eked out their "own sustenance and that of our families" by selling pulque in city plazas, and none of them wanted to lose what was in fact a very lucrative business. Moreover, the assault on alcohol threatened the tradition of ritual drinking that accompanied religious celebrations in many parts of the state. (Boyer 2003, 209)

In many areas of Mexico, militant federal *maestros* took a proactive role in closing local liquor shops, breaking up Catholic fiestas, even arresting intoxicated villagers. Krauze comments that the government's war on illiteracy was "much more successful than the campaigns to defanaticize and dealcoholize," citing reports of schoolteachers disillusioned with endemic drunkenness and adultery in their villages (1997, 449). Mary Kay Vaughan pictures the federal teachers of Tecamachalco huddled together in their Centro de Cooperación, consoling themselves with sober socialist rhetoric, "beleaguered by village hostility and indifference" (1994, 228).

The land distribution program of Lázaro Cárdenas (1934–1940) did not solve the problem; local drinking cultures would remain cyclothymic and prone to violence throughout the twentieth century. When Lola Romanucci-Ross interviewed the more prosperous and progressive citizens of her research site in 1973, they still gossiped about the bad time-allocation habits of their social inferiors — former peons of the great hacienda nearby: "The families attached to the hacienda were supposed to have been lazy and to have adopted the work habits of the [*agrarista*] immigrants only reluctantly. Many were said to have been heavy drinkers or alcoholics; they liked gambling (especially cards), fiestas, rodeos, and bullfights" (1973, 152). She discovered male violence to be closely correlated with alcohol use. There were 165 men over twenty years of age in her village. Twenty-nine or 17.6 percent of them were on the list of "alcoholics," while twenty-seven or 16.3 percent were on her list of "heavy drinkers." The overwhelming majority of village men with a record of violent aggression came from this same alcoholized 34 percent. Romanucci-Ross pointed towards the bullring as "the symbolic center of the machismo subculture," and pointed out the inadequacies of local fantasy-identity construction. The original role models were bullfighters and gun-toting charros, but "those who now molded themselves to the image were farmers and field hands who depended upon the bullring to support their pretensions" (1973, 153). This latter observation is important. The particular binge-drinking subcultures in question were characterized by corrosive identity insecurity, a kind of surrogation anxiety that inexorably led to violent acting-out. Impulse control was nonexistent among the most completely "macho" types; violence was an automatic response "almost beyond their control" (137). Their sober and drunken states were as different as day and night. Sober (perhaps hungover), they seemed sullen, depressed, and misanthropic. They became quite animated, sociable, and generous during a binge, but their euphoria had "aggressive and dangerous overtones" (146).

In *Social Character in a Mexican Village* (1996/1970), Erich Fromm and Michael Maccoby found most alcohol lovers incapable of cultural appreciation: "When our project brought movies, musical performances, and readings to the village, 60 percent of the abstainers, 36 percent of the moderate drinkers, 27 percent of the heavy drinkers, and only 7 percent of the alcoholics attended at least one of these events" (161). Maybe it was better that they stayed away: the typical village drunkard had a Jekyll-and-Hyde personality, eager to dominate people, ready to lash out, fight, and kill; he was a sadistic man, an explosively aggressive man. Why? — because he was "passive, bored, and empty" (167). "Like all sadistic impulses, those of the alcoholics are rooted in the sense of powerlessness which is engendered by the passive-receptive orientation" (Ibid.). One might think that in dealing with a male population characterized by high levels of aggression, low levels of constraint, poor harm-avoidance skills, less self-control, more impulsiveness, and so forth, the *last* terms an investigator would use would be "passive" and "receptive." Why were they not "receptive" to the movies, concerts, and readings? K. J. Sher and his team argue that "cohort, regional, cultural, and social-class factors that influence exposure and availability of different substances might greatly overshadow subtle but theoretically meaningful personality-based effects" (1999, 88). In other words, it would make more sense to derive the drinking personality from the environment. Perhaps the drunkards so accessible to cursory outside examination were not essentially passive, but essentially poor and situationally passive. Why not describe them in terms of "poverty-induced hypersensitivity" or "diminished ability to nurture positive self-images due to low social status?" Why not describe their drinking as "self-medication for psychosocial sequelae of the hacienda system?"

In emphasizing characterological passivity, Fromm and Maccoby join hands with other scholars of their generation who were busily constructing and strategically containing "the peasant" (Kearney 1996, 35). But note that the Mexican peasants in question were addicted not merely to alcohol but to wild pastimes that staged time- and death-defying male assertiveness. Taylor points to the central Mexico area "as being more influenced by the less sociable aspects of drinking and masculinity that relate to the adoption of Spanish attitudes in exaggerated forms" (1979, 111). The Spanish attitudes were quite exaggerated to begin with. The hypermasculine performance venue of bullfighting, for example, first reached its modern virulence in Sevilla, smuggling and vice capital of Europe, gateway to the Indies, home of the *bravo* or tough guy. Bullfighting was nothing less than "a pragmatic theory of machismo, a clearly comprehensible dramatization of it available to all" (Araúz de Robles 1978, 78). The basic drama or plot was endlessly repeated: small-but-brave-man-with-blade-defeats-apparently-unstoppable-brute. This storyline was and is addictive for disenfranchised and racially suspect males in several different nations. Should we not at least understand the mental or behavioral oscillation (from nobody to somebody, then back to nobody) as a thymic system, rather than deriving all from the "passive-receptive personality orientation?" Even Octavio Paz described Mexican machismo in terms of *willful* negation (2000/1950, 225–27). In this he echoed José Revueltas, who had portrayed his archetypal peasant Adán in terms of "vigorous impotence, passionate indifference, and active apathy" (1990/1943, 20). Perhaps Fromm and Maccoby should have attended the identity performance formats of their village alcoholic, instead of trying to foist more "cultural" events upon him. A large percentage of the peasants had better events to attend, performances more rewarding or more essential to their psychological well-being: bullfights, gambling sessions in the tavern, trips to the local bordello, and/or masculinist imposition events in their huts.

Thanks to bullfighting and *jaripeos*, hacienda peons were constantly reexposed to a radically nonbourgeois brand of time-mapping, a testicular brand of heroism in which one's whole future could be gambled and lost in a second. This privileging of event-time was reinforced by folk Catholicism: rural festivities were typically held in honor of a patron saint, a sort of supernatural cacique in touch with the celestial *Supremo Gobierno*, hence in a position to do favors for his or her local clients. Such beliefs were reinforced by generations of ecclesiastical orators in both Spain and Mexico. In other words, we are dealing with a web of complicities: taurine time-mapping was inseparable from local belief systems, local power structures, local economic circuits and labor markets, local drinking customs, and local gender stereotypes — each component enhancing the other, century in and century out. It would be a mistake to *reduce* bullfighting to machismo or male domination, therefore. Any male mystique involved cannot be considered apart from patterns of power and power-abuse that rural Mexicans adapted to or died (Sotelo Inclán 1970/1943).

Intergenerational transmission of trauma is facilitated by the continual reproduction of abusive milieux. Though Lázaro Cárdenas still enjoys the esteem of many historians, *cardenistas* at the local level did their best to emulate the armed petty tyrants of pre-Revolutionary days (Becker 1993, 159). The *tierra caliente* communities of southern Morelos acculturated accordingly, and in the 1980s they were still paying the price: "Villages there tend to be riven by strife and factionalism. Alcohol consumption is high, and aggressive, even murderous, displays of machismo are commonplace. Indeed the homicide rate in the hot country of Morelos is one of the highest in the world" (Ingham 1986, 12). Things were even worse in agave zones like Jalisco, if we can trust the memory of a former mezcal harvester named Macedonio:

> When I was a boy I saw how poor people got drunk on tequila. Poverty made them drink to forget. Over there, in Degollado, I saw so much blood in and outside the cantinas that it made me want to vomit. Peasants and ranchers, full of mezcal, cut each other to pieces with their machetes, coas, and axes. They shot each other just because they were looking for a fight. You could see the blood fill their shirts as they were hit. (as cited by Martínez Limón 1998, 131)

In the 1980s and 1990s, violent young men from rural areas moved to the vast downscale *colonias* surrounding Mexico City and took their bad habits with them (Gutmann 1996, 203).

Alcoholism and machismo are facile, "blame-the-victim" strategies that deflect our attention from the truly large-scale abuses of the powerful. "No Mexican ruler has ruled democratically for the simple reason that the Mexican people are not democratic," wrote the Porfirian *científico* Francisco Bulnes (cited by Krauze and Zerón-Medina 1993, 26). In full control by 1876, Díaz initiated his pacification, "friendification," and *pan o palo* (bread or the stick) policies. In time don Porfirio became Mexico's "King of Favors," as evidenced by thousands of petitions from his subjects preserved at the Universidad Iberoamericana in Mexico City (Cruz 1994). If Spain was home to the "peaceful rotation" of two corrupt political parties, Mexico was a land of ineffective suffrage and endless reelection. By 1898, Spain was headed for a devastating encounter with the United States; Mexico enjoyed very good relations with its northern neighbor, and Mexican industrial and economic growth was robust and sustained. In the opinion of Francisco I. Madero, the regime had gone too far in its enthusiasm for industrial development: "We are especially referring to factories that manufacture alcoholic beverages" (as quoted by Krauze and Zerón-Medina 1993, 59). One of those plants deserves a blue ribbon, however. The Cervecería Cuauhtémoc of Monterrey (Nuevo León) was one of the great success stories of Porfirian modernization:

> The policy of Porfirio Díaz's administration of simultaneously encouraging direct foreign investment while protecting local capital constituted one of several key factors in the success of the brewery. . . . When production began in 1891, the Cervecería was the first wholly Mexican-owned brewery in the nation; the others were controlled and operated by Europeans. The proprietors of the Cervecería were pround of its Mexican ownership, even though the prejudice existed in the country that foreign beers were of better quality. They deliberately named the company Cervecería Cuauhtémoc after the last Aztec emperor as an act of nationalism. (Hibino 1992, 27–29)

The upstart beer-brewing barons of Monterrey, the owners of the great *pulque* haciendas, and Guadalajara's tequila tycoons competed for the precious time and bodies of Mexicans. The Cervecería Cuautémoc was destined to become a powerhouse of technological development in northern Mexico, but in the beginning the beer it brewed was too expensive for the working class and was considered "an aristocratic drink" (26). Even as his policies strengthened the hacienda system and made Mexico safe for bullfighting, don Porfirio deftly accomodated his iron hand to modern communication technologies like the telegraph. A new sort of urgency came to characterize drinking in places when workers were subjected to "forced progress," the apt title of William French's 1994 study of the attempt to make mineworkers stop drinking and swallow capitalist chronopolitics. Yet clandestine liquor consumption did not flag even in areas that managed to create new police forces (197). In *Disorder and Progress* (1992), Paul J. Vanderwood established that police forces created before, during, and after the Porfiriato were as plagued with problems of drunkenness as the societies from which they were recruited. The same holds true for an infinity of local political bosses, called *caciques*, who combined alcohol abuse with the constant abuse of their powers and prerogatives. Porfirian modernization was beyond a doubt alcohol-friendly, at the macro level of supply and in every despotic microcosm.

Wild drinking sprees were not only disturbing but "illogical" for middle-class observers of the time (French 1994, 199). When it comes to the men of the mining camps of Chihuahua's Hidalgo District, the logic can be reconstructed. People proceed in accordance with their degree of certainty about the future; a high degree of certainty leads to health conservation and long-term, stable investments of time and energy; if there is no certainty, the truly rational course is to live life moment by moment, maximizing pleasure with no thought for the morrow (Gil Calvo 1989, 91–101). French underlines the constant dangers miners faced: "Mines claimed the lives of workers in premature explosions, late explosions in drill holes, equipment failures, inexperienced winch operators, falling timber and rock, floods, and falls. Three or four workers died each month of 1905, for example, in La Palmilla's mine alone" (1994, 194). Thus it would have been highly illogical for them to adopt the future-oriented Porfirian ethos, the same speedy developmental ideology they associated with the end of their *lifetimes*, so they deliberately mocked it whenever possible. "In cantinas, billiard halls, and brothels, working-class drinkers rejected the time restrictions advocated by middle-class moralists and municipal officials and imposed their own schedules" (197). Mezcal and *aguardiente* were essential gateways to a more intense temporal consciousness, a fulfillment of the need to make every second count, in quite realistic anticipation that their drinking days were numbered.

We are in no hurry here, so let us pause to ponder a more pessimistic perspective on the issue of drunken miners' resistance to modernizing industrial tempos. Suppose we picture alcoholism itself as "forced" upon the workers, seeing it not as the enemy but as the *accomplice* of "forced progress." From this perspective, the workers would have unwittingly contributed to their own domination via dipsomania, through compulsive acting-out in cantinas and bordellos. Perhaps at some deeply embedded or embodied level of their unlucky habitus, they had already internalized the time concepts foisted upon them by the powerful. Perhaps they were not really imposing their own schedules at all, just unconsciously replicating the ones assigned to them by power. Maybe the miners' drinking bouts that seemed so voluntaristic were really involuntary, in the final analysis, a kind of "somaticization of social relations of domination" (Bourdieu and Wacquant 1992, 24). Such an argument would be very tempting, almost persuasive, if somaticization were not a two-way street. Recall that "compulsive" colonial drinking took place in *pulquerías* that were subject to external surveillance by viceregal authorities, and yet the powerful could not spy the inner states of Certeau's "local authorities," nor control the self-experiencing thereby instantiated, nor hope to understand its radically different temporal coordinates. The limbic system is always calendrically virgin territory, to paraphrase Hassig. The portals of access to *kairos* may be monitored, but *kairos* itself escapes scrutiny. Baudelaire would have understood: "Always be drunk. That is all: it is *the* question. You want to stop Time crushing your shoulders, bending you double, so get drunk — militantly" (as quoted by Dardis 1989, 46).

How else can we explain why men far from the mines of Chihuahua drank just like miners? Back in Mexico City, under upturned Porfirian noses, the sacred escapism of binge drinking continued. Elite dreams of progress were matched by the alcoholized dreamwork of *pulquerías* and popular festivals. Thanks to nineteenth-century novelists like Guillermo Prieto (1818–1897) and Manuel Payno (1820–1894), we know just how dependent Mexico City had become on two reality restructuring systems — pulque and popular Catholicism — exemplified by the vast inebriated crowds that took over streets in honor of the Guadalupana. Demand drove supply in properly Keynesian fashion: there were sixteen hundred *pulquerías*, many of which were legal, some of which could serve a mind-boggling six hundred customers at a time (Pilcher 2001, 6). The political consolidation of Mexican liberalism under don Porfirio was accompanied by the social consolidation of *San Lúnes*, Saint Monday, whereby the capital city's vendors and artisans prolonged their festive binges into the work week and "imposed their own schedules" — pouring *pulque*, drinking *pulque*, eating foods stewed in *pulque*. Payno and Prieto saw and smelled all this with a mixture of horror and fascination, never failing to take note of the violent crimes that resulted from public drunkenness (Lameiras 1998). Intoxication does not mean apathy, passivity, or lack of sociopolitical awareness: "Emilia 'La Trujis' Trujillo gave memorable performances in the Porfirian era of a working-class woman being dragged off to jail for

drunkenness, cursing the hypocrisy of policemen who arrested poor people for consuming pulque and tequila while ignoring the rich fops getting
soused on champagne and coñac" (Pilcher 2001, 23). Julio Sesto, one of
don Porfirio's *científicos*, wrote that "the common people of Mexico have
two idiosyncratic ailments that are most unpleasant: ragged, dirty apparel
and an extreme inclination to intoxication" (*extremosa inclinación a la
embriaguez*) (as quoted by Krauze and Zerón-Medina 1993, 63). He felt
threatened by popular tactics of resistance but, in retrospect, he should
have felt more threatened.

Chapter 6
Death-Wish Aesthetics

The psychology of Mexican drinking in the twentieth century cannot be separated from the social and cultural unfolding of the Mexican Revolution. It is well known that combatants and their caudillos were extremely fond of drink; *borracheras* were emblematic of the liminal nature of the Revolution itself — a chaotic series of civil wars that decentered Mexican society, traumatized vast segments of the population, drastically altered lives, life-expectancies, identities. Alcohol's role in helping uprooted citizens adjust to their plight or construct their new revolutionary selves has not been adequately explored. It is a fact that Mexicans trying to make some sense of the Revolution have been very dependent on binge drinking for metaphors, concepts of time and causality, ideas about death, and modes of memory. The nationalistic regime that eventually emerged out of chaos found a rich source of legitimacy in cultural alcoholization, once Callista fantasies of prohibition proved a dead end.

The majority of Revolutionary leaders secured the loyalty of their undisciplined peasant-soldiers by drinking as hard as they did and cannily permitting mass *borracheras*. Pancho Villa may have been a teetotaler, but his troops were not (nor was he in later life). When Villa's celebrated División del Norte occupied Ciudad Juárez, the city became an even more transgressive place than usual, a vast cantina/casino/bordello. Successive waves of troops occupying Guadalajara consumed huge quantities of Cuervo tequila, then took wagonloads with them when they departed (Orellana 1994, 34). The soldiers did not drink this type of mezcal straight, but preferred *toritos* ("little bulls") that tamed the tequila with sweet soda. "The men of General Julián Medina drank an infinity of *toritos* before blowing up a railroad bridge" (34). In the civil war that followed Russia's 1917 Revolution, both Red and White troops engaged in binge drinking and fought for control of vodka storage warehouses (Erofeyev 2002, 58). In Mexico, *revolucionarios* drank as frequently as they could and used alcohol to impart a festive, anarchic, death-flouting spirit to military maneuvers. As a young doctor traveling with Medina's troops, Mariano Azuela never failed to take note of the drunken comportment of his companions. In Azuela's *Los de abajo* (1915), considered to be the first and best documentary novel of the Revolution, we actually witness more drinking events than military events, with snorting horses present at each.

From the very first pages Azuela demonstrates intimate familiarity with the thought and speech patterns of mezcal-swigging officers and troops, recreating their exalted libidos, their stream-of-consciousness mixture of songs and curses, their *voces aguardentosas* (firewater voices). The impoverished doctor published his story of revolutionary hope and disillusion in the pages of an El Paso newspaper. Eight years later it was rescued from oblivion in the course of an ongoing Mexico City debate over whether or not there existed "a virile Mexican literature" (Englekirk 1935). *Los de abajo* proved there was, and for many decades thereafter the genre known as *novelas de la Revolución* would dominate literary production and consumption in Mexico. Mariano Azuela was the one who made it possible to write modern novels in Mexico, according to Carlos Fuentes (1992, 139), but few writers matched Azuela's convincing identification with popular lifeworlds and experience. His much-praised stylistic innovations were designed to short-circuit any sort of intellectual distancing from the emotional consequences of fighting, drinking, feuds, malice, betrayal, and violent death. In succeeding decades, numerous Mexican authors continued to work within thematic coordinates established by Azuela, adding new techniques and perspectives derived not from empathy but from mistrust of the masses and an understandable disgust for ignorant, capriciously brutal caudillos.

Racially mixed *rancheros* of the high sierra are the one social class that comes out ahead in Azuela's seminal novel, at least symbolically. Their intimate knowledge of the gullies and ravines of their natural habitat give them the initial guerrilla advantage. Add to this their fierce independence, code of honorable conduct, poverty, ingenuity, marksmanship, and expert distillation techniques. Their habit of punctuating song verses with piercing yelps of underdistanced emotion continues to this day in *ranchero* music. In *Los de abajo*, the *rancheros'* charismatic leader is Demetrio Macías. Though reminiscent of Emiliano Zapata, this character is mainly a composite of the star-crossed caudillo of Jalisco, Julián Medina, and an impetuous colonel named Manuel Caloca. Macías is simultaneously a *ranchero* and "a copper-cheeked racially pure Indian with hot red blood" (Azuela 1992/1915, 40). His blood boils over in a cantina squabble with the local cacique, thereby precipitating his personal entry into the national conflict. The racial markers do not add up to an indigenous social identity, however; like Zapata, Macías is a *caudillo mestizo* (Portal 1980, 312).

In *Los de abajo* and all other novels of the Revolution, no agreement is sealed without an alcoholic beverage, and each type or brand signifies. Demetrio's stated preference for "the limpid tequila of Jalisco" rather than champagne and its "light-scattering bubbles" underscores his purity of heart and stands the Porfirian taste system on its head. Ironically, during the years of upheaval from 1910–1940, the industrial infrastructure that made tequila possible was seriously disrupted. In 1910 there were eighty-seven agave distilleries in Jalisco; by 1930 there were thirty-two (Blomberg 2000, 76). Land reform under Cárdenas would cause further problems for tequila tycoons. Throughout these disorderly decades, clandestine production of mezcal boomed; mules carrying barrels were seen emerging from ravines in remote areas of northern and western Mexico (Luna Zamora 1999, 157). In the hottest phase of the Revolution, alcohol is both the congealer of group solidarity and its dissolvent. *Borrachera*-related deaths are accepted as stoically as deaths on the battlefield. One night the men of Macías and those commanded by Pánfilo Natera seal their union just as the two leaders had done, clinking their glasses together countless times:

> "For the pleasure of having met," plenty of mezcal and aguardiente was drunk that night. Since not everybody gets along and sometimes alcohol is a bad adviser, there were of course some differences of opinion; but everything was taken care of in good form outside the cantina, the inn, or the bordello, without bothering anyone. The following morning there were a few dead [*amanecieron algunos muertos*]: an old prostitute with a bullet in her navel and two recruits of Colonel Macías with their skulls full of holes. Anastasio Montañés reported this to his chief, who shrugged his shoulders and said: "Psch! . . . Well, somebody bury them. (Azuela 1992/1915, 52–53, my translation)

Wild drunken feasts at mansions abandoned by the wealthy provide the perfect carnivalesque mockery of the Porfirian "smart set" (this is long before tequila becomes the basis of a new kind of snobbery). In Azuela's world, heavy drinking is a prime weapon of class warfare, on a par with vengeance, burning, and pillaging. A phrase from the French Revolution comes to mind: "What were a few looted mansions compared to their looted lives?" The increasingly self-indulgent small-group dynamics of Demetrio and his followers constitute a "ghostly premonition" of the future corruption of the Revolution itself, says Fuentes (1992, 138). When victories become few and far between, alcohol becomes ever more crucial to psychological well-being, a scarce and treasured commodity. "Thus, the discovery of a barrel of tequila by one of the officers was an event of the magnitude of a miracle" (Azuela 1992, 110). The main body of troops is sent forward in order to leave the officers' staff one final *borrachera*, one final cockfight, and one final opportunity for Macías to mourn the violent death of his mistress (her throat had been slashed by a hard-drinking *soldadera* named La Pintada).

Just as don Porfirio had validated his status by supplying his adulators with fine cognac, the sponsorship of mass drinking episodes made the charisma of many a Revolutionary caudillo more convincing. In *El águila y la serpiente* (1926), Martín Luis Guzmán describes the nine-day *borracheras* orchestrated by General Juan Carrasco, the Sinaloan guerrilla leader who rose like a rocket at a fiesta to eventually fall before a firing squad. This account is not fictional. Normally the drinking would begin with the occupation of a new town or city with fresh supplies of alcohol. On his way to interview the carousing general celebrating his conquest of Culiacán (Sinaloa), Guzmán found himself immersed in the spree, struggling to hold onto his ego boundaries after the soldier-peasants had already surrendered to mezcal and multiplicity. For him the scene was grotesque:

> Strange intoxication of the mass, as sad and noiseless as the shadows which folded it around! Herd drunkenness, like that of ants, happy in their reek and contact. It was the bestiality of the mezcal filling the most rudimentary need of self-liberation. Floundering about in the mud, lost in the shadows of night and conscience, all those men seemed to have renounced their quality of human beings on coming together. They seemed the soul of a huge reptile with hundreds of heads, thousands of feet, which crowded, drunk and sluggish, along the walls of a cavernous, dark street in a deserted city. As my companion [the one forcing Guzmán to drink] and I turned a corner, I managed to get away from him. How long was I held in that nauseating embrace — one hour, two, three? When I jerked myself free, I seemed to rid myself of a greater oppression, both physical and moral, than if all the blackness of the night, converted into some horrid monster, had been resting on my shoulders. (Guzmán 1930, 60)

Note how Guzmán's mezcal trip took place in an impossible to calculate time-out-of-time. His nightmarish encounter with fellow citizens incapable of self-government will be echoed by many other intellectuals, the better to highlight their own moral fiber and clear-sighted capacity to guide Mexico's destinies (Doremus 2001, 39). Marta Portal notes that *El águila y la serpiente* was sarcastically subtitled *los de arriba* (the ones on top) for concentrating on the big names of the Revolution to the exclusion of lower-class combatants (1980, 112). Top generals do not escape Guzmán's poisoned pen, however; he continually mocks the speech patterns and rudimentary cultural tastes of important figures, Alvaro Obregón in particular.

As seen earlier, the original markets for *vino mezcal* emerged in consonance with the symbolic opposition between whites and Indians and the qualities presumed to belong to each stock. Central Mexico's indigenous communities remained on the margins of revolutionary hopes and disappointments alike, and, in the opinion of José Vasconcelos, the reason was *pulque*. In one of the first issues of his influential journal *El Maestro* (1921), Vasconcelos affirmed that the "strong and sober" peasants of the north and the "vigorous Indians of the south" made much better soldiers than the *pulque*-drinking ethnic groups of Hidalgo or the State of Mexico:

> Revolutionary chiefs knew all too well that in order to recruit people they had to go north, south, or to the coasts, but that it was useless to attempt recruiting in areas close to the Federal District because the majority of men in this zone are no good as soldiers. To become convinced of this, it was enough to go up to one of the huts in areas where the maguey is cultivated and ask for the name of a town or the location of a road. Invariably, a man with a small body and an opaque gaze would come out; a man who breakfasts on pulque and keeps on drinking pulque all day long and gives pulque to his children. ("Aristocracia pulquera," reproduced by Blomberg 2000, 42–43, my translation)

Throughout the 1920s, before his wine-soaked decades of exile in California (Blanco 1977, 79–128), Vasconcelos firmly believed that Mexico's downtrodden Indians could be redeemed right out of existence through education and a mysterious racial alchemy. The indigenes would continue to prefer their old modes of redemption, however, and their old techniques of resisting the capture of their energies by ambitious statists.

We do find a rather smooth adaptation to the "fiesta of bullets" among the miners and *rancheros* of northern states. The former, as seen earlier, had lived and worked with death on a daily basis; with heavy doses of mezcal they had mocked the future-oriented ethos of the Porfirian bourgeoisie; when Villa called, they came by the thousands (Muñoz 1935; Katz 1998). *Rancheros*, for their part, were already accustomed to a seminomadic, manly life in the saddle, defending their land and cattle-raising rights with rifles. Notorious for their vicious tempers, neither hungry nor exploited, they threw in their lot with clientelistic warlords like Medina or Carrasco out of pure opportunism and an innate hatred of centralized power structures. The taste for quick-acting distilled liquors encoded distaste for government itself, and the same political psychology Deleuze and Guattari called "the war machine." Typical symptoms include "a fundamental indiscipline of the warrior, a questioning of hierarchy, perpetual blackmail by abandonment or betrayal, and a very volatile sense of honor, all of which impede the formation of the State" (1987, 358). From several different social classes, revolt and civil war generated armed nomadic gamblers celebrating their liberation from hard work and sobriety, from the chains of the past and from future consequences as well. For every prominent regional caudillo, there were a dozen so-called *cabecillas* (ringleaders) or *bandolhéroes* (a combination of *bandolero* and *héroe*) who avenged themselves on their neighbors or simply stole all they could under cover of the Revolution. As a result, any number of local caciques organized armed bands to defend themselves *from* the Revolution. Mass *borracheras* like the one sponsored by Carrasco in Culiacán were commonplace throughout the period; the eyewitness accounts of Azuela, Guzmán, and other writers compel us to foreground binge drinking against the "tapestry of cadavers" strewn across provincial Mexico. In *La sombra del caudillo* (1929), Guzmán's other novel of the Revolution, both the great and the humble impatiently rush to keep their date with death. Octavio Paz summarizes a theme common to the *novelas de la Revolución* genre when he describes the Revolution as one giant, suicidal, drunken fiesta (2000/1950, 294). Immersed in such a liminal zone, knowing that their own lives might be over very soon, some used alcohol to close their eyes and others to enhance their vision as they danced on the edge of the cliff, pre-dead leaves blown by the Revolutionary hurricane.

The caudillos who ended up on top of the rubble believed they could stay there by retiring or shooting their fellow generals and strictly enforcing the anticlerical articles of the new constitution. Resistance to forced secularization was found at all levels of Mexican society, and a genuine war machine emerged in areas where ultra-Catholic values and attitudes were deeply entrenched. Grievance-nurturing peasants became mounted guerrilla warriors overnight, as in the early days of the Revolution. Some twenty-five thousand peasants would lose their lives during *la Cristiada* (1926–1929), but they fought the *federales* to a standstill. Shortly after winning the presidency in 1928, Callista ally Alvaro Obregón was assassinated by a militant Catholic, temporarily postponing the peace process begun by the chastened Calles himself. The negotiated end of the Cristiada was not the end of the government's dechristianization campaign, however, which continued all over Mexico and blazed with singular fervor in Sonora. Catholic schools were outlawed, Catholic teachers in public schools were purged, and atheistic schoolteachers were expected to organize "Proletarian Bonfires" of religious images, sculptures, clothing, and books (Bantjes 1994, 269). In 1935 the governor "took the extremely unpopular action of decreeing complete prohibition in the state" (276). As Bantjes notes, the Callistas lacked understanding of the society they presumed to save from drinking and superstition.

In the beginning, ideologues and novelists portrayed the Mexican Revolution as a radical rupture with a previous epoch of monotonous stagnation and decadence. Time did not flow during the Porfiriato, in this trope, immobilized as it was by oppression and *caciquismo*. Even when the unrestrained Revolutionary impulse ends up betrayed, the Revolution is initially portrayed by politicized novelists as "the time of transition, the possibility of arriving not at another identical day, but at the future itself" (Portal 1980, 320). If Don Porfirio's regime was the origin-world, the

Revolution was the escape vehicle. This image of Porfirian time as static or suffocating may be psychopolitically significant but quite inaccurate in historical terms. Neither Díaz nor what Mexicans sardonically refer to as *Díazpotismo* were stuck in the past. On the contrary, the Porfirian governing elite had sought to control and secularize the populace with dreams of progress and new modes of time reckoning. In her study of patriotic festivals in late-Porfirian Tecamachalco, Vaughan notes that they "elucidated a state ideology mobilized around the future and the concepts of progress and change. The ubiquitous clock installed prominently on the town square and in all the municipal schools by Porfirian officials symbolized a new notion of time's use and mobilization, all fixed on the future" (1994, 218). The railroads that would carry Revolutionary troops all over Mexico were, after all, the legacy of an exploitative but forward-looking regime. Such facts would be quickly forgotten by the new generation of writers, who thereby anticipated "the exceptionally grandiose sociomnemonic practice of explicitly resetting a mmemonic community's 'historical chronometer' at zero" (Zerubavel 2003, 91). The tendency of novelists to portray the Porfiriato as stagnant and the Revolution as a heady dash into the future provided excellent cover for the new regime's continuation of national projects begun by the despised previous regime. "The very continuity of practice demanded some abrupt changes of rhetoric" (Knight 1997, 83).

At a deeper level, the born-again mnemonic strategy in question was symptomatic of the bipolar political psychology that emerged during the armed phase of the conflict and spun itself out in the cultural realm for decades thereafter. Generally speaking, in Revolutionary experience and representation alike, compulsive drinking and risk-taking are common symbols of the manic pole, while depression manifests itself in post-drunken remorse, horror, or disillusion. Each pole has its own way of producing truths about the meaning of life and death, chance and fate, love, hate, alcohol, and what it means to be Mexican. Individual works of fiction or nonfiction replicate the general cyclothymic parameters as they follow the triumphs and defeats of a given Revolutionary caudillo and his fatalistic soldiers. The most relevant Mexican settings include Chihuahua, whose anarchy was chronicled by Azuela, Guzmán, Nellie Campobello, and Rafael F. Muñoz; Michoacán, as portrayed by J. Rubén Romero; the *pulque*-producing *magueyales* of Hidalgo, as seen by Magdaleno; Jalisco, as documented by Juan Rulfo and Agustín Yáñez (for the exhaustive list of regions and novelists, see Aub 1969). Several novels take a caudillo — Pancho Villa is a favorite choice — and follow him in a journalistic or dark-humorous vein as he crisscrosses the republic. Vitalistic recklessness was an amazingly effective military tactic for a while, but the turning points in the civil war were precisely those days in Celaya, León, or Aguascalientes when a logical and patient Obregón outmaneuvered Villista impulsivity. As a sociopsychological phenomenon, the cult of the "man on horseback" ("*caudillismo*") had less to do with military triumph than with the mastery of death and gender anxieties. The last moments of life constituted one final opportunity to display virile aplomb, as seen in an example drawn from Pancho Villa's brief sojourn in Mexico City. There the legendary Centaur of the North "went to banquets, courted cashier girls, flirted with the actress María Conesa, and ordered Fierro to kill young David Berlanga for daring to criticize him. Berlanga is remembered for smoking a cigarrillo before dying with so steady a hand that the intact ash never fell till after he was shot" (Krauze 1997, 325). Berlanga was an intellectual and military officer affiliated with Carranza. Knowing "how-to-die" had remained one of the great aboriginalities of Mexican culture, an apt example of the slow evolutions of human history that French scholars call the *longue durée* (Braudel 1980, 25–62; Vovelle 1990, 126–53).

In Azuela's seminal novel, the manic pole of the dialectic is personified by a character whose problem drinking is the most problematic: a mentally unstable vagabond poet named Valderrama. Like a Mexican Dylan Thomas, Valderrama articulates his ecstasy through song or with observations of an almost Zen-like pithiness and mystery. He can drink half a bottle of mezcal in one swallow. He takes the news of Villa's defeat at Celaya with scornful indifference, gesturing like an emperor: "Villa? Obregón? Carranza? X . . . Y . . . Z! What's it to me? I love the Revolution as I love the erupting volcano! As to which rocks end up on the top or the bottom after the cataclysm, what does it matter to me?" (Azuela 1992, 110, my translation). Valderrama uses mezcal to avoid or postpone the inner dialogue with trauma, much like the manic French artist Alfred Jarry used absinthe — "Fueling one's mind with crushed, confused fragments relieves the memory's secret dungeons of their destructive work" (as quoted by Conrad 1988, 73). The delight Valderrama takes in chaos contrasts with his caudillo's growing melancholic fatalism. Azuela's two characters anticipate the findings of existential analysis: "The manic lives in a world of complete irresponsibility where he is bound neither by the past nor by the future, where everything happens through sheer chance; the melancholic, on the other hand, feeling himself crushed under the weight of his past, acts without feeling that he could change anything, because almost nothing is left to the realm of chance or free will" (Ellenberger 1958, 115). In an oft-cited passage from *Los de abajo*, the wife of Demetrio Macías asks him why he continues to fight. He simply tosses a small stone over a cliff and says, "Look how that rock can't stop itself" (Azuela 1992, 117).

The wind that blew through Mexico slowly died down, its veterans slowly died off. The intergenerational transmission of trauma ensured that near-death experiences would continue to inspire every modality of cultural creation in Mexico. The depressive end of the manic-depressive continuum achieves dominance in one small but influential field: avant-garde narrative. Here the world that was supposed to be a new beginning turns as stagnant as the Porfirian origin-world. A former *vasconcelista* named

Mauricio Magdaleno paves the way by introducing a narrative time designed to convey the psychic time of Otomí communities victimized by white "progress" both before and after the Revolution. *Resplandor* (1937) may or may not replicate the inner workings of Otomí time-mapping (rigidly cyclical, in Magdaleno's view), but it convincingly recreates the type of destructured consciousness Henri Ey called "the oneiric-confusional state" (1978, 64–67). The warping of narrative space and time is at its best in Magdaleno's rendering of collective *borracheras* in the maguey zone; and in their last minutes of life, liminal Otomí characters employ the drunkenness metaphor to describe their delirium or bewitchment. Having joined up with a local *caudillo* in the hope of obtaining more land and food, the Otomíes of *Resplandor* are finally left in absolute desperation and scepticism, one-dimensional figures in a desolate landscape of saltpetre and lime.

Magdaleno was not an Indian, of course, nor an ethnographer, but his novel's movement from vertigo to inertia prepared the way for a more important student of alcoholized pessimism in Mexico: José Revueltas (1914–1976). First jailed at age fourteen for militant communism, Revueltas would become Mexico's most famously incorrigible radical while producing a huge body of essays, novels, movie scripts, and journalism. As a reporter for *El Popular* in 1943, Revueltas visited the area of Michoacán devastated by the lava flows of Paricutín, a volcano that had erupted the year before. Revueltas found a "black shroud" covering the village of San Juan Parangaricútiro. Suffering under their volcano, the peasants kept shifting from one defense mechanism to another: resignation and stoic indifference, prolonged binges in the cantinas, the fanatical teachings of the Unión Nacional Sinarquista. Hypnotized by the spectacle of their own disaster, numerous peasants were ready to raise the *sinarquista* banner just to ward off further divine punishment. Revueltas was obsessed with the forces of negation weighing down upon the Tarascans, according to his biographer Alvaro Ruiz Abreu (1993, 312). He found one peasant in a state of extreme inebriation and realized that the man was "not just out on the town but the very incarnation of the sickness that dominates the blood of Mexicans" (313). The campesino was truly "dead in life," an orphan crying like an animal. Revueltas finds black dust, soldiers, liminality, and capricious forms of humiliation everywhere, and they will remain important elements of his creative universe. His first novel, *El luto humano* (*Human Mourning*, 1943) became a national bestseller. The work explores the despair and brutality of mestizo peasants caught up in a flood, with numerous flashbacks of *Cristero*-era violence. As in the real village of San Juan Parangaricútiro, Revueltian personae are situated at different points along Mexico's alcohol-messianism continuum. Sometimes the prose is as manic and unsteady as the characters themselves:

> Jerónimo, already drunk, was talking about the river, about how long Ursulo was taking, about a thousand things, with a monotonous, obstinate rhythm. His intoxication was total, as desperate, one might say, as all the intoxication of his people. A people on the point of abandoning everything, a suicidal and deaf people who were not only threatened with disappearance but who actually wanted to become lost and die despite the fact that their infinite compassion prevented them from doing so in gestures, words, savage and desired revolutions, and in what majestically and gracefully came from their hands. (1990/1943, 35, not my translation)

For Revueltas, natural disasters were apt metaphors for the many historical traumas suffered by the marginalized echelons of Mexican society and by outré writers like himself. To recognize that so many people "actually wanted to become lost and die" is a far cry from the programmatic optimism of the 1920s. Though committed in principle to Marxist ideology, Revueltas the writer found creative inspiration in folk Catholicism and his own alcoholized explorations of the collective death drive.

The Revueltian universe clears the way for the one created by Juan Rulfo (1918–1986). It is somehow fitting that Mexico's most lionized literary pessimist produced the tiniest body of work, one whose "absolute negation of time and life has no precedents in Latin American literature and has never been equalled" (Lorente-Murphy 1988, 73). In connection with his work at the Instituto Nacional Indigenista, Rulfo spent long periods of time in some of the most miserable Indian and peasant communities of Mexico; their harsh life was captured by his black-and-white photographs, while his prose portrays rural Mexico in hellish or at best purgatorial terms. Alcoholism was certainly endemic in the zones Rulfo visited, and he chooses a loquacious drunkard to convey one of his blackest visions, "Luvina," from the collection *El llano en llamas* (1953). The more the ex-teacher narrator drinks, the more he magnifies his memories of a place "where smiles are unknown" and the alcohol is of very poor quality:

> "But drink up your beer. I see you haven't even tasted it. Go ahead and drink. Or maybe you don't like it warm like that. But that's the only kind we have here. I know it tastes bad, something like burro's piss. Here you get used to it. I swear that there you won't even get this. When you go to Luvina you'll miss it. There all you can drink is a liquor they make from a plant called hojasé, and after the first swallows your head'll be whirling around like crazy, feeling like you had banged it against something. So better drink your beer. I know what I'm talking about." (1983/1953, 28)

The chatty one ends up drinking the quiet listener's beverage, continues to order more, then decides to ask for mezcal, then passes out on a table covered with flying ants (34). The drinking binge has been overlooked by critics; they focus on the ex-maestro's bleak but poetic description of Luvina rather than his mode of truth-production. One can forgive the critics for this lapse, perhaps, but not for crediting Rulfo with an accurate picture of "the Mexican." In fact, most of "the Mexicans" are not even there in the deserted villages Rulfo evokes, having slipped across the border in the *hope* of a better life. But Rulfo was drawn to the aesthetics of hopelessness and predisposed to mine the ravines of his own psyche, which were dark indeed. He was the son of an *hacendado* of Jalisco who was murdered during the Cristero war — Rulfo was six. "Our Hacienda San Pedro was burned four times, while my father was still alive. They murdered my uncle, and they hung my grandfather by his thumbs, which he lost; there was much violence and everyone died at the age of 33. Like Christ. Thus I am the son of moneyed people who lost everything in the Revolution" (Rulfo 1983, 9). As Gilbert Rose shows in *Trauma and Mastery in Life and Art* (1987), the act of writing has the power to transform passively experienced violence into an active mode that permits all manner of poisonous affects "to be attributed to fictional characters, elaborated, and transmuted" (44). That Rulfo was aware of the cathartic nature of his writing seems apparent. In conversations with Marta Portal, he chided the Mexicans of his generation with no desire to communicate their "intimate conflicts," nor to think about them at all, preferring to leave them "discarded and neglected in the subconscious, closed to further experiences, *incomunicados*" (Portal 1980, 215). Rulfo certainly communicated his conflicts, and infused them into his narrators. His creative universe is eerily similar to the petrified world of depression as described by existential phenomenologists (Ey 1978, 80–81).

Post-Revolutionary artists were like distillers searching for the right formula in which to convey their version of history, their class anxieties, *their truths*. Rulfo unerringly bases his literary enterprise on the depressive mode of being-in-the-world; this determines which topographic or ethnographic details he will ignore and which he will use as grist for his mill. In this he resembled creative mental patients studied with great empathy by Christopher Bollas: "Although they have converted the anxiety of annihilation into the excitement of its representation, it bears the weariness of the compulsory" (1995, 209). This fairly summarizes the experience of reading Rulfo, whose compulsively negative narrators finally rob his work of ethnographic credibility and take it close to black humor. Example: The town of Talpa de Allende (Jalisco) has a Virgin who is not as famous as that of Guadalupe, but famous enough to attract believers from all over Mexico since 1644; the miraculous Marian icon is housed in a basilica much prized by art historians (e.g., Wroth 1979). Whom does Rulfo choose to narrate his story "Talpa" in the 1953 *Llano en llamas* collection?

Not one of those millions of devout peasants, but a nonbeliever who sleeps with his sister-in-law during the pilgrimage and waits for his ulcerated brother to walk himself to death, which he does. Although Talpa is close to Puerto Vallarta, every single physical characteristic of the countryside is presented in the bleakest terms, and the beautiful chapel is compared to a lunatic assylum. Like Paz, Rulfo went out of his way to delegitimize Catholic Mexico and its traditional ritual systems. Victor Turner's travels to Mexican pilgrimage centers are much more empathic in this regard (1974, 166–230).

   Pedro Páramo (1955), Rulfo's one novel, recreates the thoughts of a dying/dead/undead cacique, murdered by a desperate drunkard. It is here, finally, that we begin to understand our author's true and positive contribution to Mexican nation-building, strange as it may sound to those who see his work as the "absolute negation of time and life." Recall that the memory engineers of the first generation had actively promoted historical discontinuity, the better to mark the Revolution as the decisive watershed in Mexican life; they were "explicitly resetting a mnemonic community's historical chronometer at zero" (Zerubavel 2003, 91). Rulfo's celebrated masterpiece works in the opposite direction, building an "existential bridge" that links the past to the present through narrative/mnemonic procedures akin to mourning. This was half a century ago, remember, a long time before the "Healing the Memory Workshops" of modern South Africa or the much-debated truth commissions of Chile or Argentina studied masterfully by Priscilla Haynor (2001). Today's experts stress the importance of public narrative frameworks for achieving symbolic closure in societies traumatized by human rights violations. "Survivors and victims for whom they grieve inhabit a liminal space, which is both part of society but removed from society; it could be called an experience of 'the living dead'" (Hamber and Wilson 2003, 147); furthermore, they argue that it is therapeutic for people to tell stories about this psychological experience of the uncanny (150). This is precisely what we find in Rulfo. A survivor of atrocities, he finally healed his loss through literature, made a memorial to his father and his uncle, then wrote no more. He had already done his country a great favor. To have a "sacred nation," in the view of Pierre Taminiaux, you have to develop "sacred texts" that reopen lost lines of communication:

> The return to the dead creates the perception of the wholeness of life. It is of course the revolutionary concept of progress that is reversed here, inasmuch as it creates a break in the chain of human generations and prevents the individual from being completely rooted in the earth that has given birth to him. What is at stake here is . . . the power to worship the dead and *the Fathers*. . . . The construction of a national identity, therefore, demands a kind of

regressive progress: man no longer belongs to the public sphere and its concrete necessities. (Taminiaux 1996, 92–93, my emphasis)

There were many other Mexicans whose memories needed healing; it was important to them and to the very meaning and value of "Mexicanness." If a culture does not provide reparative frameworks, what good is it? For personal or generational healing, the ultimate sacred roots of identity need to be conjured up in some way; the memory nation thereby becomes stronger — as an idea, a figure, a myth, or a highly useful fantasm. Michael Taussig's explorations of "State fetishism" are enlightening in this regard (1992, 111–40). In sum: we should take all of the walking and talking *calaveras* we find in Rulfo or Revueltas, and the writers' practices themselves, and the invisible tactics of millions of readers too, as the "everyday forms of spectral state formation," which helped to stabilize Mexico throughout the twentieth century.

Creative use of the death-in-Mexico motif culminates in the work of Malcolm Lowry, whose muse was mezcal. Living near Cuernavaca in 1936, Lowry penned a short tale about a drunken Englishman watching a drunken *pelado* loot a dead Indian. Lowry obsessively rewrote *Under the Voclano* for a decade, published it by 1947, and in the latter half of the twentieth century critics became enthralled with the novel's multiple levels of meaning. Stephen Spender sees it as the best tale of a drunkard ever written, and paradoxically a triumph of lucidity (1965, xxv). Another reader finds cosmic implications in the *borracheras* of Lowry's alter ego, Consul Geoffrey Fermin: "He drinks as if he were taking an eternal sacrament, often regarding mezcal, his favorite drink, as the nectar of immortality. Obviously there is something amiss with his mysticism" (Dorosz 1976, 16). The mountain ranges, volcanoes, and abrupt ravines of Oaxaca and Morelos were endlessly evocative for Lowry, and he was keenly sensitive to the moods of the people who populated this dramatic landscape (Woodcock 1978). As could hardly be otherwise in a book about a drunkard, time is of the essence in *Under the Volcano*. The novel's "plot-time" is one day, November 2, 1939, the Mexican *Día de los Muertos*, and its movement is cyclical, like the vast ferris wheel that forms part of Day of the Dead festivities in Quauhnahuac (the fictionalized Cuernavaca). Geoffrey Firmin's road to hell is punctuated by cantinas, each more sordid than the last. The Mexican men and women who supply the Englishman with alcohol become mother and father figures "through his drunken apocalyptic vision," and the Mexican beers enjoyed by the Consul's ex-wife stand in refreshing contrast to "the spirits which destroy Geoffrey" (Bareham 1989, 62). But to see truth beat fiction, flash forward to June 26, 1957:

Drunk and angry, Lowry had chased his wife, Margerie, away with a broken gin bottle at the close of yet another of their drawn-out, violent fights, brandishing it as wildly, as drunkenly, as the Consul did the machete he snatched up from the bar table. . . . Lowry set one bottle down after his wife fled the house to seek refuge for the night at the landlady's and picked up another, one containing Margerie's sleeping pills. . . . During the night he began to regurgitate and choked to death on his own vomit. A dingy death indeed. He had written the book and was following it like a script, though, student of the occult that he was, he might argue the book was actually writing him, that he was trapped in his own pages. (Seinfelt 1999, 231)

Mark Seinfelt's gripping account of the addictions and suicides of world-famous authors should be read in the original. Although alcohol was the first choice of the creatively self-destructive, men and women alike, their massively punitive superegos must bear much of the blame as well. Like Hemingway or Sylvia Plath, Lowry could never "get over himself."

The daemonic Lowrian writing-machine tapped the negative sacred in post-Revolutionary Mexico to become a perpetuum mobile in its own right (still whirling in Canada). Here I wish only to suggest that the influence of Mexican drinking cultures on the novel can be overlooked by critics who focus on the Faustian or Cabbalistic levels. While it is possible to argue that Lowry merely projected his vast European culture and occultist interests onto Mexico, the opposite argument is more plausible: his vast culture fell under the gravitational sway of Mexican cantina space-time. Lowry confesses his own prodigious thirst for local spirits as well as his remarkable alcohol tolerance in "Thirty-five mescals in Cuaútla" (Lowry 2000, 56–59). Perhaps he did not invent the alcoholized, death-wish psychogeography of *Under the Volcano* — perhaps he drank it in and recycled it. This would bring him into line with the other authors dealt with above, who fashioned their "own" semiotic worlds out of materials abundantly present in Mexico. Lowry set out creatively to process a genuinely impinging environment in poems like "Death of a Oaxaquenian," "Delirium in Veracruz," and "Sestina in a Cantina" (2000, 46, 50, 74–83). Alcohol seems to have been the poet's black magic shortcut to the more occult zones of the Mexican political unconscious; his works might be *our* shortcut. Lowry gives us an hour-by-hour recapitulation of a civilized man's tragic fall from grace into a refuse-filled ravine; in Juan Rulfo's fiction there is less movement, as if all important collapses had occurred ages ago. Now the ruins slowly rust and ghosts wander about, bedeviled by rancorous thoughts.

Literature provides key insights into Mexico's drinking cultures, but never affected them directly or played a hegemonic role in their psychology. Rather, the drinking cultures produced lore and attitudes eagerly chronicled and recycled by talented writers. Logically prior to an elaborate system of "national character" clichés, we have a body politic traumatized from every direction, therefore inclined to pursue happiness with any cheap but powerfully molecular means available. This coping style was well anchored in cultures that were "born in blood and fire" (Chasteen 2001). As we cast our gaze over the past five hundred years, it appears that the best that could reasonably be hoped for, in numerous Mexican lives, was a precarious balancing of positive and negative delusions, the transmutation of trauma into folk art or high-cultural death-wish aesthetics. People who have never read one page of Juan Rulfo can come up with the most elaborate representations of their own misery or Mexican misery in general, spellbinding and often quite humorous. Naturally there are vast differences in habitus and cultural capital between the intended readers of an avant-garde novel and a cantina crowd listening to *el Corrido de Juan Charrasqueado* (glossed in chapter 8). Yet both "markets" draw sustenance from Revolutionary psychodrama and its relentless exploration of near-death experiences. Both seek to make sense of Mexican history, as well as causality in general, and ideas from other nations are imported in accordance with these specific needs. The seeds of Sartrean existentialism, for example, themselves derived from war and radicalism, fell upon extremely fertile ground in Mexico (Romanell 1954, 32–36).

The Díaz dictatorship had favored positivistic, scientific justifications for its existence; following the deadly chaos of the Revolution, the sources of Mexican "spectral state" legitimation would be much more liminal and death-magic oriented, at macro and micro levels of society. Rancor and grievance-nurturing were strong, the sacrifice of the martyr constantly commemorated. As the life of Zapata proves, feeling connected to a grievance-nurturing transhistorical communitas has its own rewards, no matter what the surface bitterness or morbidity might seem to imply. The people did not wait for intellectuals to come around and *anatomize* their melancholy — they had their own tools and criteria. The power-drinking forged and consolidated in the early twentieth century was a technique of consumption that paid attention to the dead, to the truth, to unofficial memories; drunkards had their own devices for stripping away the Mexican "masks" that troubled so many intellectuals. Much like Spain's Generation of 1898, Mexican authors suffered from an identity crisis, with much "existential anxiety" about their own place in society (Doremus 2001, 18–26). They observed the many fixations in themselves and others. They saw the centuries-old symptoms, critiqued them, denounced them, parodied them, parasitized them, wrote innumerable essays and *crónicas* about them, and misinterpreted them in classist, often racist ways. From his *Cage of Melancholy* (1987), Bartra battles with the many writers who caged and straitjacketed Mexican identity with all manner of depressive or regressive stereotypes — suicidal fatalism, resentment, love of pain and violence, inferiority complex. Bartra seeks to show how the many works that define "the Mexican" form a system of elitist myths, a collection of class prejudices that facilitate domination. More Gramscian than Gramsci, Bartra imputes vast powers of manipulation to the book-publishing intelligentsia and takes it for granted that their constructs were obediently introjected by campesinos and proletarians; "national-popular" spaces in culture are created by intellectuals or not at all (1987, 191).

This nonsense is quickly refuted by reference to the aesthetic representation of Mexico's alcoholized spirit cultures, where it is abundantly clear that no artist, artistic field, or social class enjoyed a monopoly, ever. Long before the "cult of death" authors dealt with above, a vast number of stylistic decisions had already been made by artists of all ethnicities and income levels. These strategies were available to be incorporated and subsumed in, for instance, the "Posadan" universe — the visual/semiotic system associated with José Guadalupe Posada, a lithographer in touch with popular sentiments and their historical sediments. The number of folk and popular artists who make a good living off death through their aesthetic *calaveras* or *ofrendas* is simply staggering. Every single culture harbors beliefs about the dead and how best to keep in touch. Deep Mexico's Indians, *castas*, and poor whites had always specialized in ritual drinking sprees "which blurred the line between the living and the dead" (Viqueira 1999, 117). Perhaps for them, as for other disaffected groups in other countries, the death-wish drinking harbored antibourgeois fantasies of power or revenge (Goldman 1992, 149). With these socially powerless adherents of spirit cults keeping the liminal gateways open, other agents and groups were able to mine the sacred ore in creative, more marketable ways. But no peasant stopped going to the Virgin of Talpa because of Juan Rulfo, whose intended readers were the same federal schoolteachers discussed earlier, the ones checkmated by endemic village drunkenness, adultery, and Catholic recalcitrance (Vaughan 1997, 449). And pace Bartra, it is perfectly legitimate to associate Mexico with drinking and thinking about death in ways that were *originally* morose, not morose by fiat of the "dominant culture." Michael Taussig's visionary blend of Bataille and Marx conveys a better image of cultural circulation in Latin America — "that great cycle of stuttering translation of meaning and force siphoning upward through the class and race hierarchy, alchemically converting the literal into the metaphoric, there to descend to the masses to be recirculated once again 'bathed in the fires of labor'" (1997, 143).

In every social class, schooled and unschooled, we find creative individuals harnessing psychic pain in order to generate new visions: her name can be Frida Kahlo or Consuelo García — the woman who makes sugar animals for Toluca's Festival of the Dead (Carmichael and Sayer 1995, 108–11). Consuelo had her life problems too, but Frida's are much better known because that is how late capitalist art worlds work. But note: Mexico's less-privileged artists have been (1) at least as vulnerable to trauma as name artists; (2) just as creative, if the necessary adjustments are made for their lesser cultural capital in Bourdieu's sense; and (3) much more trustworthy when it comes to preserving and reworking the full bipolarity of alcoholized death culture, the entire manic-depressive continuum, the complete legacy of popular beliefs, fears, genres, and mystical hopes. When well-known author Octavio Paz wrote that "Mexican death is sterile, it does not engender like that of Aztecs and Christians" (2000/1950, 195), he could not have been more mistaken. Bartra rightly condemns such foolish pronouncements about "the Mexican" but continues to practice an amazingly disembodied, great-books anthropology, exaggerating the influence of literati (his father was Catalan poet Agustí Bartra) until it reaches truly oppressive magnitudes — enough to make anyone melancholic. I would recommend less time in the library and more time spent with old photo albums, tombstones, calendars, vintage television shows, eulogies, high school textbooks, guest books, folk fairs, war memorials, pageants, parades, posters, and other sites of social memory (Zerubavel 2003, 6). And by all means let us add "*pulquerías*" to the list.

Why should it be so hard to grant agency to Mexico's masses, so hard to hear the poetry flourishing in what Gramsci should have called "national-popular alcoholism?" Consider the excellent memory site explored by Jeffrey Pilcher: urban theatrical shows that were cheap enough for everyone in the barrio to attend. As soon as don Porfirio had gone into exile, men of comic genius arose to supply a surprising new demand for political humor among people lacking doctorates:

> After changing from his smartly tailored summer suit into white cotton pajamas, [Leopoldo Beristáin] went out on stage to be greeted by affectionate cries of "Cuatezón" [Big Drinking Buddy]. Beristáin acted the part of the inebriated Indian from Xochimilco, a theatrical village idiot and the prototype for Cantinflas's character. "El Cuatezón" delighted audiences with trenchant political commentary slurred into his drunken discourse, but the crowds were no mere passive recipients of his satire. They boisterously joined in the conversation, helping to make the so-called frivolous theater one of the most influential and democratic voices of Mexico's revolutionary society. (Pilcher 2001, 13)

Surely we are dealing with a Mexican "truth commission" avant la lettre, with laughter as the best medicine for history's abuses. The ungovernable drunken *pelado* humor associated with the name Cantinflas was destined to trouble Mexico's power brokers and Europhile cultural elites for decades, Bartra included. Until the end of the 1920s Beristáin appeared six nights a week at the Teatro María Guerrero, better known as the María Tepache, since the surrounding neighborhood was awash in *tepache* or *pulque* (Ibid.).

As we have seen again and again, the mestizos of Mexico City needed a lot of eternity to withstand the march of time. Truly they were survivors. Nevertheless, symbolic closure in traumatized societies has "a darker side" (Haber and Wilson 2003, 158). Having now established that drunkards were culture creators and activist consumers in Certeau's sense, it would only be fair to turn our attention to the actively destructive behaviors that give the word "*borracho*" its bad connotations.

Chapter 7
Spousal Assault Rituals, Then and Now

Though aware of their actions, ostensibly in control of them, and certainly responsible for them from a judicial perspective, wife assaulters are not particularly insightful nor aware of the predetermined, scripted quality of their acts. For indeed they are actors, and their wives and children play supporting roles whether they want to or not. In some ways, the whole family is type-cast by a gender role system that tends to give males, drunk or sober, a general sense of entitlement. This role system and its negative consequences are quite old. The traits of the typical batterer make him sound very much like Spanish dramatist Pedro de Calderón's classic husband: traditionalist, believer in male supremacy, insecure and jealous unto paranoia, most unwilling to second-guess his righteous rage storms. The straying wife was the immoral one, in dire need of correction or death in numerous Golden Age plays and a sizeable number of Golden Age families (Bennassar 1979, 178-180).

Many American abuse experts downplay alcohol or even discount it as a *cause* of domestic violence. Drunkenness is a lowly number ten on Lenore Walker's list of myths about battering behavior, although she allows that "The most violent physical abuse was suffered by women whose men were consistent drinkers" (1979, 25). Another American study affirmed that not drunkenness but *moderate* levels of drinking were "most closely associated with domestic abuse. . . . Individuals who never drank or got drunk often were the least abusive partners and parents" (Gelles and Straus 1988, 46). This study, like others that focus on overall quantities consumed, effects a statistical "smoothing out" of drinking episodes that can make the actual drinking patterns invisible, for example, the binge pattern, which a recent study found to be *more* conducive to aggression in cross-cultural perspective (Wells and Graham 2003). Another researcher has pointed out a number of suspicious parallels between so-called alcoholic families and families characterized by violence (Franzer 1993). They are indeed over-lapping populations, Franzer affirms: secretive, timid, loyal, blame-accept-ing, emotionally enmeshed by autocratic men warding off threats to self-esteem as best they know how. "The alcohol-involved family life is skewed toward short-term stability at the expense of long-term growth. . . . The [alcoholic] restructuring of family life establishes a milieu that tolerates and accomodates to violence" (1993, 173). This violence-accomodating restructuring is aided and abetted by the larger society's celebration of sports aggression or warfare. For Franzer, alcohol is a key causal agent of violence; for other investigators, drinking is only "associated" with spousal sparring (Gelles 1993). Experts in intimate violence are understandably reluctant to allow men any kind of mitigating excuse, perhaps equally dis-inclined to see their field as a mere extension of alcohol studies.

Can scholars of Mexican cultures and gender roles shed any light on the issue? In Chamula, reported Ruth Bunzel, episodes of domestic violence were only taken seriously if they occurred in the *absence* of alcohol. If peo-ple could say of a man that he had struck his wife while sober, then they knew he truly had evil in his heart (1991/1940, 227). Periodic episodes of *aguardiente*-induced violence were resolved when both partners apolo-gized, embraced, and exchanged brand new bottles of *aguardiente*! Chris-tine Eber devotes considerable attention to alcohol-related spousal abuse in her updated look at Highland Chiapas. In the bustling Mayan town of Chenalhó, the bad example set by non-Mayan males seems to be the prox-imate source of the problem:

> The stresslines along which alcohol facilitates violence toward women in Chenalhó are women's growing participation in the cash economy and an overall breakdown of traditional conceptions of community and alcohol's role in expressions of those. In general, it seems that as Pedrano society comes to look more like Ladino soci-ety — fragmented, competitive, with many different ideas of how one can drink and act when drunk — problems with alcohol and domestic violence have intensified. When drunk, Pedranos often imitate Ladinos. Part of their imitation involves speaking Spanish and being focused on dominating women. (2000, 205)

Back in the more fully mestizoized Tlayacapan (Morelos), John Ingham presents other cases that indicate links between masculinist lore, the eter-nal question of spousal time-control, and the cyclicity of beatings:

> One man has beaten his wife regularly throughout the many years of their marriage; he thinks it is her duty to provide him with a decent meal and his duty to teach her a lesson when she fails. He throws bowls of soup back at her when the taste does not please

him, and on one occasion he beat her severely with a length of bamboo simply because she did not bring his lunch to the field precisely at the agreed-upon time. Another villager, who continually found fault with his wife's cooking, beat her almost daily. On his return home one day, Doña Petra overheard his wife remark, "Do you beat me now and we eat later, or do we eat now and you beat me when we finish?" (1986, 62)

It is not Ingham's intention to make light of such episodes, nor mine, but let us marvel at the incredible endurance of women in the face of something that goes far beyond Bourdieu's symbolic violence. Every Mexican woman with whom I have spoken has a story about some other woman who stayed with her abusive *borracho* husband through thick and thin and apologized for him when some neighbor called the police. How long can women put up with a beating script in Mexico? A very long time, and some women even pride themselves on their ability to bear up. "A woman who is beaten and quits is not a real woman," said Dolores G. to Ingham (62). Standing by her man was a virtue she possessed in abundance; Dolores never "betrayed" her husband by filing a complaint, not even after a severe clubbing with a handstone. Perhaps we are dealing with bona fide examples of "traumatic bonding" (cf. Dutton 1995, 189–217). Social anthropologist Rosa María Osorio interviewed a large number of Mexican women in connection with her research into "alcohol as an instrument of family relations" (1992). A story told by one of the women, Isabel, provides a good example of how wife-beating episodes have both moral and sensual motivations for the *golpeadores* (batterers) and sometimes enact a grotesque nocturnal parody of the dominant chronopolitical regime:

Once, I remember, Miguel had been drinking a lot and told me I had done something to make him angry. He told me that before the day was over he was going to beat me three times and he recommended that I put down the baby girl I was carrying. He grabbed a really thick power cord and folded it into four equal parts. When I saw that, I quickly put the baby in her bed and that was when he gave me the first big whack [*fregadazo*]. That was at 8 o'clock at night and he said my next turn would be at 10:30; by then I just wanted to go to bed but he gave me another whack. I was crying and telling him to let me sleep, but he said not until I got my third beating at midnight. When midnight came he told me to take my clothes off so he could give me the third one. I didn't want to, but he insisted so much that I took them off, everything except panties. Then he gave me my third one and he told me to take everything off so he could see how he'd left me. When he saw how banged up I was, he said "Forgive me, *mi reina*, I don't want to hit you, I just want you to behave yourself so that I won't have to." The problems

> with Miguel are really ugly for the kids, since later they grow up
> traumatized and full of hatred. Miguel went to see a psychologist
> who told him he had a childhood trauma and for that reason he
> hates women. That's why he hits me, because he hates women.
> (Osorio 1992, 38, my translation)

Note that Miguel's intoxication did not keep him from having a very clear
plan for the evening, all the way through to the admonitory catharsis. At
the very least he masculinized the normally female space-time of the
home. Perhaps Isabel intuits how much Miguel depends on her for the
(re)enactment of his whole scenario of erotic hatred.

Is Miguel the author of his script, or is he nothing more than an "*hijo
de la Chingada*?" In other words, are his actions in some way motivated
by longstanding Mexican personality problems derived from the Spanish
conquering and subsequent utilization of Indian women? *Hijo* = son, *la
Chingada* = the "Raped Mother" whose passivity disgusts and alarms. As
represented by Octavio Paz, "Her passivity is abject: she offers no resistance to violence, she is an inert heap of blood, bones, and dust. Her stain
is constitutional and resides in her gender" (2000/1950, 223). Paz goes on
to identify this horrific archetype as "the atrocious incarnation of the
feminine condition" (224), thereby joining hands with every illiterate
cantina crawler who ever projected onto women his own anxieties about
humiliation and penetration. Nevertheless, in the ethnographies seen
above, it is indeed possible to find Mexican women who do not actively
resist sexualized beatings or avenge themselves afterwards in any way. In
Woman Hollering Creek (1992), Chicago-born writer Sandra Cisneros
portrayed an amazingly passive battered woman named Cleófilas, living
in Seguín, Texas with her hard-drinking, acne-scarred Mexican husband;
she escapes with the help of a lesbian truckdriver. Paz's *seminal* myth-
making, perhaps the literary equivalent of machismo, has spawned a
large body of Chicana feminist writers who repudiate his heterosexist
passivity projections and strive to show how spunky and inventive the
first truly Mexican woman was, Hernán Cortéz's translator Malintzin,
also known as La Malinche (Alarcón 2003). Historians have also taken
issue with popular views of Mexican women as somehow complicit in the
violence practiced upon them. Steve Stern's *The Secret History of Gender*
(1995) documents that subaltern women were willful and contentious
even in the most patriarchal of colonial climes. Stern's examination of the
Novohispanic trial records is even more exhaustive than Taylor's 1979
effort, and enables him to list the major unresolved gender-conflict issues
that led to domestic battles:

> Did a woman have an absolute duty to have tortillas, the end prod-
> uct of arduous female labor, ready for her husband on demand, or
> was this duty conditioned by her view of her husband's reliability as

an economic provider? Might a woman tarry on her market, water-fetching, and church rounds without special permission from her husband? Was her latitude of semi-independent movement stretched if her husband proved irresponsible or unaccountable for his diversions and whereabouts? Did a woman have a duty to submit to physical punishment by her husband-patriarch as a private matter under his jurisdiction, or did she have a right to judge whether punishment was measured and proportionate? (1995, 300)

As the reader might guess, all of these questions, and several more related to sexual infidelity, children, and chores, produced answers in the direction of female empowerment and agency. At the worst, Indian and peasant women were only strategically submissive. Certainly we would not want to assume that every single Mexican woman has simply taken it on the chin, so to speak, eschewing all thought of revenge, incapable of violence or selfishness herself. What about alcohol? Although his readers cannot fail to notice the omnipresence of heavy drinking in late colonial incidents of domestic violence, Stern is most unwilling to assign alcohol any intrinsic qualities, causality, or even importance. His chain of causation is long, in a gender-politicized, social-structuralist direction, but comes up quite short vis-à-vis the more embodied or sensual aspects of domestic violence. His approach could not explain the case of Miguel and Isabel presented above, nor many others. In my view, Felipe Castro Gutiérrez is on the right track when he notes that in colonial Michoacán the normal and expected ritual prelude to a beating was a drinking bout (1998, 17).

I think there are times in the domestic lives of men and women when gendered micropolitical conflict is merely the surface pretext for a satisfyingly sadistic round of beatings. These assaults clearly are facilitated *in some way* by heavy drinking. The "dark eros" of alcohol-related violence will not be ferreted out by the sort of questions asked and answered by Stern, simply because such questions do not bear on the cognitive or affective levels that are most closely linked to the neurochemistry of the substance itself. This shortcoming is not Stern's alone, of course, but is shared by all approaches to social phenomena that rely on conscious, accessible "human guidedness" for their theories and methods (cf. Pernanen 1991, 19–20). For this reason, Alasuutari goes too far in writing that "Alcohol does generate effects within the human metabolism, but it does not convey meanings to the human consciousness" (1982, 49). Doesn't alcohol help a man to *select* among the available cultural meanings? Shouldn't we postulate the existence of terrains in the brain where emotions are first assembled and then marched to the beat of a very different drummer? The beat, and the resulting beatings, would still be connected to the local moral economy and its messages.

Initial hypothesis: at some point in the slow or quick destructuration of consciousness wrought by strong drink, preexisting patriarchal cognitions find convincing emotional/chemical validation. Possible evidence: in many parts of Mexico, heavy drinkers themselves delineate progressive stages of mental disorganization and metaphorical movement toward the animal during the course of a typical *borrachera*. The folk model has many variants — I present a composite in table 7.1.

TABLE 7.1 Drinking Stage: Male Behaviors

Sangre de chango (monkey blood)	Trusting, sentimental, open, friendly, joyful, uninhibited
Sangre de león (lion blood)	Belligerant, argumentative, drinking faster, resorting to cuss words
Sangre de cochino (pig's blood)	Clumsiness, dizziness, staggering, vomiting, falling, passing out.

These categories are also used to describe the type of behaviors that predominate in a particular drunkard. In some local versions the monkey blood is replaced by mockingbird's blood, thereby explaining why some men burst into song after the first few drinks (or the first fifteen or twenty, in the José Alfredo tune cited in chapter 3). God-the-Winemaker should never have allowed the devil to irrigate his divine vineyards with animal blood, according to another folktale (retold by J. Frank Dobie in 1935 and Coulombe 2002, 3). The four hundred rabbits of Nahua folklore, flushed out in chapter 1, were a pre-Christian ethnotheory of alcohol's depersonalizing effects. Any *borracho*, therefore, can metaphorize the progressive destructuring of consciousness via alcohol, thereby proving Pernanen's point: "A drinker's own cognitive functions will not cease until the final comatose stage, at which point the individual is not of much interest to the study of the determination of behavior by alcohol use anyway" (1991, 222). In their own colorful way, folk typologies allude to a cerebral zone that might come into play sometime *before* the comatose state but sometime *after* a Mexican wife comes home late from the market wearing too much lipstick. In this zone, a different sort of "guidedness" takes over in the brain of her hard-drinking husband. Can we locate this sociopsychological short-circuit, this external/internal relay station where certain switches are finally turned on and others bypassed? Can we ferret out this crucial secret in Mexico's "secret history of gender?"

Every town and village boasts a local moral economy comprised of psychocultural scripts or "schemata" that supply the props of rationalization and motivate the appropriate acting out. The importance of the motivational aspect is underlined by Roy D'Andrade: "To say that something is a 'schema' is a shorthand way of saying that a distinct and strongly interconnected pattern of interpretive elements can be activated by minimal inputs" (1992, 29). Holly Matthews applied this theory of mental templates to the folk morality of her Oaxacan villagers, of mixed Zapotec and Mixtec descent (1992). She discovered that tales of *La Llorona* (the Weeping Woman) were constantly used by the people in their everyday lives to interpret and explain male-female behavioral differences; the tales were not only guides to what actually happens "in real life" but also to what should or might happen as well (127). *La Llorona* cautionary tales vary in terms of the context in which they are told, the specific lesson about marital obligations being taught, and the gender of the person telling the tale. Shame and exposure are of the essence: A man feels *pena* or *vergüenza* and his honor is on the line when he hears negative or unflattering comments about his wife in the cantina. Women, for their part, are bitterly disappointed when their men use family funds to pursue pleasures like drinking, gambling, whoring, or, worst of all, when their husbands establish more permanent resource-consuming liaisons with other women (148). Regarding the eternal problem of money lost on booze, we find tale motifs like

> F-11   One day he lost all their money when he passed out in the street. And La Llorona had much *pena* (shame) because the money was all gone from his drinking. And so she said to him, "Why should I work hard to give you money to waste? I will not work anymore until the drinking stops."

> F-28   But he kept drinking and one night he lost all their money when he passed out in the street. And so she killed herself so that he would have no one to care for him and no one to help him. (Matthews 1992, 149–50)

In these folktales, violation of marital expectations by one spouse leads to just three emotional reactions on the part of the other: shame, sadness, anger. "Each of these emotion words is itself a schema with embedded goals," notes Matthews (151). Revenge-by-suicide is one such embedded goal. Some kind of violence is never far away, and the legendary weeping woman always gets the worst of it:

> M-1   La Llorona was a very evil woman. She roamed the streets and visited other men in the fields. Her husband did not know, but everyone else did. When he found out, he beat her. She killed herself and her children. Now he has no wife, no home, and no pride. (153)

> M-31   La Llorona was an evil woman married to a good man. They lived together and were content. She worked hard and had children. But then one day she went crazy and began to walk the streets. Everyone knew but her husband.

> And then his mother told him that his wife had been walk-
> ing the streets and that other men were laughing about
> him. He had such a great *coraje* (anger) that he went to
> look for her. He found her with her lover and he killed
> them both so that she would never make a fool of him
> again. (154)

The stock of generic scripts studied by Matthews would seem to indicate that Oaxacan wife-beating is associated with, perhaps anchored by, a finite num-ber of strong emotional schemas. We are driven to assume, additionally, that the actual schemas that trigger the beating in real life would be found near the bottom of psychologist Mardi Horowitz's cognitive hierarchy:

> The mature schemas would tend to keep the primitive schemas in
> check just as more advanced brain systems keep primitive spinal
> reflexes in check. With any reduction in use of higher-order sche-
> mas, the lower-order forms might gain primacy in organizing
> responses to a drive. Instead of using well-differentiated role-rela-
> tionship models for expressing sexual desire or aggressivity, the
> person may organize experience and action by primitive schemas
> for expressing lust and rage. (Horowitz 1988, 182–83)

From this perspective, the *Llorona* folktales themselves could be seen as more mature schematic structures, counseling caution and warning of the consequences of surrender to those lower-order passions. Alcohol, in the meantime, would be the chemical facilitator of schema reduction, moving mental organization from more differentiated to less so. Hundreds of years of alcohol-induced homicide and wife-beating in central Mexico have not gone unnoticed by the people, far from it, but "when push comes to shove," no amount of wise folklore keeps the deeper script from being replayed, century in and century out. Moreover, there is something in alcohol intoxication that fuels men's worst fear: betrayal. While research-ing the judicial archives of Parral (Chihuahua), William French came across fascinating collections of love letters written during courtships that went awry and ended in murder-suicide. The 1919 case of Pedro and Enri-queta gives us food for thought:

> As she found herself accused of being untrue and having to deal
> with Pedro's insecurities every time he got drunk, Enriqueta made
> him promise not to drink any more; in other words, she set limits
> on his behavior and on how he was to treat her. This was somewhat
> unusual, as a constant theme of the middle-class press and popular
> almanacs of the time was that women, especially wives, were to
> offer love and understanding, not limits, as the means of keeping
> men away from vice. Pedro, admitting that he was the most humble

and vice-ridden man alive, initially agreed to stop drinking. When he returned to the bottle, however, and she ended the relationship, demanding the return of her love letters, he was astounded. "How can you say I am the only one responsible for the end of the relationship," he protested, "when you knew all along I was a drinker?" (French 2003, 132)

Indeed, Enriqueta had known from the beginning that Pedro belonged to Chihuahua's most seriously alcoholized group: mineworkers. The tragic end of their five month courtship made headlines and "served to instruct women in the consequences of sullying male honor and to define men as willing at all costs to act, either in order to take what was theirs or to preserve their reputations" (133).

If not the *producer* of real-life dramas of sexualized violence, alcohol is surely their traditional *sponsor*. The cultural dramaturgy is very much on display during religious fiestas in Santa María Atzompa (Oaxaca), the municipal seat for six colonias and three ranchos with a total population of 5200. According to anthropologist Ramona Pérez, "The fiesta, as a safe haven for candid behavior, becomes a theatrical production of individual stories played out against the community's story" (2000, 367). We are not in the realm of fiction, she emphasizes; the large quantities of alcohol consumed guarantee that whatever happens is believed to express "the 'true' feelings of the participants" (367). Pérez studied some thirty religious and secular fiestas over a four year period, with approximately two hundred people in attendance at each. The fiesta format — men sitting and women serving — enabled the men to get a major head start on the drinking. Male privilege was enhanced by

> the responsibility given to unmarried daughters for taking care of their fathers, grandfathers, and childless uncles during the fiestas. The girls, ranging in age from seven years to adolescence, are at the beck and call of the men. They run errands, help them off to the side to urinate or vomit, drag their passed-out bodies out of the way of other participants, and help them stumble home at the end of the night. Twice I witnessed young girls being slapped and castigated by their mothers when they refused to cater to their father's demands during a fiesta. (369)

In each of the sixteen religious fiestas she attended, Pérez observed one outbreak of violence: "Husband and wife abuse accounted for 10 of the 16 violent disruptions (63%) while male/male abuse accounted for six (38%)" (365). Then she makes a startling assertion: "The movement of gendered physical, emotional, and mental abuse into a public space, such as the fiesta, is a clear indication that such behavior is not only acceptable to the larger social unit, but sanctioned by it, albeit hidden behind notions of uncontrolled behavior resulting from excessive drinking" (369). But the relatively small number of fights she observed would not seem to support such a drastic conclusion; indeed, the typical pattern of the outbreaks of man-on-woman violence actually served to give women a prominent and quite public opportunity to indicate their disapproval:

> In almost every incident of husband/wife abuse, the attacks are provoked by the man verbally, followed by fist blows directed towards the face as soon as the woman responds in any way. The pattern is so predictable that a woman will normally not suffer from more than a few punches before she is swarmed by her female relatives and children. They form a ring around the woman, and the dominant older female, in many cases the mother of the husband, becomes the spokeswoman pushing him away while chastising him loudly and crudely. (367)

It is truly upsetting to see a woman getting punched by her man, but the immediate closing of the ranks and the vocal castigation would not seem to indicate community "approval" of spousal assault. At the same time, we can see how the festal format itself — men sitting and drinking, women serving them in every way — would tend to reinforce the male sense of entitlement and male impatience with delayed gratification or hints of female disconformity. With this in mind, the genuinely startling datum is: there is only an average of one violent incident per fiesta!

Pérez relates male frustration to the globalization of Santa María Atzompa's crafts industry and the emergence of economically independent women with new priorities and outlooks. But since spousal abuse is nothing new in Indian/peasant Mexico, but something quite traditional, this explanation cannot suffice. Village women "did it all" in colonial times too; despite never-ending domestic and child-bearing duties they were deeply integrated into community life, as shown by their participation in collective rebellions or their central role in pulque elaboration and distribution. The village community was everything in this world, and Indian/peasant marriages were primarily "conjugal arrangements" for purposes of production and reproduction (Taylor 1979, 155). There could be no broken homes in such a world, by definition, and little globalization, but the women were getting regular beatings anyway during or after masculine *borracheras*. Like Steve Stern before her, Pérez wants to trace alcoholized wife-beating events *away* from the alcohol, in a conscious and indeed conscientious social-structuralist direction. We can agree that changes in the global economy influence the local one; we might even be in the midst of a "global masculinity crisis," as someone called it. But transnational or local economies have no direct bearing on the preconscious schemas to which alcohol reduces men.

If instead we follow the flows of the *libidinal* economy, searching for less conscious schemas and motivational templates, the question of unwitting female complicity in violence reappears. To begin with, the earliest known intrapsychic structures in infants are created by females known as mothers. This psychic foundation can be cracked from the start if the mother or the childrearing methods are of the teasing, frustrating, aggressive, or abusive type. Then the early object relations are forged first in irritation, then under mounting anger, and finally by rage, the peak affect state that simultaneously instantiates the all-bad schema and the wish to restore the all-good one. Such fantasies or early self/other schemas can be powerfully fixating; through a number of transformational mechanisms described by Otto Kernberg, the primal, acute, rage-formed schemas eventually coalesce into the chronic, stable, cognitively elaborate phenomenon we call hatred, and on from there to "aggressive but well-rationalized systems of morality and justified indignation" (Kernberg 1992, 223–24). Misogyny is a good example of such a righteously moral system, and heavy drinking might well facilitate the return of the archaic rage scenarios from which it developed. Consider again the case of Miguel and Isabel cited at the beginning of this chapter. The reader will recall that Miguel wanted to give Isabel three *fregadazos*, with the last at the stroke of midnight. More was at stake than control. As we have seen ad nauseum, alcohol is a time-negating psychotropic drug. Miguel's domestic chronopolitical imposition was neither spontaneous nor linear but cyclical, hence a kind of ritual protocol. Following psychiatrist Sheldon Bach, Miguel's spousal assault ritual was a magical conjuring of "the fantasied world of the idealized merger where the laws of space, time, and logic, which promote differentiation, are suspended" as well as "a manic assertion that he can be omnipotently powerful by himself" (Bach 1991, 81–84). The end result, however, is just "a primitive identification with the aggressive, omnipotent, and androgynous mother of pain" (84). Thus Miguel could not have been an "*hijo de la Chingada*" if his archaic maternal imago was aggressive, not abjectly passive, which obviously undercuts Paz's explanation of Mexican misogyny.

Evidence indicates that the sins of aggressive-yet-all-consenting mothers are visited first on the sons, then on the son's wives. Maternal overprotection or overindulgence, frustration of early dependency needs, ambivalent attitudes to authority figures, inability to cope with stress, an unfavorable home environment — all these are mentioned by Boris Segal as conducive to the growth of heavy drinking in cross-cultural perspective (1986, 156). Mexican women who were themselves raised in fatherless or father-ineffective homes are especially prone to nurturing future wife-beating alcoholics in their own nest, according to Fromm and Maccoby. "With their sons they are both indulgent and sadistic, overprotective and intolerant of independence or disobedience. Fiercely they defend their sons from the outside world, but they crush initiative and self-confidence. . . . Depending on the strength of the mother fixation, there are two types of alcoholic, one who drinks to maintain symbolically and independently the "symbiotic" ties with the mother and another who drinks to repair the damaged image of male force and patriarchal power" (1996/1970, 172, 178).

The dysfunctional family ties Fromm and Maccoby find in their "matriarchal alcoholics" are an eerie echo of the sacred family scenario brought to Mexico by the minions of the Church. The core Catholic myth has to do with a Son trying to measure up to some very high Paternal standards, with emotional support from his compliant, self-effacing Mother. Jesus, as both the Bible and Erich Fromm would attest, was not "characterologically oriented to the ethic of material accumulation" (178), and on several occasions he expressed doubts about his "ability to carry on the patriarchal tradition" — two characteristics of the archetypal matriarchal alcoholic. Christ's distant *Padre Eterno*, like colonial power itself, was not disposed to let mere sentiment stand in the way of cosmic justice. Ibero-Mexican advocations of María hypostatized the maternal role as one of total abnegation, dutiful self-sacrifice, and dependable forgiveness for almost any crime, and Mexicans of both genders retain an impressive array of trance-induction techniques for contacting the mother goddess.

The heavy symbolic legacy of the Catholic Church is undeniable, but it is still necessary to explain how people in a given culture could be *motivated to act out* a Madonna complex or a Holy nuclear Family phantasy. For a symbol to become truly powerful it must enter into a *regime* of signs, a real-world socioeconomic desiring assemblage (Deleuze and Guattari 1987, 399). Christ's sacrifice might have continued to be understood in *less passional* terms of community responsibility had Amerindian lifeworlds remained intact, but they did not. The faster indigenous communities could be disintegrated, the sooner their men could be converted into a cheap supply of agrarian labor. A very similar process was crucial to the origins of the Blessed Mother cult itself in the latter years of the Roman empire, according to Michael Carroll (1986). With the decline of *calpulli*-like multifamily groupings all over Mexico, increasing mestizoization, the Oedipalization of Indian-peasant emotionality, growth of latifundios, women's increasing marginalization, and so forth, Holy Family cultural symbols crossed a critical threshold to become internal cultural models with the power to produce truths and motivate behaviors. In newly restructured lifeworlds, theoretically, the María cult helped divide and conquer the minds of Mexican women and, through them, men. The Virgin Mary became the beneficiary of the split-off idealization of the archaic mother, and *La Llorona* occupied the psychocultural space thereby created for cruel compulsions and filicidal thoughts. "Odd though it may sound, motherhood provides an excellent vehicle for some women to exercise perverse and perverting attitudes toward their offspring" (Weldon 1992, 63). Marian sanctity is a fertile seedbed: precisely those women with the most intense devotion to the Mother of God might have felt empowered *only as mothers*, therefore unwilling to relinquish the one thing that empowered them: the utter dependence of their offspring. Male children forced to "seduce the aggressor" just to make it through childhood can develop serious problems with core gender identity, and in later life they have scores to settle (Galenson 1988). The psychic splitting associated with Mexican mariology is on display in a popular song:

> *Yo te vengo a pedir, Virgencita de Talpa,*
>
> *que me vuelva a querer, que no sea ingrata.*
>
> *Tú que todo lo puedes, haz que regrese,*
>
> *que vuelva a ser como antes y que me bese.*
>
> *Y si no me la traes, vale más que se muera,*
>
> *ya que su alma no es mía, que sea de Dios.*

> [I come to request, little Virgin of Talpa,
>
> for her to love me again and not be so ungrateful.
>
> You who can do anything, make her come back,
>
> to be like she was before and kiss me.
>
> And if you don't bring her back to me, better that she die,
>
> since her soul is not mine, let it belong to God.]

This does not seem like Christ's kind of Christianity on the face of it, but more like instrumental magic, sentimental devotion to a celestial Mother icon alternating with an archaic rage/revenge scenario. Perhaps Juan Rulfo was on to something after all in his 1953 story about the less-than-noble motivations of the Virgin's peasant pilgrims.

Miguel and Isabel, the couple we met earlier, made their home in an old rural community undergoing rapid absorption by Mexico City. In 1992, the ancient ranchos of Huixquilucan still harbored numerous agaves; *pulque* production and consumption were robust. Distilled beverages had also become essential to any type of family gathering or event celebration, and indeed to any meeting between old friends, a wake, a Sunday, even for adults attending a children's party (Osorio 1992, 28–29). The male population was characterized by occupational instability due in part to shifting demand for labor, but much exacerbated by alcohol. Heavy drinking, including celebrations of "Holy Monday" that could last until Wednesday, were behind numerous missed workdays, firings, and job changes. In Huixquilucan, just as in Naucalpan or Tlanepantla, a typical "alcoholic family" experienced several drinking-related financial crises per year, which caused additional drinking, and underlying gender conflicts flared up accordingly. Consequences included intimate abuse and domestic rape; separation, divorce, or simple desertion; neglect and mistreatment of children; battered woman's syndrome; colitis, mental illness, menstrual disruption; and, last but not least, high levels of female alcoholism (30). Osorio hypothesizes that a woman's binge drinking might begin with the family of origin, perhaps to protest or escape from parental conflicts, but after marriage it only serves to increase the husband's already high levels of drinking. Such problems were less visible at greater educational and income levels (25). How did the proletarians attempt to deal with alcohol problems? Osorio cites the fledgling local AA group, the occasional conversion to one Protestant sect or another, and the vows made to the Virgin of Guadalupe (which in her view work better). Personal testimonials from women who have suffered at the hands of their hard-drinking mates enable Osorio to see a common pattern: daughters of alcoholic fathers usually have alcoholic brothers and end up with alcoholic husbands who give them children to do it all over again (39).

In Mexico, as in the United States, battered women tend to have strongly traditionalist attitudes about family unity and male privilege. "Ileana," a Mexican woman discussed by Jessica Kreimerman Lew (1997), went through an eighteen-month engagement with a handsome young man of *buena familia* that included one rape and several beatings. After the worst incident she pleaded for help from her prospective sister-in-law: "*Tu hermano me madreó*" ["Your brother beat the crap out of me"], to which the other replied, "You'd better get used to it, all of us women must" (Lew 1997, 131). In the view of sociologist Gabriel Careaga (1984), violent episodes were as common in Mexican middle-class homes as they were among the lowly strata described by Oscar Lewis (1959, 1961). In the more affluent world examined by Careaga, tequila-loving Mexican fathers had serious problems with anger management: they broke things, kicked down doors, threw telephones against the wall. The mothers were depressed, self-denying, obsessed with keeping their distance from the underclass, and proven experts at *chantaje sentimental* (emotional blackmail). The result was a family dynamics that resembled nothing so much as a Spanish-language telenovela (1984, 69–95). When sons and daughters grew up and began to exhibit desires for individual autonomy, "the mother recurred to everything imaginable to keep them close to her bosom" (74–75). Parental emotional dynamics were also behind the amazing generational continuity in drinking patterns. Despite the whippings they receive for it, male sons commenced binge-style drinking at an early age; the boozing-and-abusing pattern was particularly common in prosperous *ranchero* families in cahoots with the PRI (202). This provides support for the view of Américo Paredes, incidentally, for whom Mexican "machismo" was an essentially middle-class male fantasy complex (Paredes 1993, 215–34).

Bearing such data in mind, can we continue to see alcohol as associated with battering but in no way causative of it? It seems to me that (1) if violence is both a psychological *precursor* of alcohol use and an expected *consequence* of its use in several different social classes, and (2) if family discord leads directly to pharmacological vulnerability in later life, then (3) we cannot simply drop drinking from the causal chain. Certainly not in Mexico, where "negative as well as positive feelings about the mother may be displaced onto the wife" (Ingham 1986, 73). "Wives are scolded and beaten precisely because they seem to fall short of the ideal of the virginal, all-giving mother." They do not only *seem* to fall short, they *do* fall short, inevitably, even as they scurry to help their grandfathers urinate or vomit during the town fiesta. And let us not forget "the effect of an abusive father shutting off any meaningful affectionate relationship with his son, leaving that son no other alternative than the mother for emotional gratification. . . . The added possibility that the mother also might have had an abusive streak herself would only complicate his emotions" (Shupe, Stacey, and Hazlewood 1987, 36). Behind every wife-assaulter, in other words, we might find some youngster forced to "seduce the aggressor" and expect all needs to be met by mamá — without ceasing to idealize his hard-drinking, hard-hitting father at some level of the psyche. Learning to drink and learning to beat are inextricably intertwined in the unconscious search for an absolute provider who will never disappoint. At this level we discover structural connection and intergenerational reproduction, not mere association.

We have come a long way from the sociohistorical surface pretexts for domestic abuse, whether they be "The tortillas are cold" or "Your success in the global crafts market unnerves me." We are much closer, however, to the drinking rationales endlessly repeated in the Mexican song corpus. Examples abound in *las canciones rancheras*: "Despite my being really drunk, I keep drinking thanks to that woman"; "Between glasses of tequila I weep for your betrayal and all the lies of your cruel and false love"; "All women can go to hell, all they are good for is to cause us pain"; "She was a woman and she lied, just like all women"; "If I live drunk it's to forget the pain she stuck into my heart"; "I spend my nights staring at her portrait, surrounded by bottles." In the world according to the *corrido* innumerable Mexican big men get rubbed out in cantinas while drinking to forget some treacherous female. Other, more manic songs encourage men to tame the stubborn "mules": "I'm gonna ride her bareback, and break her and tame her, and though they say I'm a fool, some day I'm gonna humble her."

A common place to listen to such lyrics was the neighborhood cantina of the kind studied by Brian Stross (1991/1967). The typical woman who worked in such cantinas was an unwed mother who "drank, smoked, blasphemed, sold her body, and sexually flirted with men without feeling *vergüenza* [shame]" (290), all for a percentage of the drinks purchased by the men. "The symbolic negation of feminine attributes by the women of the cantina must be very satisfying for the client who might have gone there to forget his frustrations with some woman on the outside made pure, austere, and passive by cultural norms and the Church" (300). Thus it was impossible for a man to be "disrespectful" to such a woman, and indeed she was obliged to put up with "all manner of indignities, hostilities, and aggression" (Ibid.). In a cantina, additionally, one is more likely to hear the classic Mexican *mentada de madre* (denigratory mentioning of another's mother for purposes of humor or violence), or proverbs like "*Asnos y mujeres, a palos entienden*" ("Donkeys and women understand through beatings"). Misogynistic rationales are everywhere to be found, and every portrayal of spousal assault in humorous terms reflects the cultural weight of male psychic needs. Readers of Jesús Acosta's comic strip "*Chupamirto*" were treated to decades of funny proletarian machismo. The hero, a petty thief from the notorious neighborhood of Tepito, specialized in clubbing his *vieja* (old lady) under the very noses of the police (Pilcher 2001, 31).

There can be no beating without rigid defensive schemas, and aggressive maternal overprotection might be the proximal instrument of schema rigidification in Mexico. Ingham found numerous cases of girls raised in father-ineffective families who grew up to become possessive and controlling of their sons to a phenomenal degree (1986, 75). Their female offspring, meanwhile, were more vulnerable to the folk-medical diagnosis of *susto*. Let us keep in mind the sociopsychological matrix — the Oedipalization of Indian-peasant emotionality, the cult of the Blessed Mother that divided and conquered Mexican psyches. In this context, heavy drinking can be seen as a kind of balancing mechanism. Too-much-mother would be the psychological equivalent of ravenous sharks; here alcohol would function like a liferaft, the all-important vehicle of separation and individuation. Yet too-little-mother seems undesirable too, and here alcohol becomes a bridge back to the primordial love connection. Not everyone can be Roland Barthes, entering his mother's Paris apartment through a trapdoor, powering his high-cultural writing machine with an umbilical cord referent (Mavor 2003). For the heterosexual, low-cultural men studied here, alcohol is the emotionally incestuous "satellite position" that keeps them locked into orbit around the maternal imago (Stein 1994, 135). In the words of an old song:

> Si te odio y te quiero no puedo explicarme,
>
> si a veces yo siento deseos de matarte
>
> y a veces llorando me postro a tus pies.
>
> [Why I love you and I hate you I can't comprehend,
>
> why sometimes I feel desires to kill you
>
> and sometimes weeping I fall down at your feet.]

Our brothers walk a dangerous emotional tightrope while inebriated, in other words, but get no applause or prizes for it. A mother or a sister or a wife, meanwhile, constitutes the "obvious" symbol of primeval chaotic engulfment and simultaneously the refuge from the same. In the end we have no trouble linking the dynamics of sobriety/intoxication with cyclical wife-beating/pardon-begging. They intersect in the same spatiotemporal zone, the one in which the chemical determinism of a distillate activates one crucial schema of a script that does not belong to men alone. As they go through the lifecycle, women become the unwitting facilitators of the Oedipalized "mestizo" psychodrama south of the border, that is, the oscillating sadomasochistic object relations that men drink down with their first shots of mezcal.

Now we can understand why the beating urge can emerge all of a sudden, in men who seemed to be exemplary fiancés, husbands, or fathers in every way. Kearney wrote of an Ixtepeji villager named Celedonio Juárez, age forty-five, good husband, father of nine, hard worker, well-respected. Mezcal, at one time the source of his greatest happiness, had turned him into a village Jekyll-and-Hyde: "Now I can't drink so much as I used to. Until I was 37 I could drink night and day and I never forgot what happened. But now after a couple of drinks I forget everything, and when I'm like that I try to hit and mistreat everyone around me" (1991, 345) — especially his wife and children, a source of great *pena* and mortification for him. Having not yet become a member of AA, Celedonio did not blame alcohol for his difficulties; instead he was convinced that "an evil woman" had hexed him via "black magic" (345–46). Celedonio's ethnotheory of his malady parallels the psychoanalytic approach outlined above. The evil female apparition personifies Freud's famous "return of the castratory moment." As explained by Lawrence Kramer, "Sexual violence is precipitated when the awareness of one's negative condition — that one does not possess the phallus, after all, and never can — assumes a haunting positive form, an apparitional form. . . . Maddeningly, this someone else almost never appears in his own person. He hides behind a symbol, a persona, or an emissary — the last typically a woman — who mercilessly exposes one's imposture" (1997, 28–29). As seen throughout this book, apparitional modes of thought characterize the binge drinking cultures of Mexico. Perhaps dissociation derived from drinking finally "empowered" Celedonio directly to vent his anger on evil forces (the wife, i.e., the witch, i.e., the archaic androgynous mother of pain, i.e., the inner double of the mother who once threatened his bodily integrity with spankings, forced feedings, or invasive toilet training). Like the Mayan couples who pour more *aguardiente* on wounds caused by *aguardiente*, the people of Ixtepeji blamed witchcraft and paid no heed to the town's normal, obligatory, peer-enforced *borrachera* patterns.

At what *conscious* point will the schema for wife assault be activated in an unfolding morality script? Usually the trigger is some real or imagined female sin of action or omission that threatens the man's alcohol-supported sense of entitlement and requires a balancing "correction." During his time in Mexico City, Matthew Gutmann observed numerous group-therapy sessions at the Centro de Atención a la Violencia Intrafamiliar (CAVI). Men who had been reported to the police for beating their wives were organized into groups and encouraged to discuss their violent episodes. "I'm the victim here" was a defense Gutmann heard time and again:

> Thus, these men use terms like *ninguneado* [nothinged], *minimizado* [slighted], *humillado* [humiliated], and *descontrolado* [out of control] to describe how they feel as a result of how their wives, mothers, and other women treat *them*. . . . The violent tempers and eruptions of the CAVI men were consistently rekindled, the men said, when they received less respect and obedience than they knew they deserved. Such challenges to their authority were personified by the women in their lives, often regardless of the immediate sources of rancor. Jealousy was cited as a particularly sensitive problem, provoked by wives wearing "extra short" skirts or more makeup than usual, or coming home late and refusing to explain where they have been. One woman filed a complaint with CAVI stating that her husband inspected her vagina whenever she got home because he was sure she had a secret lover. (Gutmann 1996, 211–12)

With grievances strongly reminiscent of the colonial complaints studied by Taylor, Stern, and Castro Gutiérrez, Gutmann's men were equally frustrated by their wives' alleged lazy streaks — especially if those confounded tortillas were not hot and ready at suppertime (209). The men of the AA group studied by Brandes seemed better able to take responsibility for the many times they had assaulted their wives or children while intoxicated; their main difficulty lay in apologizing for the beatings without seeming unduly feminized: "Whatever they feel inside, it is rare for men openly to express guilt over mistreatment of women. In Alcoholics Anonymous, by contrast, men feel free to abstain from drink and ask women in public for forgiveness" (Brandes 2002, 107). Such public, emotional displays of repentance are seen as a sign of masculine strength by the members. All is not well in the *Distrito Federal*, however. Brandes finds that "a hyper-masculine atmosphere prevails in the Moral Support meeting room" (127); in addition, attendance at AA homosocial bonding sessions is so time-consuming that "the actual number of hours they spend with the family is probably not much greater than it was prior to group membership" (117). Small wonder, then, that "the majority of married men in the group continue to suffer problems with wives and children" (122). In keeping with the trends of modern scholarship, Brandes insists that the Mexican AA movement promotes "a redefinition of traditional gender roles" (198). The men he studied are certainly not in denial about their booze-inspired violence and penchant for *fregadazos*; indeed they seem rather adept at self-recrimination (118). What they have suppressed, I would wager, is how appropriate the spousal assault seemed at the time, how righteously moral, how strangely enjoyable.

All drinks are mixed, figuratively speaking. It matters not whether the *pulque* is fresh, white, and bacteria-free, or whether the aguardiente has been distilled in hygienic conditions. Even the purest drink enters into a dynamic relationship with a bodymind that might harbor other kinds of toxins. Some are known, some are only suspected. All consciously held "justifications" for beatings can be traced to public/private gender hegemonies, the gendered moral economy, misogynistic traditions. This approach is legitimate, possibly emancipatory, safe, and academically well-covered at this point. A more challenging research option, in my view, would explore the less familiar spatiotemporal zones of a destructured, desubjectified consciousness that somehow manages to reproduce itself through history. Despite all the changes in Mexican markets, patterns of ownership, relations of production, and so forth, wives continue to be beaten. To conclude this chapter, let us travel to the strange zones where the necessary motivational schemas survive, century in and century out.

John Ingham paved the way in choosing to discuss Tlayacapan drunkenness in terms of its transformational possibilities (1986, 151–55). The town's binge drinkers (i.e., all the men, including Ingham while he was there) were identified not by name but by nickname: Goat, Parrot, Heron, Bird, Pig, Parakeet, Badger, Fly, Rat, Cow, Scorpion, Snake, Toad, Monkey, Squirrel, and so on. Alcohol also facilitated a more dangerous mixture of man and beast in Tlayacapan, the *nagual*: "Men who see naguales often are drunk at the time, and naguales seem predisposed to attack drunks. In one instance, what was thought at first to be a nagual turned out, on closer inspection, to be nothing more than another drunk. Indeed, drunken men and naguales are suspiciously alike. Both undergo temporary transformations, usually at night. Naguales rarely are women, and women rarely drink to excess" (153). In colonial times, so-called *nagualismo* was a subversive mode of magic folk medicine (Aguirre Beltrán 1963), but let us focus on the psychogeography of the transformations and the apparitions. Ingham found that both desired encounters with loose women and undesired encounters with evil beings took place in the liminal zone of the *barrancas* (ravines, canyons, or gullies) — "intrusions of unruly wilderness amid an otherwise civilized landscape" and veritable "passageways to the underworld" (103). Ravines were the sites of clandestine alcohol distillation for many centuries, as we saw earlier, and *barranca* metaphors were much favored by authors like Malcolm Lowry and composers like José Alfredo Jiménez. So let us make the most of the *barranca* metaphor — there may be none better for the unconscious wellsprings of intimate violence, and it jibes perfectly with studies of traumatic networking in the brain (Bollas 1992, 1995). Picture, then, a scarred psychic landscape, a chain of formidable ravines carved out in Mexican minds by their intergenerational drinking cultures. A child growing up in Tlayacapan or Huixquilucan amidst alcoholized parental discord learn to banish his anguished, rage-filled ideas to unconscious holding areas where they acquire their own psychic gravity, their own ramifying coherence, and begin to live a life of their own (cf. Bollas 1992, 77–81). The fear of damage to the self animates the inclination to damage another's self. Hell, as Lowry or Rulfo well knew, is a place in the mind where one never forgives and is never forgiven. Through a sinkhole present in every neighborhood, one can slide into a deep canyon where idealization is relentlessly pursued by degradation, where rage storms sweep across the terrain unpredictably but inevitably. Ravines of the mind have fractal or strange-attractor shapes that are self-similar at different time scales — one man's one-day *borrachera* might recapitulate one culture's drunken centuries. Mental ravines are cavernous, twisting, dendritic spacetimes of negative desiring production, bizarre progeny of the founding Oedipus. There is flow, but not autonomy; one is swept away by the forces of negative affect, the winds of pain whirling chaotically around stony accretions and thorny dead cacti, old humiliated/humiliator paradigm scenarios, sterile gardens of grievance-nurturing and resentment.

In Mexico, the intimate violence of spousal assault defends against the threat of castration represented in literature by famously perverse archetypes (*La Llorona, La Malinche, La Chingada*). Seemingly motivated by the shortness of the skirt or the excess of the lipstick, ritual spousal assault's true aim is that of "capturing the lost object, aggressively punishing it for straying, and maintaining a sexual excitement that will keep both self and object idealized, libidinized, and alive, so that his mother will never again be lost or dead to him" (Bach 1991, 83). In keeping with their assigned roles in the sociocultural script, women learn to occupy the moral highground, to suffer with rather exhibitionistic abnegation and console their damaged insecure men, just like La Virgen de Guadalupe. Feminist scholars take it for granted that Mexican popular piety disempowers women: "If newer racial and gendered identities are to be forged, the insight arrived at in [Chicana feminist] writing needs to be communicated to millions of women who still live under such metaphoric controls. How are they to be persuaded to accept those insights if they still exist under the ideology 'Guadalupe-Malintzin'?" (Alarcón 2003, 44). In a radical recent development noted by Patricia Zavella, "Lesbian theorists also claim La Virgen de Guadalupe as their icon, reconfiguring her as a symbol of indigenous liberation and women's empowerment" (2003, 230). Sometimes the regestalting works, sometimes it doesn't, as illustrated by cases of lesbians unable to avoid the whole script in their relationships, right down to the battering behavior (241). Just like men, women can compulsively identify with the archaic androgynous mother of pain and become perfectly capable of every malicious trait they routinely attribute to men — with the possible exception of that classic masculine sense of entitlement. As several women have explained to me, a Mexican mother is always more likely to (1) *endiosar* her male children (make them feel like little gods who can do no wrong), and then (2) short-sightedly present herself as the only answer to their prayers. This is exactly what my Mexican sister-in-law is doing with her two sons, as I look on helplessly.

For the time being, therefore, in marriage-minded Mexico, the sins of the mothers will continue to be visited upon their daughters-in-law. Idealization and denigration, guilt and contrition, libidinal battery-charging, and men charged with battery: these are all real and probably unavoidable consequences of keeping alcoholized links to archaic imagos intact. Drinking itself is a legal activity, bars are licensed, but let us remember that the real business is eternity. An unknown number of cantinas are situated along the road to hell, or under the volcano, while others have purgatorial locations and still others lead to psychic terrains of forgiveness and redemption. Demon-creatures do not monopolize Mexican drinking cultures, thank God, but for magical power to exist at all the whole continuum of trauma-processing object relations must be kept operational. For every cost there is a benefit. As I establish in the next chapter, the same "psychological cantina" that sets the stage for domestic violence played an important role in Mexico's *recovery* from Revolutionary violence, and continues to be instrumental to the perpetuation of the cosmic race itself.

Chapter 8
The Pedro Infante Generation

Mexico's post-Revolutionary governability was facilitated by enthralling representational formats that did not demand literacy: mural painting, patriotic festivals, radio shows, records, and movies of the so-called Golden Age of Mexican cinema (approximately 1935–1955). Despite a state-orchestrated cult of indigenism, the racialist values and gender polarities of *ranchero* Mexico became more salient than ever due to the political clout of cattle barons and enterprising media barons who gave the public what it wanted: the best of both worlds. Rapidly modernizing men and women wanted to keep one foot in their idealized provincial origin worlds, but also wished to avoid stigmatizing identity-attributions of rusticity and backwardness. Thus the public's idols of identity could never be *indios* (a word often used pejoratively), but talented exemplars of the folk-urban symbiosis with modest backgrounds, predominantly European features, strong vocal chords, and sexual charisma. Male movie stars were magnetic for both women and men, according to Yolanda Moreno. "The idol is above all the idealized image that the Mexican would like to have of himself. Several generations desired, and not very secretly, to be like Jorge Negrete, Pedro Infante, or Javier Solís" (1989, 200).

Not all scholars have viewed this phenomenon with Moreno's nostalgic ecuanimity. The more popular the movie, in general, the greater the embarrassment felt by academic film critics, foreign and domestic. Joanne Hershfield is typical in tracing the origins of the most successful films — *ranchero* romances — to the wrong racial, religious, and gender politics: "Through the image of the *charro*, this singularly Mexican film genre glorified the machismo of the nation, drawing a link between the patriarchal hacendado, the state, and paternalism. The *comedia ranchera* may be read as a thinly disguised challenge, in the form of a musical love-story, to

149

Cárdenas's social and economic reforms" (1999, 91). Hershfeld lists a number of classic 1930s *ranchero* pictures and then asks how such "reactionary films" could be released during the very presidency of Lázaro Cárdenas (91–92). This way of framing the question is both naïve and unproductive; Hershfield and the critics she relies upon prove themselves incapable of accounting for the psychology of the people who flocked to see the movies. Let us explore the issue without bias, therefore, because it does lead to a better grasp of the dynamics of alcoholic nationalism promoted by Mexico's mass culture industries. As a perquisite, we soon discover that *ranchero* movie idols and Cárdenas were nothing less than strategic allies.

The *comedia ranchera* was, first and foremost, an efficient vehicle for the propagation of *música ranchera*; it was the music video system of its time and place. As the media barons soon grasped, people were primarily addicted to the nostalgia encoded or encapsulated in the songs, so they structured the movies around them. Other elements had the status of an afterthought, and usually looked it. Artists were singers first and actors second, if at all. The well-known mariachi Vargas appeared in approximately two hundred films (Burr 1999:145), but it would be misleading to analyze them in "filmic" terms. They will only look like a silly collection of stereotypes, vintage Mexican calendar art in motion. The music must take center stage, but to carry out this regestalting requires a different set of critical tools, a minimum degree of empathy with the emotionality of bygone generations, and at least grudging admiration for the talented composers who renovated Mexico's vast corpus of regional song styles.

Regarding the Catholic elements that Hershfield hastily identifies with Cristero reaction (1999, 90), it is vital to know that Mexican urbanization "certainly did not result in the kind of progressive secularization which the revolutionaries had favored (and which certain theories might have predicted)" (Knight 1990, 256). Knight offers several vignettes that show urban life *reinforcing* certain kinds of religious practices. Although Lázaro Cárdenas had participated in anticlerical and anti-alcohol initiatives as governor of Michoacán, his love of indigenous traditions kept him from the worst sins of the Callistas, and even these never matched the fanatical extremes of 1930s Spain (Mitchell 1998, 63–93). Shortly before he sent Calles into exile, Cárdenas announced that "The government will not repeat the mistake committed by previous administrations in considering the religious question a preeminent problem" (as cited by Krauze 1997, 459). At the end of his term in office, Cárdenas even thanked the Church for supporting the oil expropriation. As with General Alvaro Obregón's marriage with the Catholic sacraments, Porfirian-style pragmatism prevailed in the end. Indeed, why make enemies out of 80 percent of the population? The Church did not have to be destroyed, after all, simply plagiarized — "recast as political theology on its original footing of violence, sacrifice, and spectacle" (Taussig 1997, 12). Part of the PRI's (and

Mexico's) stability was based on the successful assimilation of this lesson by the film industry of the 1940s. In *Río Escondido* (1948), the legendary director Emilio Fernández elevated a humble federal schoolteacher (played by María Félix) into a Christ-like figure, ready to suffer martyrdom on a sacred educational mission from a God-like Presidente (Pérez Siller 1998). Such relentlessly didactic films provided a kind of legitimacy for the ruling group that Calles could only have dreamed of, although the Mexican picture industry itself was soon pinned down by Hollywood's hegemony (Seth Fein 1999).

Film scholars eagerly point to the racialist aspects of *ranchero* comedies. Let us recall that every other discourse of Mexican identity formation was racialist or simply racist during the period under discussion. Each discourse proposed solutions, each competed for ultimate legitimacy, each sought to overcome one shameful legacy or another, but none was ever Hitlerian in scope. José de Vasconcelos confidently predicted in *The Cosmic Race* that one day his country's "ugliest races" would voluntarily cease to reproduce — for purely aesthetic reasons! (1997/1925, 72). *Indigenista* writers like Ricardo Pozas or Mauricio Magdaleno damned the white world for its abuses, not without cause: de-Indianization had truly been the dream of Mexico's middle-class *gente decente* for centuries. Mexico was home to "an intractably racist society," Knight notes (1997, 87). De facto racist assumptions crept into or lurked behind many manifestos — even the best intentioned: "The *indigenistas* could shake the bars of their conceptual prison but not escape from it" (100). My point is that *ranchero* comedies were neither more nor less racist than other cultural products. Many mestizos learned to value their mixed blood following the Revolution; many more kept on striving to differentiate themselves from impoverished or "backward" groups; but note that even those closest to European standards of beauty and appearance did not wish to be identified with the always unpopular Spaniard. In cattle-raising country, this surrogation anxiety had pre-Revolutionary and post-Revolutionary solutions: The *hidalgo campirano* or "country gentleman" was a prosperous, mestizoized creole who steered a middle course, taking care to distance himself from the *gachupín* hacendado class targeted for elimination, and naturally from the unflattering image of lowly peasants and Indians (Alfaro 1994, 12). For large parts of the population, however, the *hidalgo campirano* was too distant socially, too much a part of the establishment, still too Spanish. During and after the Revolution, popular tastes favored charismatic mestizo rancheros like Pancho Villa or Emiliano Zapata. The latter, erroneously or strategically portrayed as a peasant in many murals, was actually the most celebrated *charro* of his region before joining Madero's revolt. So regardless of the actual skin color of film idols like Jorge Negrete or Pedro Infante, the roles they built their fame upon were still prototypical mestizo fantasies, and the public idolatry was a better vindication of racial hybridity than anything Vasconcelos had to offer. Following Negrete's death, one popular *corrido* praised him for so ably "representing your Aztec blood" (Jiménez 1995, 542). To this very day, tellingly, Mexicans inordinately proud of their whiteness will sometimes refer to a *ranchero* spectacle or concert as *cosa de indios* (strictly for Injuns).

Racial hybridity was on display in a different theatrical venue — bullfighting, the former propaganda machine of Iberian hegemony. Rodolfo Gaona's combination of Navarrese and indigenous blood fueled the exoticist fantasies of taurine journalists on both sides of the Atlantic; he was called "the Caliph of León." Silverio Pérez came to be called, just as absurdly, "the Pharoah of Texcoco." The idea was to emphasize the non-Western majesty of their bullring performances (Claramunt 1989, 2:226). Perhaps most interesting is one critic's fanciful attribution of Silverio's killing style to his mixed blood:

> It is undeniable that in Silverio Pérez, more than in any other matador, we have seen the heir of the ancestral feelings of the American Indian, the echo of a terrible and sublime world that seeks above all its purest expression. Being so indigenous he can at the same time be deeply Hispanic and unite the two dispositions, improving with *mestizaje* like the Mudéjar art of the Iberian Peninsula that achieved new and unsuspected qualities through a similar process. (Daniel Medina de la Serna as cited by Claramunt 1989, 2:226, my translation)

The matador Silverio Pérez was the physical opposite of Manolete, his lanky Iberian contemporary. With short arms, stubby legs, and bright little eyes set in a gigantic head, Silverio "exuded a charming ugliness." Alone with a bull in the ring, however, he changed into a portentious and insolent figure, took charge in a terrifying way, got so close to the bull with every pass of his cape that fans were simultaneously electrified and anguished (Néstor Luján as cited by Claramunt 1989, 2:230). The oscillation from shamed inferior to cocky superior, built into the very drama of the bullfight itself, was a perfect script for the mestizo success story.

Land reform is next on our list of rebuttal points. It is a commonplace among film critics that *ranchero* melodramas conveyed a tacit rebuke of the agrarian policies of General Cárdenas (e.g., García Riera 1969, 130). If this is true, then the movies anticipated the explicit rebuke of many intended beneficiaries of those policies and future generations of economic historians. But it is only a half-truth. What critics overlook is that the most popular film genre in the country routinely demonized *hacendados*, thereby providing tactical support for the governmental dream of liberating peons from the hacienda system. "*Tata*" Cárdenas carried out his agrarian program in paternalistic fashion — "like a vast ceremony of moral restitution to the Mexican poor" (Krauze 1997, 515); that the *ranchero* movies did not question or perturb the fundamental peasant faith in hierarchies was therefore quite useful to him. As Marjorie Becker explains, the Presidente and his allies "refused to believe that campesinos could in fact shake off habits of deference to the powerful. Consequently, the cardenistas constructed an ideology calling for social control and then proceeded to imitate the old elites' techniques of control" (1993, 159). Far from being a reactionary rebuke to *cardenismo*, therefore, musical comedies that portrayed charismatic *charros* standing up to evil landowners provided fantasmatic support for it. Keeping the people focused on the old love-hate relationship with the hacienda was the best possible smokescreen for a land distribution plan that either failed miserably (Fallaw 2001) or turned the state itself into what Krauze calls "a new and all encompassing 'hacendado'" (1997, 463).

What about booze? As it happens, the tequila industry offers the best example of the disruptions wrought by agrarian reform and the eventual reassertion of a proper business economy in all its asymmetry. Between 1930 and 1940, most of the agave lands of the great tequila dynasties of Jalisco were confiscated and distributed among several thousand *ejidatarios* (cooperative farmers). The population of maguey plants declined by 65 percent, what Luna terms the "disarticulating effect" of the *ejido* land distribution program and a "harsh blow" to the tequila industrialists (1999, 153). Don Eladio Sauza, son and heir to don Cenobio Sauza (chapter 5), had sought secretly to portion out his estates to trusted compadres, but to no avail. By 1937 he was truly an ex-hacendado, though retaining ownership of the family distillery. He had already transferred most of his money to the urban real estate market of Guadalajara. He founded that city's first commercial radio stations, XED and XEDQ, started a trendy nightspot known as the Colonial Club, and participated in other ventures alongside other ex-hacendados. In the meantime, numerous *ejidatarios* had set up clandestine distilleries in the same places and with the same techniques that had been used in colonial times! Both illegal and legal tequila concerns benefitted from the boom in U.S. consumption during World War II; gringo demand for the product was so great that the tequila had to be watered down by Mexico City middlemen in the very trains that carried it north. Thereafter, the famous brand dynasties reasserted their control of the tequila industry through a number of indirect financial and marketing strategies, all perfectly legal (Luna 1999, 155–58). Tequila is now sold and consumed as the authentically Mexican drink, best appreciated by connoisseurs, pushed most aggressively by educated young businessmen in a position to alcoholize whole new generations on both sides of the border. As one expert tequila taster explains, "We produced Tequila Campanario to penetrate a very crowded high-end market. . . . When we sell bad tequila abroad, as people used to do, it reflects badly on the industry and we get a reputation as an *albañil* [worker's] drink" (Gabriel Espíndola as cited by Orozco 2003, 233). God forbid.

Alcoholization proceeds in dialectical, chicken-and-egg fashion. Demand increases supplies, better supplies stimulate demand, good marketing strategies encourage alcohol-related practices and philosophies to emerge or reconfirm themselves. On the supply side, the whole infrastructure necessary to keep cantinas and corner stores stocked with beverages was constantly upgraded in the 1920s and 1930s. The proprietors of Mexico City's bars banded together in 1939 to better defend their commercial interests, and the nationwide Confederación Nacional de Comerciantes de Vinos y Licores dates from 1945 (Garibay 1997, 146–53). Beer became big business for the first time. Monterrey's Cervecería Cuauhtemoc, born during the Porfiriato's alcohol-friendly modernization, became tremendously successful in post-Revolutionary Mexico. As Hibino relates, "only two industries, the state-owned railroads and oil industry, surpassed the brewery in size in the mid-1950s. The Cervecería brewery, however, was distinct from state-owned firms because it grew to thirty times its original size without financing from the exterior and eventually developed its own technology" (1992, 23–24). This mode of alcoholization was not economically parasitic; the nationalistic brewery generated a number of spin-off industries (bottles, malt, cardboard, plastics, steel) "that own more than one hundred U.S. patents and have exported their technology to more than twenty countries" (24). The brewery's intimate involvement with Mexican higher education will be discussed in due time.

Tequila baron don Eladio Sauza and General Cárdenas had something in common: an enthusiasm for radio. Station XFX, run by the Secretaría de Educación Pública, became a key conveyor of the government's perspectives and policies. Its musical programming, according to Joy Hayes, "created a model of nationalist discourse that influenced both government and commercial broadcasting in Mexico throughout the twentieth century" (2000, 42). But demographic and marketing forces unleashed by modernization outshone the government in framing Mexican identities: "As rural audience reactions to XFX broadcasts indicate, the most popular and lasting radio discourse of the 1930s was not the programming disseminated by government stations but the programming produced by Mexico City's dominant commercial broadcasters, especially Emilio Azcárraga" (Hayes 2000, 62). Azcárraga was destined to become the owner of the most powerful radio station in the Western Hemisphere, XEW. Azcárraga, also known as el Tigre, maintained friendships in high places for many decades and generously helped the PRI to build the post-Revolutionary status quo. It could be argued that, in the long run, men like Azcárraga were more important than men like Vasconcelos or Diego Rivera. Writes Knight: "Pervasive and appealing, radio and cinema far outstripped, in terms of mass cultural impact, the static visual didactics of the revolutionary muralists" (Knight 1990, 260).

Unlike the "transfer of sacrality" from Church to State clumsily attempted by Calles (or the young Cárdenas), the identity-constructing forces of the private sector energetically promoted alcohol and religion — hence their success and subsequent accomodation by every PRI adminis- tration of the twentieth century. Gender identity was at stake in all this, naturally: drinking strong Mexican liquors in a cantina signified genuine manliness (often regarded as machismo), and anything that fortified virile self-confidence was good for business and good for governance (Doremus 2001, 97). Let us not imprison our paradigms in a top-down model of cul- tural circulation; instead let us give pride of place to a gendered ethnona- tionalism strongly pushed at the grass-roots level of local cultural worlds. With the State consolidated and less anxious, villagers previously victim- ized by anti-alcohol and anticlerical schoolteachers reasserted themselves with *charreadas*, *jaripeos*, horseraising, cockfighting, brass bands, and noisy Catholic festivals. Tecamachalco (Puebla) was typical:

> By popular acclaim the festival shed the Spartan character it had in the sanitizing 1930s under the teetotaling school inspector González. Expert *charros* sauntered along in the parade on their horses with their silver spurs and broad-brimmed, velveteen som- breros with brocade. Village women prepared great vats of *mole*. Villagers danced until dawn and enjoyed elaborate displays of fire- works. (Vaughan 1994, 230)

Vaughan views the combination of the hedonic and the patriotic not in terms of state imposition but of "hegemonic articulation" (230–35). Dur- ing the business-oriented presidencies of Manuel Avila Camacho (1940–1946) and Miguel Alemán (1946–1952), the ruling party hastened to put itself at the head of such nationalistic parades. With its own radio network and its monopoly on school textbooks, the Secretaría de Edu- cación Pública helped to consecrate emblematic figures of patriotism and progress. National cultural synergy was achieved when private-sector media networks "articulated" with state-financed programs and initiatives. For example, as soon as the literacy levels of the population reached opti- mum levels, the market for mass-produced comic books exploded. Anne Rubinstein finds this genre playing a huge role in the dissemination of modernist ideals in Mexico; comics were "as ubiquitous as radio and more common than cinema" (1998, 13). Jean Franco asserts that comic-strip novels known as *libros semanales* transmitted "the same modernization story: the family is a drag and has to be left behind" (1986, 132). "Precisely because the *libros semanales* are so unglamorous and are so clearly intended for women who are integrated or are about to be integrated into the work place, they need a different kind of modernization plot — one that cannot simply hold out the carrot of consumption" (131). Chro- molithography, meanwhile, was an identity-constructing Mexican indus- try that worked in just the opposite way, purveying a much more idealistic or nostalgic worldview than the *libros semanales*. According to noted calendar collector Jim Heimann:

> The imagery printed on these calendars borrowed heavily from a romanticized version of Mexican life and mythology, idealizing native customs, dress, and folklore. The calendars, which were freely distributed by businesses, often were a household's primary piece of art and became a central piece of interior decoration surrounded by family photos and religious icons. The subject matter of the calendars ranged from religious icons, such as Our Lady of Guadalupe, to those images drawn from Mexico's vibrant history. The power of the *cromos*, as the calendars are known, is undeniable. They fulfilled, through illustrations, a past and present that was understood by all levels of society. (Heimann 2002, 4)

The alluring image of the *china poblana*, a kind of small town girl-next-door, was popular even in the United States, according to Jeanne Gillespie: "The dark-haired, dark-eyed young Mexican woman named 'Rosarita,' with a white blouse, often decorated with lace, and a full green skirt adorned with colorful ribbons, represents one brand of Mexican food products. The *china poblana* also appears in Corona beer advertisements and on tavern serving trays popular in the 1950s and 1960s" (1998, 36).

Many of the subjects and images in question are beautifully rendered, but we have to eschew the standard art vocabulary used when discussing the "long" production cycles of the "anti-economic economy of pure art which can acknowledge no other demand than one it can generate itself" (Bourdieu 1996, 142). The less intellectual, more commercial enterprises cited above follow an inverse logic of "short" production cycles, since they "minimize risks by an advance adjustment to predictable demand" (142). Mexico's cultural elites played but a small role in the businesses and formats that arose to supply this demand, so Roger Bartra's approach is of no use to us here. There was nothing remotely "melancholy" about national heroes or those famous gendered icons, *charro* and *china poblana*, especially when pictured together dancing the *jarabe tapatío*. It is certainly the case that drunken, adulterous, and violent fathers were portrayed in a bad light by modernizing comic-strip novels (Franco 1986, 132), but in calendars, music, and the movies, wild drinking by handsome *charros* in cantinas was portrayed in a joyous, patriotic light. Inside this folk-urban discursive universe we find no inferiority complex, no labyrinth of solitude, no existential angst — just old-fashioned ethnocentrism and romanticism as reworked by middlebrow folklorists like Rubén Campos, Higinio Vázquez Santa Ana, or Fernando Ramírez de Aguilar. These men never enjoyed the literary cachet of Rulfo or Paz, obviously, but they did enjoy the backing of an immense state pedagogical bureaucracy that circulated their works to every school in the country (Pérez Montfort 1998, 385).

Back in the private sector, *ranchero* and *ranchero*-emulating drinking cultures were an eternal source of inspiration for those who made Mexican movies or penned their plots. Many an ex-Vasconcelista jumped on the bandwagon. Mauricio Magdaleno, author of the dark indigenist novel *Resplandor* (1937), found that he could reach a much larger audience with scripts for films like *Flor silvestre* (1943), *Río escondido* (1948), or *Duelo en las Montañas* (1949), all of which feature attractive, binge-drinking *charros* in starring roles. Even the melancholy Indians undergo a makeover. Anne Doremus notes that Magdaleno's script for the 1943 film *María Candelaria* completely reverses his earlier representations of indigenous communities (2001, 78). We are forced to conclude that the livestock-raising *ranchero* world had its own sort of cultural hegemony — disturbingly preindustrial, unfashionably Catholic, festive to a fault, and much concerned with breeding. It favored racial hybridity, in fact or in fantasy, and it fetishized gender roles. Lola Romanucci-Ross was right to see the bullring as the center of Dionysian machismo in her village, and we can well understand why she preferred upwardly mobile neighborhoods with their basketball courts, businesses, sobriety, and English lessons. Though she did express pity for the poor village macho whose subculture "shrivels around him" (1973, 154), she vastly underestimated the resistance harbored by that subculture, and somehow missed its remarkable swelling and expansion via mass-mediated formats. If she had turned on the radio in 1973, she would have heard all the evidence needed, countless songs commemorating crowded rural get-togethers, ranchos grand and small, fine horses, woman-taming, gambling, tequila, mariachis, cockfighting, words of honor, saloon brawls, *compadrazgo*, and wound-licking binges. Long before 1973 her restless village machos were migrating to join their plucky urban counterparts in Mexico City's saloons, all under the smiling auspices of a cleverly inclusive one-party system already in bed with beer barons, tequila tycoons, big ranchers from every state, caciques at local and regional levels, and predatory media giants like "*el Tigre.*"

Can we find multimedia Mexican melodramas that showcase the articulation of alcoholized Catholic erotics with the needs of the post-Revolutionary ruling class? Yes, or I would not bother asking. One such story, recounted in every possible format, was that of Juan *el Charrasqueado* (John the One-Slashed-with-a-Knife), who began his mythic life in 1942 as the hard-drinking hero of a *corrido* by Victor Cordero. The song was a huge hit for Jorge Negrete in 1947, and a movie with Pedro Almendáriz in the starring role appeared in 1952. In the meantime, off and on, Cordero transformed his *corrido* into a vast, rambling novel that would remain unpublished until 1998. This posthumous book is of great interest not for its manifest literary quality, which is nil, but for its disturbingly clairsentient presentation of the fantasmatic, rather obscene underside of Cardenist and PRI legitimation strategies.

Like a museum designed to inculcate reproductive and revolutionary ideals into the young, *Juan Charrasqueado* is set up as a series of dioramas. Violent death in the context of heavy drinking is the motor of narrative action — true to the world of the cantina *corrido* itself. The insistent boozing is motivated by (1) mestizo status-seeking and manhood affirmation and (2) guilt over sexual transgressions. The story begins when the vast Hacienda de la Flor is purchased by don Angel del Campo, an exiled Republican Spaniard who quickly takes to the despotic ways of his colonial forbears. He vampirizes the lives and labor of his peons, forces them to buy goods in his own *tienda de raya*, even falls upon their barefoot virginal daughters with uncontrolled lust (he had been a classic don Juan in Spain). His devout Catholic wife, doña Chole, and his own virginal daughter, Flor, educated by nuns, know nothing of his sins. Every time don Angel appears, he seems more and more like Satan — just the sort of *hacendado* demonization Cárdenas might have enjoyed — and of course the mindset is thoroughly preindustrial. In Mexican folklore, the devil "uses money and a parody of contractual relations to appropriate a person's soul, his or her essence. In this respect, his behavior mimics that of the Spaniard who appropriated the labor of Indian peasants and took advantage of them in commercial transactions" (Ingham 1986, 108). Popular street festivals throughout Mexico underline the Spaniard = Satan equation. Cordero's diorama is equally reminiscent of a class-conscious mural by Orozco or Siqueiros: we see the barely-repressed rage in peasant eyes, machetes trembling in their hands.

At the same time, however, we are constantly invited to admire the many Iberian cultural seeds that took root and flowered in the valleys and sierras of Mexico following the early decades of depopulation by disease. The local priest, Father Bernardino, is gratefully loved by all for his charity and "his humble patriarchal character" (Cordero 1998:41). There is nothing about the young Juan Bravo del Monte that does not correspond to the Ibero-Mexican, fertility-favoring, phallocentric honor code. At age twenty-three he is the best horseman, the best *charro*, the best dressed, the best armed. In the Zapatesque iconic tradition, Juan simultaneously boasts a splendid mustache and bronzed Amerindian skin. A graduate of the fourth grade, Juan knows many secrets denied to the more educated: cards, cantinas, the misery of the peasantry, all livestock activities, the ins-and-outs of cockfighting. We first glimpse Juan when he rides into the hacienda and hurls don Angel's money in his face, along with an endless litany of ethnic and economic grievances. As don Angel impatiently fingers his riding crop, Juan explains how he changed his destiny by mastering games of chance: "That's why the horse I'm riding is mine, don Angel, and I enjoy the luxury of getting drunk whenever I want" (28). But the setting for this oedipal mise-en-scène is too private: Cordero will reserve his best ink for the tableau scene of the *pelea de gallos*, wherein a silver-colored cock raised personally by Juan will best the champion golden cock of

Aguascalientes in a savage encounter. Like the Balinese cockfights famously glossed by Clifford Geertz (1973), Mexican *peleas de gallos* are not about "money gambling" so much as "status gambling." Our protagonist is destined to emerge triumphant in these moments of phallocentric *deep play* that are so irrational from a utilitarian standpoint (rather like bullfighting). Prior to the match Juan rides through San Miguel holding his cock aloft, daring the rich merchants to wager against it, triggering waves of enthusiasm in the women. He maneuvers his proud steed Azabache into an elegant bow before the virtuous Flor, chaperoned by her haughty *hacendado* parents. After the match, loaded down with silver, status enhanced, Juan proceeds to San Miguel's best cantina "to celebrate the triumph of his cock" (46).

Cordero credibly inserts himself into the narrative's cantina scenes in the character of Victor, a poet and composer playing piano for the pretty prostitutes who surround their free-spending "John." The romantic music is always a prelude to tears, more drinking, truth emergence, quarrels among the women, and sexual commerce. Although Juan's way of drinking himself into oblivion is irreproachably virile, it usually leads to a desire for lacrimose melodies played by "musicians with hangover faces." A few binges celebrate one stroke of luck or another, but most are motivated by Juan's endless capacity for self-torture. He feels remorse for having besmirched the honor and marriage potential of one virgin or another, and regrets his burning urge to keep on doing it. (The drinking itself elicits no guilt whatsoever). Juan gets his eponymous *charrasca* or knife-scar from don Angel, the devilish *hacendado*, for having (1) impregnated his daughter Flor (2) with mestizo blood (3) out of wedlock. Fully in keeping with the harsh real-life consequences of Catholic patriarchy, the "dance-token" women of the cantina are all *sinvergüenzas*, having lost their *vergüenza* or shame, thus their marriageability, through the abusive lust of men just like Juan. As noted by Brian Stross, men who find libidinal outlets in cantinas and bordellos are not obliged to change their notions of the "ideal" woman (1991/1967, 301). Just as Stross would have predicted, Cordero's saloon women drink heavily and oscillate between scandalous flirtation and self-pity. The omniscient narrator's endless ramblings about virginity, sin, Eve, flesh, and hookers are priceless and help us to understand why female singers were destined to play such a pivotal role in the evolution of ranchera music — less of the sin, more of the guilt, and greater believability as traumatized sexual pessimists. They are all *scarred*, one way or another, although Juan's scar can also be seen as an archetypal symbol of achieved masculine identity — "the trace of a flaw that is displayed, and meant to be read, as a sign of wholeness" (Kramer 1998, 250).

Machismo *strictu sensu* is the product of political despotism. Becker affirms that "The cardenistas entered the black-and-white picture of the past that they themselves had painted and began to impersonate the elites within" (1993, 159); at lower levels of power, this surrogation strategy used "local petty tyrants to impose *cardenismo* on the population. Since the revolution Cárdenas had been allied with such armed strongmen" (161). The new political bosses did not demonize themselves, obviously, but thought of themselves as benevolent, charismatic, truly popular caciques — just like honest Juan, founder of the Agrarian Party of Guanajuato and de facto Big Man of San Miguel de Allende. Too pure of heart and way too virile to stay alive for long, Juan's love of strong drink sets the stage for the final betrayal-and-sacrifice motif so essential in Mexico. The cockfighting hero will be cut down in his prime by a revenge-minded cacique and his *tejano* henchmen. Lest there be any doubt about the element of phallic worship, also known as worship of the generative powers, Cordero puts his readers into the shoes of Catholic schoolgirls who accidentally come upon the morgue where Juan's lifeless body lies in all its naked glory, nothing left to their or to our imaginations. No movie of the period would feature such a salacious episode, of course, since it makes far too explicit the homoerotic exhibitionism of Ibero-Mexican phallocentric aesthetics. Cordero's morgue scene accidentally shows post-Revolutionary *caciquismo* milking power from the phantasy reservoir of Roman Catholicism. The Church Fathers themselves unwittingly guaranteed the survival of pagan genitalia worship in forms of disguise and denial — Marian masochism, celibacy, the crucified nude Christ, prurient confessional manuals, and so on (Carroll 1986, 49–89; Drewermann 1995, 327–584).

This is all very regressive, and yet exploitable. With no little help from alcohol, a recalcitrant population had preserved a colonial reservoir of psychic algorithms and associations that were unexpectedly useful to the institutionalized Revolution. The "golden age" of Mexican movies made old fantasy elements more attractive than ever; they were then recycled and reactivated by the nation's network of real-life cantinas and their "cocky" denizens — all imitating each other in their desire to be unrivalled. This is the dialectics of alcoholization seen from a different angle. Mexico's fiestas, cantinas, and corner bars were permanent liminal spaces for creative performance, socially sanctioned sites for the ecstatic recovery of local and regional gender identities. Imagine being a migrant proletarian in Mexico City with all manner of hardships, but still able to drink *comiteco*, the much-honored rum of your home town, Comitán de Domínguez (Chiapas). It would be like drinking tequila when you are a harvester or a ranchero *from* Tequila (Jalisco). Cutting to the chase, we find that, by the middle decades of the twentieth century, Mexican cultural circulation was so alcoholized that not even the AA ideology has been able to lobotomize it. In fact, many Alcoholics Anonymous groups in Mexico came into being precisely to help the generation that first *embodied* the aforementioned dialectics of cultural alcoholization, the so-called *Generación Pedroinfantesca* (the Pedro Infante Generation). Every April 15th, the anniversary of the Mexican idol's sudden death in 1957, AA members meet and recall his role in the genesis of their drinking problems. Nostalgia blends with outrage in some of their comments:

> Just imagine how many lads of that era became irresponsible drunkies, thanks to the movies of Pedro Infante. If that happened here, in Mexico City, what must have happened on the ranches or in small towns? Because Pedro was always planted in the countryside, dressed like a charro, a mariachi, a ranch foreman, a small town rustic, or a horseman. And no yellow-bellied authority figure ever kept him from drinking his fill. It couldn't have been a more powerful model to imitate. (as cited by Aguilar Siller 1997, 26, my translation)

Aguilar describes one member, "Sergio," whose out-of-control drinking had its roots in a well-crafted imitation of Pedro Infante that women found irresistible (24). Infante was not a drunkard, I hasten to add, he merely played one on the silver screen. He had risen from grinding poverty to massive box office success without alienating his rural and working-class fans, who were much impressed by his rakish lifestyle, motorcycle stunts, and passion for flying (Burr 1999, 113). Before he crashed his converted World War II bomber near Mérida (Yucatán) at age thirty-nine, Infante had recorded some 322 songs, and they remain a broadcast staple of radio stations throughout the hemisphere. At least the AA members studied by Aguilar retain some degree of cultural memory even as they dutifully anathematize it.

For the rest of this chapter, let us examine Mexican popular music as the pivotal multivocal semantic system watered and kept alive in alcoholized communitas (cf. Turner 1974, 259). We cannot limit ourselves to the many traditional songs that explicitly refer to alcohol use and its happy or sad effects — the erudite folklorist Vicente Mendoza grouped them under the heading *canciones báquicas* — (Bacchic songs) (1982, 489–97). Such songs flourished in every century and in every regional style, and lyrics glorifying regional identities are indeed a perennial favorite of cantina-crawlers. From a purely thematic point of view, however, drinking songs are vastly outnumbered by songs that refer in some way to the roller-coaster of love. Mendoza finds 126 basic themes in this swollen corpus (1982, 51–53), and we might picture them as 126 points on a continuum from mania to depression. As emphasized earlier, *ranchero* movies were *musical* comedies; audiences tolerated the flimsiest, most farcical plotlines because they knew that, sooner or later, someone was going to sing a beautiful and meaningful *ranchera* love song: a melancholy *huapango*, a *vals*, a *corrido*, a *bolero-ranchero*. Not Pedro Infante alone, of course, but hundreds of Mexican artists contributed in one way or another to this fecund cultural repertory with strong roots in regional musical cultures. Composing was Vincent Cordero's true forte: besides the well-known *Corrido de*

Juan Charrasqueado, he wrote over two thousand songs and many were recorded by the big names of Mexican music.

The powerful media industries that competed to supply cultural goods obeyed the laws of the short production cycle, as noted earlier; the paradox is that the mass demand for such quick-fix packages of cultural meaning and aesthetic pleasure was based on the very *longue durée* of Mexican social libido — that is, courtship rituals, seduction strategies, lovemaking, sexual morality, and anything that made babies more rather than less likely to appear. In other words, art forms associated with reproductive success were made available for resale in attractive new packages. Mexican culture producers hastened to use modern technology, but saw no need to reinvent the underlying sociobiological wheel. Moreover, the wind or string instruments used in romantic *ranchera* and mariachi music had specific, fairly untranslateable identity connotations, including gender identity (Jáuregui 1990; Thomson 1994; Nevín 2001; Sheehy 2000). To reiterate the paradox: radio's explosive growth since the decade of the 1930s was fed by a steady programming diet of regional musics older than Miguel Hidalgo's first *grito*. We must also mention the strategic political importance of incorporeal but loving "object voices" (Dolar 1996). President Lázaro Cárdenas himself believed that the Mexican people were "profoundly auditory" and that radio broadcasts were the key to "the integration of a national mentality" (Hayes 2000, 88). Cárdenas would not have condoned the alcoholized underside of this mentality, but he would have appreciated its pragmatic benefits — for his government had been quite keen "to develop a cultural policy aimed at unifying the country's culturally diverse and geographically dispersed citizens" (42). In analyzing the national response to the oil nationalization speech made by Cárdenas, Hayes concludes that "the paternal voice of the president provided an ideal medium through which the antimodern trajectories of radio and nation could be realized" (92). Numerous short-cycle commercial concerns reveal the government and the private sector in synergy, strategically accomodating Mexico's recalcitrant and change-resistant traditions anchored in the body itself, most particularly in its urge to merge with another body. Small wonder, then, that many middle-class parents, both to the left and to the right of the PRI, were at great pains to protect their children from Mexican popular culture in any of its formats. Folk-urban ranchera songs were deemed "*música de borrachos*" or "*música de indios*." Even the elegant bolero composer Agustín Lara was off-limits, due to his reputation as a womanizer and adultery-facilitator, and cross-dressing Cantinflas movies were completely off-limits for younger viewers.

In theory, there need not have been cross-contamination between love songs and the aforementioned "Bacchic songs" that explicitly refer to the joys or sorrows of drinking. Around 1930, however, a peculiar sort of *Volksgeist* emerged from the convergence of the many different industries that competed to supply vast new markets characterized by the desire for change and the nostalgia for the unchanged. Whatever role played by alcohol in the genesis or maintenance of the traditional folk repertory gives way, in subsequent decades, to something exponentially different. Briefly stated, the media-driven standardization of regional love songs was simultaneous with and inseparable from their alcoholization. The culture-wide corpus still included all 126 stops on the emotional rollercoaster, but certain themes began to predominate (betrayal, revenge, self-pity). A song need have no explicit mention of alcohol in the lyrics, therefore, if (1) the way it is being sung suggests that the singer is personally acquainted with binge drinking and/or (2) the song is clearly meant to be understood or best appreciated in a binge-drinking context or by an alcoholized emotional sensibility.

The basic alcohol-related stylistic elements were first synthesized and codified in the voice of a woman, María de la Luz Flores Aceves, better known as Lucha Reyes (1906–1944). A native of Jalisco, she was already singing in the *carpas* of Mexico City at the age of seven. Career ambitions took her to Los Angeles and later to central Europe, where she lost her fine soprano voice due to illness. Back in Mexico City, she discovered that her new hoarser, throatier instrument was ideal for interpreting the fledgling *ranchera* genre.

> Personality and neurosis did the rest. She gave lavishly of her voice, tearing it apart, whining, crying, laughing and cursing. No one had ever heard of such a performance style. Triumphing over critics who did not accept her lack of refinement, soon Lucha Reyes symbolized and personified the fierce and temperamental woman, Mexican-style. (Moreno 1989, 190)

The first female ever to sing with a mariachi group, Reyes would eventually be known as "the Queen of Mariachi." Reyes caused a sensation when she returned to Los Angeles in 1930. For the next fourteen years she was sought after by Mexican film directors, club owners, and composers like Alfredo D'Orsay whose song about a female tequila drinker, "*La tequilera*" became Reyes's signature song:

Como buena mexicana	Like a good Mexican woman
sufriré el dolor tranquila,	I'll calmly suffer the pain,
al fin y al cabo mañana	anyway you look at it, tomorrow
tendré mi trago de tequila.	I'll have my shot of tequila. (Moreno 1979, album VI, my translation)

Mexicans for whom I have played this ancient recording tell me that Reyes sounds inebriated, but it is certainly not a cliché, hiccuping delivery that she adopts. Incidentally, this song could not have come at a better time for the tequila industry, shrunken by 1930 to one-fifth of its 1902 production (Luna 1999, 133). Reyes confessed that every time she sang another number, "*Rayando el sol*," she got such a lump in her throat that she needed a good stiff drink (Moreno 1989, 190). It was not drink that finally silenced her, but an overdose of barbiturates in 1944 at the height of her border-crossing career (Burr 1999, 178).

The apparent death-wish trajectory of Lucha Reyes's life invites comparison with that of American singers like Janis Joplin. There are only a few strategies available to women who participate in musical rebellions: straightforward emulation of male rebellion, including its misogyny; the mystical affirmation of female strengths and passions; or the more postmodern "living-in-flux women who play with sexual personae" (Reynolds and Press 1995, 232–34). In almost any cultural field, a woman artist finds herself in a maddening double bind, damned if she does and damned if she doesn't; men are rarely obliged to make a break with accepted gender roles. In what Camille Paglia would call "poetic self-masculinization" (1991, 672), Lucha Reyes foreshadowed the dual persona of many female rock stars — "lusty hedonist and suffering victim" — but her true legacy was a long list of Mexican woman singers known as *cantantes bravías*. Each one perfected her own interpretation of the archetypal sexual persona first embodied by Reyes. They include Amalia "La Tariácuri" Mendoza, Flor Silvestre, Lucha Villa, Yolanda del Río, and Lola Beltrán, also called "Lola la Grande" for her remarkable career — seventy-eight albums and fifty films (Burr 1999, 63). Amalia Mendoza specialized in a musical weeping technique that was later used to stunning effect by Yolanda del Río in her career-launching, proto-feminist hit, "La Hija de Nadie" (1972). Whatever these women were really like in their private lives, their passionate, tormented performance personae were a serious departure from respectable middle-class norms. This is one more reason to challenge the "reactionary" label that some might hastily apply to the *ranchera* genre. We can continue using the word "regressive," however, by all means. In songs originally penned by men, female *ranchera* singers brought a powerful new note of authenticity to the obsession with lies, betrayal, and revenge; but the result was to anchor those archaic scenarios ever more firmly in the minds of music consumers, men and women alike, and this goes double if they were major alcohol consumers. Yolanda Moreno attributes the vogue of *ranchera* songs precisely to the aggressive manner in which they were performed (1989, 197); older, more bucolic styles were left in the dust, and a number of talented women singers ruined their voices trying to meet the demands of the new style. The majority settled on a "simple exaltation of the rude and boastful voice, a dry and cutting delivery clearly inspired by tequila, mezcal or comiteco" (Ibid.).

From a nationalistic point of view, the *cantante bravía* persona was definitely closer to the gender-bending *soldaderas* (camp followers) or idealized patriotic women favored by post-Revolutionary ideologues, as opposed to the stay-at-home, self-abnegating mothers praised by social conservatives (Rubenstein 1998, 166). The defiant body language of female *ranchera* singers mirrored that of proletarian women all over Mexico, especially the women who frequented or worked in cantinas. The latter had developed their own local performance styles to boost liquor sales, help men confirm their virility or confess their insecurities, and support children born out of wedlock. Were these women "reactionary" or were they adaptively creative in their own way? As will be glimpsed in short order, the unfeminine behaviors of famous *cantantes* and obscure saloon women alike might have been matched by a movement toward feminine positions in alcoholized male consciousness.

Legions of artists and composers took it upon themselves to effect the alcoholic aggiornamento of the Mexican love song corpus. Like Lucha Reyes, many of these individuals had truly magnetic personalities and awe-inspiring degrees of talent and fecundity. No scholar could be blamed for falling under their biographical spell, but detailed studies of individual trees often render the forest invisible. Bourdieu emphasizes that even the most charismatic producer of culture "owes his magic efficacy to a whole logic of the field that recognizes and authorizes him; his act would be nothing but a crazy or insignificant gesture without the universe of celebrants and believers who are ready to produce it as endowed with meaning and value by reference to the entire tradition which produced their categories of perception and appreciation" (1996, 169). In a sense, my whole study could be seen as an effort to account for alcohol's role in the genesis or maintenance of these categories. We should use the phrase "universe of celebrants" to stand for the many generations of romantically inclined drinkers who used alcohol to "suspend disbelief" and arrange to be compelled by musical magicians (if they were not already musicians themselves). Though it may seem paradoxical at first, Bourdieu's own procedure is to construct the laws of a cultural subfield through a detailed analysis of the artist at its center. The Mexican subfield in question, to recapitulate, is the twentieth-century folk-urban *ranchero* expressive complex that enabled large numbers of modernizing Mexicans to maintain conscious and unconscious linkages with a deeply desired, utterly recalcitrant identity reservoir — the heterodox Catholic *longue durée* of gender roles and love-death fantasies. Logically, the figure at the center of this field of cultural production was bound to be absolutely, phenomenally unoriginal — one of a kind.

José Alfredo Jiménez y Sandoval was born in Dolores Hidalgo (Guanajuato) in 1926. His father was a druggist who died in 1934, after which the mother moved the family to Mexico City. Jiménez had perhaps a total of five years of formal schooling; he had no musical training and played no instruments, but started composing songs at age fourteen. For a time he was a promising soccer player, then a waiter who entertained patrons with his singing. The owner of the restaurant formed a group with Jiménez as lead vocalist in 1946. By 1948 they had played on XEX and the powerful XEW, and in 1950 one of his songs was recorded by Pedro Infante himself. The tune's famous first words were "*Ando borracho, ando tomando*" ("I'm going around drunk, I'm going around drinking"). An ancient *canción báquica* begins in just the same way (Mendoza 1982, 493). Contrary to what genial New York writer Pete Hamill remembers from his drinking days in Mexico (1994, 192), Jiménez did not "growl" his songs. Nor did he indulge in the exaggerated, cliché-drunk vocal effects that appear in some other singers. What we do hear in the recordings is an occasional voiced [z] instead of the unvoiced sibilant [s], for example, with the humor and the alcoholic authenticity in perfect balance. I leave it up to the reader to confirm or dispute this observation. In any case, record executives and publicity experts like the exiled Spaniard Eulalio Ferrer Rodríguez knew at once that José Alfredo's music was perfectly commercial. With an additional four hit songs in 1951, José Alfredo's rise was meteoric — exactly what happens in a cultural assemblage characterized by short production cycles and short-term drinking episodes, *borracheras*:

> He drank heavily throughout most of his life. He wrote about alcoholism on "Llegó Borracho el Borracho," which, though banned from the radio, only helped to make him more popular. . . . . In 1968 Jiménez was diagnosed with cirrhosis of the liver. For the next few years he was on medication that helped him feel better and sing better, but he eventually began drinking heavily again. Ironically, Jiménez may have foreshadowed his own death, composing his gratitude song "Gracias" in 1972. (Burr 1999, 122)

By way of clarification, Jiménez did not merely foreshadow his own death towards the end. He was already obsessing about it in his first teenage compositions, and he took death-wish aesthetics to new heights (or depths) throughout his career. Much like the writer José Revueltas, José Alfredo embraced his creative sensibility in sacrificial or martyrological terms; *la muerte* is evoked in many of the four-hundred songs he composed before finally meeting her in 1973.

If a poetic essay penned by Octavio Paz in the 1950s is still considered relevant to an understanding of Mexico, then still more crucial should be the pithy poetic essays of José Alfredo *memorized by millions*. But due to the usual circuits of bourgeois academic consecration, we know much more about Paz than Jiménez. Carlos Monsiváis churned out a short, impressionistic piece on Jiménez and his music (Monsiváis 1998), and José Alfredo's nephew serves up a collection of random anecdotes (Azanza Jiménez 1999). Moreno (1989) and Burr (1999) provide dictionary entries. Héctor Madera Ferrón offers a few pages that not only omit the drinking but include a drawing of Jiménez, done by the author's wife, that whitewashes the singer's racial hybridity (Madera Ferrón 1993, 163–71). Some might find it scandalous that a man with the cultural weight of ten Sinatras has no biography worthy of the name, but again, our goal is to understand the coordinates of the cultural subfield that spawned him, perhaps ensnared him, survived him, and still drinks to his memory.

As it happens, José Alfredo's own life was not as important to him as the ongoing construction of a persona that was to be as profoundly romantic as possible, at one in every way with the desires and expectations of his universe of celebrants. This persona was partly a deliberate and controlled construction, yet also the product of unstoppable inspiration. Songs were in continual birth throes in the Mexican composer's brain; alcohol stirred and blended the traditional repertory of motifs and helped select among the 126 love emotions listed by Mendoza. As a composer Jiménez needed the anchor of a convincing narrator figure: a poor but proud man, alternatively lucky and unlucky in love, a guiltless drunkard, undoubtedly mestizo, enchanted by beauty and natural metaphors of time and space (mountains, skies, the night, full moons, etc.). This romantic anchor or figure of narration was not an "act," I emphasize; indeed, Jiménez's legendary lack of acting ability was precisely what enabled him to *become* a legend. Jiménez did not really invent this figure, either, any more than Mario Moreno invented the character of the *pelado* drunkard he called "Cantinflas." But in this study we do not equate creativity with originality. In what follows, therefore, by the "José Alfredo self" I mean the fictive but not false narrative figure constructed by and through Jiménez, his archetypal sexual and conceptual persona, his unconscious distillation of the logic of his whole subfield of cultural production. Jiménez used strong drink to access his muse and embody this mystical body from which all truths seemed to flow by themselves. The inspiration process in question was essentially that of trauma-mastery, through regressive concentration of emotion, similar to Rulfian catharsis but far more palatable since it was musical. Before, during, and after his *borracheras*, archaic yet enduring life issues and psychological currents were un-self-consciously orchestrated out of the flux of his depersonalized unconscious in aesthetically pleasing patterns. Inspiration came during special moments of timeless, time-out temporality that blurred and overflowed ego-boundaries. Jiménez often confessed to losing the notion of time during composition (Azanza 1998, 65). He was routinely late to important events as a result, but clocks were never that important to his core audience anyway.

Again, let us not allow this towering figure to obscure the forest that nurtured him. In and out of Mexico, the self-construction programmed into musical styles is always "sociogenic," as explained by John Shephard and Alan Wicke: "The material character of sound in music speaks directly and concretely through its technology of articulation to the individual's awareness and sense of self, an awareness and sense, it should be remembered, that is pervasively social and discursive in its mediation and constitution" (Shepherd and Wicke 1997, 164). If the human body is the principal site for the musical mediation of social and symbolic processes, then any chemical substance that enhances the material or bodily binding process must be seen as central too, rather than peripheral. Now add the all-important means of communication itself: radio. Says Hayes, "I would argue that radio voices have a materiality that ties them directly to premodern, somatic modes of speech. Despite its incorporeity, radio sound directly provokes the corporeal experiences of hearing and feeling, as well as other kinds of bodily responses" (2000, 23). Putting two and two together, we can see how broadcast alcoholized musical temporality might restore a lost somatic dimension to the words of the mother tongue. In the specific body of music we are dealing with, the José Alfredo self is encoded into each song; we find the whole code in each *canción*, like the complete DNA in one cell. The encoded self-construction is simultaneously the blueprint for a *borrachera mexicana*, an idiosyncratic but sociogenic Mexican binge, which means not passive listening to one song or another but active drinking to impersonate the narrating self branded into each song. The actual number of drinks consumed is irrelevant (as long as it is a large number). Cultured binge drinking, in this case, simply means drinking until one can totally identify with all elements encoded into the music.

We now have a more precise definition of power drinking in Mexico. To arrive at the uncanny authority of "the drunkard's truth," just follow the simple drinking rules (negotiated by the universe of celebrants itself) to become the expected self and achieve the desired powers. In other words, allow yourself to be guided by the alcoholized self-construction blueprint that each recording *materializes*. Sooner or later the powers emerge in a distinct spatiotemporal zone where anxieties (i.e., potentials for humiliation) are temporarily, cathartically mastered. The sort of musically stoked binge we are describing is like a controlled cerebral collapse that enables time-collapsing haecceities to reverberate again and again, especially as the drinkers become older. One finds much the same process at work (at play) in scores of José Alfredo love songs: an initial lyrical inspiration, subsequently packaged in a superb but equally ritualistic arrangement by Rubén Fuentes, played by the archetypal Mariachi Vargas. In each and every musical artifact one finds an ecstatic life event encapsulated, or "shelled" as Malcolm Lowry might say, with the sociomusical frame serving as a protective coating as well as a cue promising that a threatening or humiliating experience will be symbolically overcome. In these *kairos* echo chambers, a poor man's meaningful life events reverberate endlessly. An example: In *El cielo de Chihuahua*, José Alfredo's narrator figure recalls the magic night he lost his virginity in a rural setting under the stars:

El cielo de Chihuahua fue testigo

del beso que me diste y que te di.

La luna de Parral brilló esa noche

como ninguna luna ha brillado para mi.

[The skies of Chiuhuahua witnessed

the kiss you gave to me and I to you.

The moon over Parral shined that night

like no other moon has shone for me.]

In this song's endless echoing memory chamber, the self puts his best foot forward: simplified, dramatized, hypostatized, made coherent, ratified by *"ansias infinitas de adorar"* ("infinite desires to adore"). It is meant to be sung very slowly.

Earlier we met an anonymous alcoholic, "Sergio," whose luck with the ladies was based on his dead-on imitation of Pedro Infante (Aguilar 1997:24). As it happens, most of the songs associated with *borracho* role model Pedro Infante were composed by Jiménez — Monsiváis lauds Infante for not "getting in the way" of José Alfredo's melodies (1998, 22). A new idol emerged following Infante's tragic accident of 1957. Javier Solís, reputedly the son of a violent alcoholic, was rather more convincing when singing a José Alfredo song or any other song that encoded cyclothymia. "With his incredible smooth baritone and impeccable air of authority," writes Ramiro Burr, "Solís could describe the hellish torture of love's addiction or the dark fear of being abandoned, while projecting a cool, exquisite detachment" (1999, 190). His voice was perfect for sending treacherous women to the devil. When Solís died at age thirty-five after gallbladder surgery, the scepter was passed to Jalisco native Vicente Fernández. With his own superb vocal instrument, Fernández made definitive recordings of alcohol-friendly songs from several different decades and from one end of the bipolar continuum to the other. This range was crucial to success in the ranchera genre in particular, as was his concomitant ability to interpret many different "types" of macho. Contrary to cliché, some of the most successful macho stratagems are those of shyness, timidity, and apparent passivity. Numerous songs composed by José Alfredo Jiménez rely on a narrator persona who is strongly reminiscent of sociologist José Valverde's *macho melancólico*, a canny performance perfect for awakening the protective maternal instincts of the woman he wishes to conquer (1986, 190). The assumed identity (poor but proud, lucky and unlucky, hopelessly in love) necessarily promises a fair degree of reproductive success, or few men would wish to assume it.

Such obvious sociobiological benefits are potentially complemented by psychological ones. Psychoanalysts say that the achievement of love can signify a complete, harmonious resolution of contradictory developmental tasks (Kernberg 1991). Failure or success at love is therefore a powerful metaphor for failure or success in general. It follows that people who have been positioned from birth in some sort of socioeconomic "failure condition" (poverty, illiteracy, racism) would tend to obsess more than usual about love, lost love, desperate love, unrequited love, love regained, or, most commonly, love betrayed. Consider the 1919 murder-suicide of Pedro and Enriqueta (which also took place in Parral, under the skies of Chihuahua): "Whereas Enriqueta blamed alcohol, Pedro himself identified another intoxicant as the source of his problems: love" (French 2003, 132). He must have been listening to Mexican popular music, where such rationales have been legion for generations. Just as Pedro did, the narrator of many a song lyric reminds his girlfriend that

Ya sabías que era borracho,	You already knew I was a drunk,
jugador de billar.	a player of billiards.
Ya sabía todos mis vicios,	You already knew all my vices,
¿qué remedias con llorar?	so what are you crying about?

When the woman stomps on the man's heart, as she inevitably does, song lyrics can convey surprising amounts of spite:

En medio de una botella	In the midst of a bottle
enterré tu recuerdo.	I buried your memory.
Voy a quemar con el trago	With drink I'm going to burn
todo el amor que te tengo.	all the love I have for you.
Te bajaré de mi cielo	I'll lower you from my heaven
para mandarte al infierno.	to send you to hell.

Another song intones: "Go and please don't come back, follow your road gambling your love, the love that will soon be the garbage that you already are"; and others follow suit: "Your breast of woman, a hyena's lair, destroyed the heart that loved you. Now reap the harvest of your lies. You will no longer rise from the mud of your life, the world is over for you"; "Give your love to whomever you want, what do I care? When your fate catches up with you, you'll sell your affection and your kisses without love." In other words, you're on your way to becoming a cantina sex worker. José Alfredo expressed the cultural double standard quite lucidly in one of his songs: "The road that you have chosen, I walked a thousand times as well, but remember that I'm a man, and a man doesn't lose like a woman." In most of his other songs, of course, he reiterates the gendered, centuries-old addiction rationale: I'm drunk as a skunk and it's all your fault. Note that, in the general song corpus, even men who frequent prostitutes are unable to get over the one woman whose memory is *making* them drink. As heard in one bolero, "I've had one hundred women in my life, but none of them replaced your love. Many times I've tried to forget you, but you stay here inside my being." The man is not referring to his mother but, as seen in chapter 8, maternal overprotection might have played the major role in the germination of such rigidities. Clearly we are dealing with some kind of persistent attachment disorder, some inability to switch to a new love, some fixation on the nonfungible (de Sousa 1990, 261).

Having collected Mexican drinking songs like some people collect kachina dolls, I have only two or three that convey the message "Forget her, you need to move on now." And I have yet to find one that says, "Let's just have two drinks each, my friends, then go home to our wives." José Alfredo's hard-drinking narrator hits the nail on the head: "The years have taught me nothing, I always fall into the same traps. Now I'm off again to toast with strangers and weep over the same wounds" (from the song *En el último trago*). Clearly there is no expectation of recovery at the cantina, but of what T. J. Scheff called "the ritual management of emotions" (1979, 140). The songs that José Alfredo began writing in the 1950s, and those of great ranchera music contemporaries, combine symbolic mastery of status anxieties and sexual anxieties. Heavy drinking provides the crucial deterritorialization from one's "real" (daily, verifiable, surveiled, shrunken) identity into a default persona that is theatrical-historical and continues to behave with a kind of rationality inside the altered state of consciousness. Inside the Mexican community of celebrants in question, what we might call "Jose Alfredo catharsis" is brought about with musical/dramatic techniques "which provide audiences with an immediate, realistic portrayal of experiences like those of the audience, and with characters who are similar to the members of the audience" (Scheff 1979, 136) — similar above all in their desire to turn some kind of failure into some kind of success. In José Alfredo catharsis, the schema repertoire that has been reduced and made more "realistic" by alcohol consists of the basic self-other or role-relationship models of human emotional life (Horowitz 1988, 111–48), with the "self" side of each model activated and enhanced. "Under the warm glow of intoxication," wrote Herbert Barry, "the drinker feels assertive and independent, while at the same time feeling affectionate and nurtured" (1976,

253). This pleasurable juggling of "active" and "passive" self concepts is not experienced as dissonance inside the circular psychodramatic musical theater. Moreover, there may be something in music "saturated with the rhetoric of virility or gender polarity," argues Lawrence Kramer, that "ecstatically decenters" the masculine subject (1997, 111). Perhaps alcoholized musical temporality is a miraculous space of gender reversal, perfect for defusing castration anxiety while the "patients" are in a state of high receptivity, unafraid to yield. But all good things must come to an end. More than a few men stumble out of the cantina and, in their altered state of consciousness, confuse the return home with the return of the "castratory moment."

Chapter 9
Thirsty Urban Nomads

"A colossal fiction" — that's how sociologist Gabriel Careaga described life in modern Mexico City (1984, 171). In learning how to survive amidst unwashed masses on the streets or in the subway, middle-class men and women had forgotten how to relate to others except in a depersonalized, masked, deceitful way. Lacking a secure sense of identity, alienated citizens could only feign a personality they did not really have and could not construct (1984, 205). "Eventually a man realizes how he has been split between his desires to be grandiose and the reality of knowing he is a poor devil who lives on loan, on illusions and dreams that will never be fulfilled" (172). Careaga found many such men working in one niche or another of Mexico City's labyrinthine bureaucracy. Each day they would leave their drab, meaningless workplaces and escape to their favorite drinking establishments, "in an ever more oppressive and irrational dialectic" (187). Fortunately for Careaga, drinking enhanced their natural love of conversation and produced much grist for his mill. After a few *copas*, for example, Señor Miranda relates how Father Albert used to beat him with a belt in high school; how at law school he became fond of no-holds-barred drinking and whoring until he met his wife; how they fell in love listening to Frank Sinatra records; how he is now a successful lawyer and has stopped abusing alcohol, although he still gets really drunk once a week [sic]; and how he sees his new lover twice a week at his secret bachelor's pad (85–86). While drinking themselves into oblivion, Careaga's informants remember everything. Señor Saldaña recounts his origins in the lower middle class and his present place in "the middle-middle class" with a home in Colonia Prado Churubusco. Throughout his life he had taken maximum advantage of his resemblance to Frank Sinatra. "When he met Elda, he knew she would be his wife because she was docile, ingenuous, and virgin" (80). Following marriage in 1948, he went back to his playboy habits, including drunken fiestas with his friends three times a week on average. Elda began to suffer from boredom, melancholy, even suicidal impulses. Twenty-three years and several children later:

> The family continues to disintegrate. The mother takes more and more anti-depressants, and the father continues to frequent fourth-rate cabarets [*cabarets de mala muerte*], making friends with the teenaged proletarians who go to those places, buying them drinks and prostitutes because he likes group fornication. He gets drunk every day. . . . Today he is not as drunk as other days, he is neither happy nor sad, but incredibly depressed [sic], intensely pensive as he evokes his image as a 25 year old Frank Sinatra joyfully singing at parties, crazy with desires to conquer the world. Pausing at Insurgentes he asks, "What the fuck has happened to me?" ["*¿Qué chingados me ha pasado?*"]. (82)

Should the fellow sitting on the next barstool ask such a question, buy him a drink, hum a gay Sinatra tune, and coax him back to a more pleasant quasi-fictional state of mind. This would be the role of any decent *cuate*, of course, helping drinking buddies stabilize their preferred selves or at least enjoy the exquisite feeling of being failures despite their best efforts. More to the point: if the social theorist describing Mexico City has an excessively windowless concept of alienation, replace him with one of the Marxist urbanists recently studied by Andy Merrifield (2002), the ones who open up conceptual sites for spontaneity, celebration, drinking orgies, *jouissance*, laughter, mockery, passion, and euphoria (Merrifield 2002, 83–84). Imprisoned by a dour, agency-eradicating notion of alienation, Careaga overlooked daily ritual resistance inside the capitalist megacity, not to mention the creative self-construction inside the self-pity. "The mind is a problem-solving agency even if it stages the representations of self trauma-tizing ideas and feelings" (Bollas 1992, 241). Note how alienation did not keep a Careaga drunkard from reaching intense degrees of introspection; unhappiness was one of their raw materials, one of their foods for thought, the sand of trauma that produced the pearl of identity. It is as if each were saying "I suffer, therefore I exist." But above all, as seen in the passage above, he is saying "*Me acuerdo*" — ("I remember"). The total recall that Careaga found again and again in his drinkers is exactly what cracks open the otherwise implacable, deceitful megalopolis, and this disa-lienating rupture should not be missed. Practical memory is a tactical resource that "counts on an accumulated time, which is in its favor, to overcome a hostile composition of place" (Certeau 1988, 82). "Far from being the reliquary or trash can of the past, it sustains itself by *believing* in the existence of possibilities and by vigilantly awaiting them" (87, emphasis in original). From Ixtepeji to the Distrito Federal, Mexico's temporally opportunistic drinkers not only believe but know from experience that sooner or later "something alien to the present will or must occur" (87). I stress that Certeau never mentions the word alcohol, but his ideas restore agency to popular cultural time-warping and shed much light on the intentional worlds constructed by Mexican binge drinking.

Social memory studies are in vogue these days. Every great city of the world, and every lesser one too, sets space aside for monuments, museums, placards, statues, and other forms of "mnemonic socialization" — all intended to inculcate the "official sociomnemonic tour of the past" (Zerubavel 2003, 5, 31). From Certeau's perspective, these are exactly the places where memory *atrophies* (1988, 87) — "in fact, memory is a sort of anti-museum: it is not localizable" (108). Thus he reserves a special place in his theories for "the journalistic practice that consists in seizing the opportunity and making memory the means of transforming spaces" (86). Suppose, therefore, that we could locate a journalist with a strong background in architecture and civil planning, who knows Mexico City inside and out, buildings grand and monuments galore, but who instead seizes the opportunity to write a book that subversively *remembers* places that many Mexicans might rather forget: *pulquerías*, cantinas, prisons, and red-light districts. An amazing octogenarian named Armando Jiménez has written such a book (Jiménez 2000), and in some ways it is more radical than *Das Kapital*. With the help of Jiménez, we too can "remember" places like *La Gallina de Los Huevos de Oro* (The Hen of the Golden Eggs), a pulquería that opened on Pinto Street in 1920 and for the next sixty-nine years helped men evade reality, primarily the office workers of the nearby Dirección de Telégrafos. The *pulquería*'s name conveys the kind of gender-bending *albur* Cantinflas loved; "*huevos*" is a vulgar word for testicles yet somehow the owner of these eggs is female, a *gallina*. Jiménez asserts that this conundrum kept the business busy (19–21). The accompanying picture of men holding large mugs of *pulque* and urinating is tasteless but priceless — surely *this* should be forgotten, but no — it was a normal part of the homosocial lifeworld. In reinscribing the body in urban space, Jiménez follows the carnivalesque logic of drinking itself. *Cantina la Castellana*, located near the powerful radio station XEW, was responsible for comical obscenities heard throughout the hemisphere, slips-of-the-tongue made by announcers who had stopped by the bar to limber up for work (112–17). Again and again we are amazed to discover the longevity of Mexico City's portals to glory. *El Capricho* opened for business in the summer of 1897 "and delivered euphorias during the next 91 years" (70), specializing in *curados* — *pulque* blended with celery, oatmeal, peanuts, strawberries, mangos, oysters, nopal cactus, and so on, essentially anything that satisfied the customer's caprice, or his son's, or his great-grandson's. Decade after decade they all unblushingly used the same corner *mingitorio* or urinal in plain view of customers (72).

In the mid-1980s there were 1,493 *pulquerías* in Mexico City; 90 percent of them have now disappeared. The many cantinas recreated by Jiménez seem upscale, sometimes elegant by comparison. *Cantina La Reforma*, for example, boasted a beautiful, oval-shaped mahogony bar and white-jacketed waiters rushing to quench the thirsts of important men like Plutarco Elías Calles, former hypocritical teetotaling Presidente de la República and butt of many a drunkard's joke (77). These are the same elegant establishments reproduced in full color by Garibay Alvarez (1998), who wisely sent expert women photographers all over the city to persuade drinkers and bartenders to allow picture-taking. What we see are numerous clean, respectable, very well-stocked bars catering to a broad cross section of male society. Customers read the paper, play *dominó*, enjoy tasty *botanas*, buy lottery tickets, squeeze fresh limes into their drinks, smoke cigars, listen to music, and engage in the ingenious double and triple erotic word-playing known as *alburear*. Perhaps the sociologist Careaga went to such places, found the moodiest drinkers he could, and dutifully declared their glasses to be half-empty. With the help of our *cuates* Certeau and Jiménez, we see they are half-full. The populous capital's watering holes, so many oases in the urban desert, still enable people of all social classes to manage their emotions — no better and no worse than other things are managed in Mexico City.

These are human beings drinking, and being, with legitimate humanistic concerns. Certeau urged scholars to go to a city and "analyze the microbe-like, singular and plural practices which an urbanistic system was supposed to administer or suppress, but which have outlived its decay" (1988, 96). So let us not miss the disalienation going on inside the saloon network, the vast numbers of Mexico City residents (so-called *chilangos*) appropriating their surroundings, evoking their memories, playing homosocial jokes on their friends, or feeling the sweet sting of nostalgia for times lost and youth misspent. Here too we find the official members of panoptic administrations, prestigious Mexican legislators defending their jukebox rights with pistols (Jiménez 2000, 158). This tactic would fall under the heading "Get-in-touch-with-your-inner-cacique" and the locale in question was salón-cantina *El Submarino*. This was nothing compared to what happened one night in 1932. A brilliant young folksinger from Yucatán, Augusto "Guty" Cárdenas, finished his show on XEW and went to the cantina *Salón Bach*, guitar under arm, pistol in holster, and began drinking with his *cuates*. Guty's attempt to play flamenco guitar brought a sarcastic grimace to the face of a young Spaniard, José Peláez. Confronted by the angry Mexican radio star, who by then had drunk enough to have *sangre de león*, Peláez smashed a bottle on his head. Staggering and stumbling, the *yucateco* fired three shots in the general direction of Peláez. As fate would have it, the Spaniard's brother arrived just then and emptied his own gun into Guty, killing him instantly at age twenty-six. The cantina was shut down and national mourning began (85–86). Making the dead present again is yet another way to disalienate, as seen earlier, as well as an important reminder to eat drink and be merry for tomorrow you may die. Jiménez resurrects forgotten French folklorist Auguste Mignard, who travelled to Mexico in 1932 to write an in-depth study of the maguey world; Mignard worked very hard, collected impossible-to-find illustrations, and just as he completed his research he dropped dead in the pulquería *El Gorgeo Arrullador* (33).

Magical power-drinking has many ugly side effects, and, as the Spanish proverb has it, "Alcohol is a bad adviser." But let us not stumble and lose our theoretical footing. In Certeau's view, "urban life increasingly permits the re-emergence of the element that the urbanistic project excluded" (95), that is, memory in the spontaneous tactical sense outlined earlier, which is similar to a miracle — "the recourse to a different world from which can, *must*, come the blow that will change the established order" (86). Practical memory stages a slightly different comeback in the form of "delinquent narrativity" — the carnivalesque reinscription of the mortal body in ordered texts or spaces (130). Armando Jiménez is delinquent narration personified, of course, and his decision to write intelligently about cantinas and *pulquerías* replicates what was going on inside them — temporal opportunism, "coups" of memory, a delight in the basic ungovernability of the universe, the unshakeable belief in miracles and the vigilant waiting for Deleuzian haecceities. Surely one could engage in all of these "surreptitious creativities" without alcohol, and certainly Certeau did not recommend binge drinking, but the Mexicans in question prefer to do it *with* alcohol. This is one of alcohol's *cultural meanings* for them, one of the powers it is believed to have. The psychology involved is akin to that of the *Lotería Nacional*: "To play the lottery is an attempt to tune in to divine providence, to give God a chance to intervene in my life, to deny that success is due only to my effort, to pit grace against merit" (Zaid 1997, 85). Like gamblers, drinkers are firm believers in the possiblity of undeserved blessings and spiritual luck. To toss back a lot of drinks is to toss the dice in a dramatic way, sometimes fatal for the drinkers and others, since giving God a chance to intervene always offers an opening to his ancient nemesis.

Though no stranger to evil practices, therefore, alcohol must still be seen as subversive memory in a bottle, an escape route, temporal opportunism quite similar to that of village Mexico, but now fully urbanized and sharing in that "mobile infinity of tactics" that flaunt the Corbusieran/totalitarian dream of a city where surprises would be averted and "criminal tricks" eliminated (Certeau 1988, 89). Armando Jiménez's intuitive grasp of this logic leads him to conclude his subversive memoir with the prison escape tale of Joel David Kaplan, a millionaire gringo arms smuggler serving a twenty-eight-year sentence for shooting his Mexican partner. Kaplan was confined to the high-security modern penitentiary located in Santa Martha Acatitla (in the eastern cuadrant of the megacity). When money talks, no one criticizes its accent; Kaplan bribed the prison chaplain and other insiders to supply him with bottles of good rum, and made friends with other powerful prisoners like General Humberto Mariles and the Venezuelan Carlos Contreras Castro. In addition he had a beautiful smart wife for conjugal visits and cunning schemes. At exactly 6:35 P.M. on August 18, 1971, a potent high-altitude helicopter emerged from the metropolitan smog and landed on the vast exercise patio of the prison. Kaplan and Contreras Castro ran up, climbed in, took off. Not a single shot was fired from any of the prison's twelve watchtowers, since the helicopter had been painted police blue. Total elapsed time for the escape: ten seconds (Jiménez 2000, 277–79).

Kaplan was a drunkard and a murderer, but the tale of his great escape amuses our inner tricky criminal. To poach on Certeau's terminology, Kaplan had found just the "right point in time (*kairos*)" to make his break. His vigilance, obviously unimpaired by rum, had made "possible a transgression of the law of the place," by exploiting "the invisible resources of a time which obeys other laws and which, taking it by surprise, steals something from the distribution owning the space" (Certeau 1988, 85). I intend this not as a *reductio ad absurdum* but as a fair extrapolation of the former French Jesuit's approach. As noted by Jeremy Ahearne, Certeau's analyses were often inspired by and found tactical support in "forms of social autism" (1995, 182). Imagine, therefore, that Mexico City is the giant, alienating prison set up to stomp on peoples' narcissistic dreams; escape seems impossible, but no: there is an ancient, citywide network of time machines that allow people to fly away for several hours at a time, caution thrown to the winds, social consequences bracketed. Tactical memory disalienates because it is artful, opportunistic, and, let's face it, completely amoral. Thus there is no reason to feel pity for the way in which drinkers "remember" the past, no matter how much self-pity is on display. Heavy drinking can be the very emblem of social autism, metaphysical selfishness, and an every-man-for-himself attitude in the very midst of noisy camaraderie.

Certeau can be counted among the thinkers who found agency in the common people, everyday practices by which they extricate themselves from monolithic capitalist urban alienation. Subversive modes of "walking in the city" were one of his specialities (1988, 91–110). Wouldn't "walking drunk in the city" redouble the subversive nature of popular tactics, the carnivalesque impulse that panoptic power can pursue but never crush? In theory yes, though it will be hard to make ourselves feel admiration and respect for the *borracho* approaching us on the sidewalk. Fortunately, thirsty "urban nomad" itineraries can be observed throughout the social spectrum, from the lowliest stigmatized *lépero* to Luis Chico Goerne (1892–1960), renowned attorney and Mexican Supreme Court justice. While rector of the UNAM from 1935 to 1938, Chico Goerne involved numerous professors and students in his daily ritual drinking route. The rector would begin with a beer in *El Paraíso*, then it was on to *La Puerta del Sol* for a cuba libre, salted peanuts, and urinal visit. Then he would go to *La Opera* for a third highball, and the last stop would be the bar *Don Quijote* of the Regis Hotel. "In the event of urgent University business, everyone knew where he could be found" (Jiménez 2000, 105). Chico Goerne was extremely popular with the students, as was the bartender at *El Paraíso*, Natalio Raudón, for inventing a drink that combined "tequila, mezcal, anís, rum, aguardiente and other explosives" (Ibid.). Many were the teachers who tutored their students in exchange for beverages at cantinas within staggering distance of faculty offices. Inside this disalienating system, feeling low was the price one willingly paid to feel grandiose; grandiosity was usually right around the corner, at the next drinking establishment on one's customary route. Any number of cantinas boast plaques of nostalgia and gratitude from "the Class of _____" [insert the year]. This sounds much more like communitas than social autism.

While we are on the subject, Mexico provides the only example in the western hemisphere of a major university system founded upon beer. Monterrey's Cervecería Cuauhtemoc was directly responsible for the creation of the Instituto Tecnológico de Monterrey, also known as Monterrey Tech, and its dozen allied campuses throughout Mexico. Brewery baron Eugenio Garza Sada "not only wielded great power over the school's finances, but also played an influential role in its formative years as the arbiter of the institution's board of directors. With the solid financial backing from beer capital and Eugenio Garza Sada's vision, classes began in 1943 with fourteen professors and 226 students" (Hibino 1992, 32). The other great Mexican brewer, Cervecería Modelo, began in the 1920s with Spanish capital. Yet another great beer complex set up shop in Tecate (Baja California). By 1964, the annual per capita consumption of beer in Mexico was twenty-three liters; it had grown to forty-nine liters per capita by 1998 (Musacchio 1999, 555), largely at the expense of *pulque*.

Alcoholization in the business sense of the word always yields fruit in cultural realms, sometimes rotten, sometimes exquisite. In twentieth-century Mexico, it was perfectly possible to be a drunkard and a genius at the same time. The Revueltas brothers — composer Silvestre, painter Fermín, and writer José — were Mexico's premier example of an alcoholized family with unquestionable talent and radical revolutionary ideals. The sisters, the wives, and the daughters got the worst of it, naturally, as they have recounted in their memoirs. José explained to his youngest daughter Olivia that he and his brothers drank not to escape but to feel the suffering of Mexico more intensely — "that immense unexpressed pain in the hearts of the people" (as cited by Ruiz 1993, 112). In a letter to his brother, José wrote that "It is essential to understand that today's artist, in this dark stage of history, can be nothing but a sacrificial victim, a being that cries all of the tears that he doesn't want others to cry" (139). Alcohol, needless to say, helped yesterday's artist buy into this level of self-denying grandiosity, this readiness to be victim number one. Unlike the amoral every-man-for-himself escapist drinking discussed above, martyrological drinking is socially engaged and actively seeks to overturn the status quo in Christian or Marxist fashion. One thereby rises on the hierarchy of suffering while sinking physiologically. If a *borracho* is already predisposed to see his own suffering as exalted and meaningful, he will find as much corroboration as needed in Mexican cultural traditions. There was something about being in Mexico, observed Victor Turner, that turned men into Christ surrogates: "To be bloodily killed by the establishment, after betrayal by a traitor to one's own cause as Guajardo betrayed don Emiliano Zapata, and after proclaiming a message that includes support for the impoverished and exploited — these are the ingredients of a career that, following an archetypal myth, becomes itself a myth generative of patterns of and for individual and corporate processes" (1974, 123). Since "cultural symbols never have power just because they are symbols" (D'Andrade 1992, 229), we must not slight the archaic, lower-order cognitive/emotional schemas that binge drinking conjures up so effectively. This gives us the full pattern: Race and class conflicts strongly motivate power-drinking that short-circuits alternative schemas and makes it likely that status-enhancing identity elements derived from fantasmatic Catholicism and Mexican history will be embodied, quite literally, by individuals like Zapata or José Revueltas. It is still temporal opportunism, but now on a grand scale, deployed and maneuvering inside a culturewide "sociomental topography" (Zerubavel 2003, 2). "Like the Jews," says Luis González y González, "we Mexicans take pleasure in remembering calamities and persecutions" (1998, 77).

Church attendance is not required to activate this gloriously recalcitrant process. For the male members of the Revueltas family and many other talented, left-leaning, priest-baiting families of Mexico, the way of the bottle was the true way of the cross. The toxic torture liquids were brewed or distilled by powerful vested interests of the "establishment" and served up by smiling treacherous bartenders like Natalio Raudón. The ethically superior martyr role called for one to accept such Judas kisses, submit to ostracism by contemporary Pharisees, even seek it out in order to achieve a glorious hereafter — both here and after. This is no mere collection of tale motifs: we are dealing with the very machinery of social pacification. If a centralist semiotic cannot effect a capture of the war machine, turning it into a narrative episode in a more manageable passional semiotic, there will be no social peace or stability (Deleuze and Guattari 1987, 351–99). Sought-after betrayal is not only the key motif, as in Turner, but the key *mechanism*, as in Girard (1982). Emiliano Zapata, the ultimate warrior machine, eventually turned his furor upon himself in a series of heroically self-abolishing drinking events, finally agreeing to a free beer that he knew perfectly well would be his last.

Alcohol's ansiolytic and psycholytic powers work in tandem; first one is salient, then the other. "Beer helps me a lot," says one of Rulfo's narrators. "It relieves me, makes me feel like my head has been rubbed with camphor oil" (Rulfo 1983/1953, 28). As a poorly paid newspapermen with a big family and numerous debts, Revueltas used alcohol for occasional personal stress-relief, without losing sight of his larger ideological goal: not to ease the pain of alienation but to focus on it. In that sense he was very much a participant in the postwar "renaissance of interest in alienation" among leftist writers in capitalist countries and dissident intellectuals in Communist countries (Catephores 1990). After his visits to Mexicali and Tijuana, Revueltas argued that in such places it was necessary to drink "until mental clarity is gone," the better to feel the sting of exploitation and racial discrimination (Ruiz 1993, 317). This tool of sociological research was definitely not authorized by the Partido Comunista Mexicano, far more sober than its Russian counterpart, but it was good for his writing. Heavy drinking must be counted as one of the mind-splitting mechanisms deliberately cultivated by the creative, "purposefully embraced as a preferred pattern of repeated dissolution and reorganization" (Rose 1987, 110). Or in the words of Revueltas's ex-wife, "He couldn't settle down; family responsibility was alien to him. If he drew up a writing goal he fulfilled it, even if it meant the demise of his children, of his wife, of his marriage. . . . Was it a generational disease that afflicted communists of the time?" (Ruiz 1993, 280). "Look," Revueltas said to a critic, "I belong to no school, no fad, no generation, but I do believe in scepticism and doubting as great human values. I love having no direction, just opening door after door as I come to each one" (328). No great writer is a hero to his wife, but Deleuze and Guattari would surely have applauded the Mexican author's rhizomatic outlook. In the perceptive phrase of Mexican writer José Emilio Pacheco, "Revueltas constructs himself by dismantling himself" (as cited by Ruiz, 420).

During his 1950s love-hate affair with the Mexican Communist Party, Revueltas lived "beneath the empire of emotional instability, ideological imbalance, without a steady job, wandering. Perhaps that is why so many characters in his novels and stories are tossed about on wild seas, lost in the fog or in the obscurity of remote cities" (297). Most of these characters drink heavily, and their thought patterns oscillate between incoherence and indignation. Revueltas could see as much "alienation" as any UNAM sociologist, but he also saw and elaborated the crucial element of dark farce. Here is the plot of *El abismo*, cogently summarized by Sam Slick:

> Martínez, an office worker, suffers from the boredom and meaninglessness of life. Seemingly trapped, he turns to alcohol for escape; progressively he falls into the clutches of alcoholism and eventually begins to suffer from blackouts. Shortly after one such episode, Martínez's fellow workers maliciously convince him that, during a drunken stupor, he has killed a man. Martínez, believing

the cruel hoax, is struck with fear and awaits the arrival of the police at his office. Giving way to paranoia, however, he pathetically tries to escape. In an effort to disguise himself he borrows some clothes from one of the hoax's perpetrators. Purposely trying to carry the hoax to new heights, the latter gives Martínez clothes that do not fit him. As Martínez exits the office looking perfectly ridiculous, his colleagues laugh uproariously. But Martínez is unaware of any of this and emotionally thanks the man for helping him to escape. (1983, 108–9)

Note how the storyline hinges on mockery and victimization, in true Passional or Girardian fashion. Revueltas himself was extremely conflicted about alcohol, convinced that his political and literary enemies, real or imagined, delighted in his inability to "control" his drinking. The archetypal drunken principal appears again and again in the Revueltian universe, showing up at school utterly smashed, saddening and confusing the children with "the grotesque spectacle of a good and decent man losing everything to alcohol" (Ruiz 1993, 294). Revueltas was painfully aware that his brother Silvestre (1899–1940), one of Mexico's foremost composers and an accomplished violinist, had drunk himself to death. Ruiz believes that binges kept José in touch with his deceased brother's *sombra* or ghost, and I am compelled to agree. The alcoholized state of consciousness is the "linking object" par excellence, the perfect token of triumph over loss; ritual drinking sprees that reunited the living and the dead were an ancient Mexican specialty (Stein 1984, 136; Viqueira 1999, 117). It can come as no shock to us that Mexico's most cultured binge drinkers replicate, in their own lives, the psychological coordinates or semantic systems of Mexico's binge-drinking cultures. Fully aware that many had mocked his brother's *borracheras*, Revueltas penned a spirited defense in which he dismisses the snide comments of the "Pharisees" and identifies alcohol as a tool of vision used only by the bravest and most honorable artists. José writes that his brother Silvestre

> had chosen the road of self-devouring (*autodevoración*), painful but nevertheless provident and terribly fertile. There is something very humble and barbarous, inexpressibly humble and accusatory, in the alcohol of Verlaine, in the alcohol of Silvestre, in the alcohol of Mussorgsky, in that of Whitman, in the saintly, criminal alcohol of all solitary men, that makes us feel as if we had just been slapped in the face. (as cited by Ruiz 1993, 393, my translation)

During the final decade of his life, José used alcohol for both ansiolytic and psycholytic reasons and finally achieved his own "global vision of the tragedy of contemporary man" (398). His ideological maturity was reached just as his marriage was crumbling after twenty-five tempestuous years. The student movement of 1968 was the writer's finest moment, beloved as he was to young radicals of many different schools. Following the massacre of Tlatelolco and harrowing months of hiding, Revueltas was caught and imprisoned in Lecumberri prison — the notorious "Black Palace." Lacking outside friends with helicopters, Revueltas approved the construction of a crude *alambique* to distill whatever was available, usually potatoes, apples, or guayaba (27). Chilean poet Pablo Neruda penned a plea to *el Señor Presidente*, Gustavo Díaz Ordaz, attempting to get Revueltas out of the Black Palace. Neruda describes his fellow writer as "contradictory, hirsute, inventive, desperate and mischievous: a synthesis of the Mexican soul. He has, like his country, his own orbit, free and violent" (as cited by Ruiz 1993, 29). Revueltas was finally freed in the spring of 1971, his liver and pancreas already ruined from the bad prison booze. "He was a young man in speech and in thought, but prematurely old at age 57," says Ruiz (407). To celebrate his release, his student friends threw him a splendid *borrachera*. Revueltas resumed his writing, drinking, and drifting, but by 1974 he was simply tired of living. The 1976 transfer of his brother Silvestre's remains to the *Rotonda de los Hombres Ilustres* sharpened the ailing author's death wish: he intuited that his own "crucifixion" was near at hand, since he explicitly identified himself with a rebellious, revolutionary kind of Christ. A tall glass of vodka drunk quite deliberately during Holy Week was enough to send him to meet his brother Silvestre (35). It was another sacrificial Mexican love-death, literal and not just literary.

As could hardly be otherwise, the *historiales* or personal histories told by recovering Mexican alcoholics are indebted to the larger narrative formats of the culture. AA narratives "resemble the archetypal Catholic cycle of transgression, guilt, and confession as means to moral cleansing and repentance" (Brandes 2002, 45). This broad cultural connectivity aside, Brandes draws sharp distinctions between his ex-drinkers and normal male society in Mexico: "The men of Moral Support differ from many other Mexican men in that they are openly repentant" (106). And again: "It is highly unusual for a Mexican man to cry in front of other men. This display of personal weakness — so uncharacteristic of *macho* behavior in the outside world — represents bravery and sincerity in the context of the group" (176). By now we know, however, that inside any given drinking culture of Mexico we find endless opportunities for men to weep, express repentance, ask women for forgiveness, exhibit morose remorse, cleanse themselves pychologically — all in front of other *cuates* and with their corroboration. Men in cantinas are actually less concerned about the maintenance of masculine identity than anonymous abstainers, for the simple reason that the culturally sanctioned cantina format provides the unquestioned gender security that is lacking in an AA meeting room. The better to convince themselves that they can apologize, sob, and still stay men, "a hyper-masculine atmosphere prevails in the Moral Support meeting room" (127), complete with obscene language and stories of prodigious masturbation. Thus it would seem premature to congratulate Mexican AA groups for redefining gender roles. Moreover, Mexico's carnivalesque drunkards carry out their festive disruption of gender stereotypes less self-consciously, with greater freedom and in a richer cultural vein — the same one that AA must wash from men's brains. The explicit deconstruction of machismo stereotypes can also be found in the very center of the *ranchera* cultural field, in numerous songs by José Alfredo Jiménez and his successors, now placed in broad circulation by pop stars like Luis Miguel or conjunto bands in the borderlands.

Something is gained in the transformation of undisciplined Mexican drinkers into disciplined AA members, but perhaps something of equal value is lost: tactical memory in Certeau's sense or the spirit of cultural resistance synonymous with the Revueltas brothers discussed above. Some of the Moral Support members studied by Brandes, "David" for instance, are strangely unable to account for the huge quantities of liquor they consumed while in the prime of life (Brandes 2002, 163). The AA mentality requires binges to be recalled and narrated in one way only, or not at all; that is why Moral Support's colonized members, victims of Zerubavel's "mnemonic obliteration," cannot be granted the last word on Mexican *borracheras*. One must listen instead to prelobotomized, guilt-free narratives of drinking. Either go to a local bull-baiting festival in Morelos or simply *turn on the radio.* "I look at life just like the froth on the beach. I can die right now or tomorrow, it's all the same to me." Another song: "I'm going around very but very much drunk. So what? What do I care if I have the vice? If today I laugh out of pure pleasure, it's my very own laughter; if I cry, very much my tears. If the world doesn't like it, it can go to hell." And another: "Aguardiente is my father, mezcal is my godfather, *refino* is my relative, and pulque is my blood brother" (*refino* is similar to Everclear). "If only you could see how beautiful these borracheras are," and "how happily I spend the hours emptying bottles," says one old tune recorded by Linda Ronstadt in recent times. Another, once a hit for Javier Solís: "How is it my fault that I like wine? In drunkenness I find joy and sweetness." Yet another: "I'm happy by nature and I do believe that being born in a carnival made me an upright man. La Llorona makes me laugh with her song of pain." Another: "My coffin should be small, small and made of pure glass, so that when my *cuates* put me inside they can fill it with pure mezcal." One humorous *corrido* narrates how the wake of a deceased borracho called "El Fufuy" turned into a raucous drunken party. In other songs, hardy party animals reassure their women that they can still perform: "If because you see me drunk you think I'll leave you hanging, don't worry, I drink, but I'll fulfill you." From a *ranchera* by Tomás Méndez, "I want you to know that I'm going around drinking like a man, not a drunkard." A man cannot possibly be an alcoholic, many songs imply, if he always pays his way and never sponges drinks. From a *ranchera* by Jesús Martínez: "If I get drunk, it's because I like drinks, and when I drink, I don't borrow money from anyone." And the hit song by Agustín Nuño: "I'm a bricklayer, it's true, and if I'm a partylover [*parrandero*] the bartender never shouts at me, since when I invite I always bring cash."

It would be misleading to suggest that somehow in every single binge a Mexican is consciously thinking about alcohol or his lifelong relationship with it. The binge is the cognitive/emotional template that determines how external and internal stimulae are registered, reacted to, enjoyed, or cursed. If all goes well, the typical drinker is immersed in a festive time zone, probably surrounded by joke-telling friends, talking about any topic with candor and enthusiasm — women, cars, bulls, politics, anything. The misleading term used by cognitive psychologists, "alcohol myopia," suggests that a drinker sees less than someone in a "normal" state of consciousness. This formulation is itself myopic and overlooks that alcohol is the great semiotizer. The narrowing and focusing of attention on seemingly trivial nearby objects can impregnate them with meaning:

Cigarro que se te apaga	If a cigarette goes out on you
no lo vuelvas a encender,	don't light it up again,
la vieja que te abandone	if a broad abandons you
no la vuelvas a querer.	don't ever love her again.
Tengo un cigarro en la mano	I've got a cigarette in my hand
que ya se me está acabando,	that's already going out on me,
son iguales las pasiones	passions are just like that
van pasando, van pasando.	always fading, always fading.

With the right kind of holy water, the most "secular" object is endowed with a cosmic glow. Back at AA headquarters, meanwhile, swallowing hegemonic notions about sobriety and bodily discipline fails to bring about career advances proletarians were led to expect (Brandes 2002, 188). They remain as marginal and as *alienated* as before, in other words, but now incapable of even clumsy modes of countering the dominant chronopolitics. And farewell to the most ecstatic types of psychic reorganization, the glorious Rabelaisian acceptance of the body and its desires and its demise. Hello to sphincteric modes of "transcendence" that replace addiction with authoritarianism (Kramer and Alstad 1993, 207–57).

While ravaging the body, every *borrachera* reorganizes the mind of a bearer of Mexican culture, constructs a different fractal-shaped self-cluster, deploys a distinct psychic defense arsenal, invokes a particular temporal gestalt. The better to deal with both historical and intimate events, a "higher" vantage point is being sought, beyond the visible light spectrum, damn the torpedoes and full speed ahead. Creative binge drinking, as seen in the lives of José Alfredo or José Revueltas, bespeaks a miraculous proficiency for mining and refining the dark matter of Mexico's scarred imaginary. A college degree is not required. Almost any man can engage in creative binge drinking if with the assistance of powerfully conjunctive symbols he "breaks on through to the other side" and reaches a state of consciousness that seems miraculous. It is like the resurrection of a Lazarus buried by those who equate time with money. A question for the Pharisees of today: Where are alienated citydwellers going to find ludic space-time or some minimal assistance with mood management? It obviously cannot be work and unfortunately cannot be home — two places designed to shrink men into humble supporting roles. Bullrings and cantinas, by contrast, are venues that inflate them with heroic starring roles.

The demand for this kind of ego-inflation is not necessarily irrational or out of touch with historical realities. Mexico's economy grew by leaps and bounds during the middle decades of the twentieth century, but a gigantic market remained for old-fashioned, preindustrial, frankly despotic notions of power that were by no means fictitious: antimodern political bosses remained essential to PRI governance for nearly eighty years (Oppenheimer 1996, 89–92). They were as essential as the nationwide network of saloons that enabled men abused by power to get in touch with their inner, revenge-minded caciques. Even the most socially autistic style of drinking does not take place in a social vacuum. The tactical turns Certeau found in popular culture can be "broadly poetic" or "retaliatory," writes Ahearne (1995, 164), and why not both at the same time? In many different genres of Mexican popular culture, political marginalization is the necessary precondition for upward movement, the scripted affirmation of bruised egos, or even the wholesale rejection of racial and social hierarchies. These elements are maintained in precarious manic balance in José Alfredo's signature song, *El rey*:

Con dinero y sin dinero,	With or without money,
yo hago siempre lo que quiero	I always do as I like
y mi palabra es la ley.	and my word is law.
No tengo trono ni reina,	I have no throne or queen,
ni nadie que me comprenda,	nor anyone who understands me,
pero sigo siendo el rey.	but I'm still the king.

Both the "good" cacique Juan Charrasqueado and the "bad" cacique who had him shot could identify with the feeling. Cacique-type role models were being actualized everywhere in modern/antimodern Mexico: imposing their wills, chasing skirts, whining about the one who got away, consuming patriotic, mestizo-status-affirming liquors, sometimes ending up dead and sung about by "musicians with hangover faces." The marginal social status of numerous cantina regulars made such fantasy role models even more appealing — like awkward mestizo bullfighters entering the ring and leaving in pharaonic triumph.

The cultural meanings of alcohol discussed in this book are very much ongoing, and they have major political and demographic ramifications for all areas affected by the Mexican "*diaspora ranchera*" — a macropattern of migratory flows now in its sixth century (Barragán 1997, 81–116). The groups that make up the diaspora cannot be reduced to traditional categories of ethnicity or social class, but they are strongly differentiated nonetheless by their nomadic practices, ambition, adaptability, and alcohol-friendly value system. Unlike city dwellers who feel lost in the country, the Mexican *ranchero* feels at home in both because he brings his familiar modus operandi along with him. That is what unites the bracero in California with the cattleman of the Sierra Madre, the female maquiladora worker in Ciudad Juárez, the goat herder in Veracruz, the distiller of mezcal in Nuevo León, the marijuana grower in Sonora, or the priest in Michoacán (Barragán 1997, 52). Not only do they share a value system: they might even be in touch with each other, forming one of the transnational migratory networks studied by Mike Davis (2001). Davis was surprised to find "that so many immigrants occupy strikingly different class positions in the parallel worlds they move between" (103). The same men of San Miguel el Alto (Jalisco) who work as waiters, busboys, and gardeners in Palm Springs (California) — "an efficient, largely invisible army of brown labor" — live in mansions back in San Miguel (103). Mexicans are the largest of the Latino groups who are engaged in *magical urbanism*, busily "turning the lights back on in the dead spaces of North American cities" (67).

This demographic dynamism was first forged in the mountains of the Great Chichimeca in viceregal times. Now, as in previous centuries, colonization and consolidation are the goals. Folklorist Américo Paredes used the term "Greater Mexico" to refer to areas settled and inhabited by people of Mexican culture north of the Río Bravo (1993/1966); he is still revered for having shown how to retrieve victims' views of Anglocentric hegemony in the borderlands. José Limón has continued this important line of research into subaltern affairs in the Southwest:

> Southerners went to Texas and the West, especially after the Civil War, and many became part of the Anglo cattle culture within the framework of a racist rage articulated literally and expressively

against the Greater Mexican male, who stood as the most powerful
representative of opposition to this intrusion. Here again we see the
projection of eroticized images of perversity in the unambivalent
degradation of the Mexican male body in Anglo cowboy song and
popular fiction. On the Mexican side of this encounter, a balladry
was born celebrating not just literal armed resistance but also the
sensuously "manly" body itself, in expressive eroticized resistance
against an official discourse that would degrade it. (Limón 1998,
211)

Limón laments that a good part of this official discourse had its origins in
Mexico's own intelligentsia, namely, the vulgar Freudian pseudo-anthro-
pology of Samuel Ramos and Octavio Paz. This approach made much of
the supposed hypersexuality of "the Mexican macho" while remaining
tone-deaf to the humor in his folklore and blind to its own bias vis-à-vis
dark-complected, vaguely threatening working-class men. Limón targets
this moribund but still influential discourse and conjectures that Paz was
as worried about the stereotypical "dirty Mexican" as any racist Texas
Ranger (81–83). Paz had written a bestseller that real, flesh-and-blood
Mexicans did not need; translating *El laberinto de la soledad* into English
in the 1960s served, among other things, to reinforce "a racialized negative
perception of the Mexican masses" that connected poisonously with the
segregationist mindset of the times (89). Limón possesses an insider's
knowledge of past border conflicts and ugly episodes of discrimination,
but he feels that the time has come to celebrate "the play of eroticism and
desire between Greater Mexico and the United States" (4). Avoiding the
edgy postmodernist performance artists of Los Angeles, he glosses simpler,
more romantic, better-known examples of borderlands encounters: songs
like Marty Robbins's *El Paso*, singers like the slain Selena, political figures
like Henry Cisneros, movies like *High Noon*, *Lone Star* or *Giant*. In a score
of mass cultural texts and icons Limón uncovers a thriving libidinal economy whose investment in mestizo bodies has paid increasing dividends
over the decades and may now herald "the passing of an archaic order of
racialized sexuality" (211).

The explosive growth of *Tejano*, *norteño*, *conjunto*, and other subgenres
of regional Mexican music should not be confused with stylistic change
within them, which has beeen minimal. Both the growth and the stylistic
inertia have ensured, in turn, that Limón's "Tex-Sex-Mex romance" worldview continues to guide the flow of desire along the Rio Grande and
throughout areas of Mexican population in the United States. Higher levels of social alienation are correlated with greater consumption of popular
music (Blau 1988). Music is the most typical, all-terrain vehicle of ethnic
and gender identity formation in Greater Mexico; listening to songs does
not require literacy or the sort of scholastic cognitive skills necessary for
reading a long novel or Chicana feminist tract. As seen earlier, song lyrics

ostensibly dealing with love's rollercoaster can encode socioeconomic failure or success in general; that said, there is no shortage of lyrics that
explicitly express economic and political concerns. The most important
norteño group, Los Tigres del Norte, made a "deliberate decision in the late
1970s to tackle within their music the controversial issues that affected the
millions of Mexicans who were migrating into the U.S. yearly — especially
anti-immigration politics and the disillusionment that is caused by living
in a hostile country" (Burr 1999, 200). Drug smuggling *corridos* have also
been a staple for the Tigres del Norte, as has the recreation of delinquent
antiheroic sexual personae like Emilio Varela and Camelia la Tejana.

Diasporic identities maintained through alcohol are giant invisible res-
ervoirs of *alternative Mexicanness*. They tap into some of the same psy-
chohistorical resources that fueled Mexico's millenarian movements; they
encode the transfer of sacrality wrought by the Mexican Revolution; they
exploit the same modes of tactical memory and time-warping that kept
urban alienation at bay. Mexican "magical urbanism" in the United States
is temporal as well as spatial, Mike Davis would surely agree. As we have
seen throughout this book, alcohol can be a way out of social insanity or
personal tragedy; it can be a serum of truth; it can resurrect a San Luis
Potosí identity somewhere in downtown Saint Louis. Unschooled binge
drinkers of and from Mexico still arrange for ecstatic memory events, subversive humor and verbal pyrotechnics, melodramatic or farcical depic-
tions of life and death. This is a personal truth revelation process, as
opposed to a more impersonal, social-science process of truth production.
This helps us to understand, among other things, why the rate of actual
stylistic change is abnormally slow inside popular "Tex-Sex-Mex" music.
According to the general rules of artistic evolution formulated by Colin
Martindale, "the more an audience is exposed to a type of art, the faster
the art should change" (1990, 52); when it does not change, we can only
conclude that it retains the "high arousal potential" of art forms associated
with the sacred. It is akin to Martindale's formula, "Meaningfulness habit-
uates slowly" (53). The irony of Greater Mexican culture, therefore, is that
the recalcitrant maintenance of portals to infinity is propelled by seemingly transient cultural forms — a defiant *corrido* from Los Tigres del
Norte, a cold can of Azteca beer, then several more of each in bars and cantinas and shacks on the corner. Just like Artemio Cruz, the archetypal
cacique created by Carlos Fuentes, migrating *rancheros* have a thirst for
"moments of authenticity uncompromised by alienation" (Smith 1989,
184).

Now, in cities across America, "Neighborhood aesthetic wars have
become commonplace as Latino carnivality collides with the psychosexual
anxieties of *Truman Show* white residential culture" (Davis 2001, 64). The
neighborhoods in question are known to all. They can be found in Cicero,
Illinois; Cotton, California; Ridgewood, New York; South El Paso, Texas;
the Cloverleaf and Roy Royall neighborhoods of Houston; any number of

neighborhoods in the Los Angeles area, and so on. As Michael J. Weiss demonstrates in an amazing study, these and dozens of other communities can be grouped into one of three basic demographic/marketing *clusters*: Family Scramble, Latino America, and Hispanic Mix (Weiss 2000:266–99). In the first, people enjoy malt liquor, pet birds, and changing their own shock absorbers. They do not go to movies or lift weights, but they do watch *Jenny Jones* and read *Car and Driver*. Most frequent purchase: "money orders bound for Mexico" (297). In the second, more middle-class cluster found most frequently in California and the San Antonio area, people drink tequila, avoid stair-steppers and easy-listening music, watch many hours of television per week, and "look to the church as a source of stability" (267). They voted for Bill Clinton in 1996. When night falls on the third cluster, "Hispanic Mix residents head to a handful of entertainment spots at high rates, among them dance clubs, basketball games, boxing matches, and video arcades. Where Hispanic Mix residents do excel is in consumption of media: their fondness for rap and especially Spanish music is off the charts. Beyond their foreign-language publications, they also buy baby, car, and TV magazines more often than the general population" (299). They do not go to Walt Disney World, their voting rates are very low, and they have amazing rates of DUI arrests (as seen in the introduction). Although the cluster approach is rather more simplistic than a Bourdieu-inspired analysis of habitus and field, it does give us an idea of the many elements that feed into identity construction in urban neighborhoods. In this brave new world, even a brazenly mass-mediated iconic Latina derriere can be "an ample trope for cultural belonging" (Negrón-Muntaner 2003, 297).

People who enjoy domestic beer, Montgomery Ward, and changing their own shock absorbers are bound to unnerve sober, stable, upwardly mobile ethnic identities with no wish to be stigmatized. If students and scholars of Latino Studies are truly committed to "diversity," however, we should be able to accomodate and perhaps celebrate all types of identity construction, high and low, queer and straight, drunken or sober. Could there really be any significant disconnect between identity construction tactics used by the disadvantaged and those preferred by the zany writers and filmmakers celebrated by academics? It seems probable. Manuel Martín-Rodríguez shows that, in texts being written by Chicanos and Chicanas,

> the key to (cultural and/or racial) survival is not seen in the *preservation* of unchanged traditions and customs (or racial or ethnic purity, for that matter) but, rather, in their constant *transformation* and adaptation, in the continual crossing of new borders and in the continuous generation of new paradigms. . . . Deterritorialization rather than territorialization, diaspora rather than settlement, "becoming" rather than being are the key elements of this new discourse. (Martín-Rodríguez 2001, 94)

We actually came upon this discourse earlier, in 1915, embodied by Manuel Azuela's mentally unstable vagabond alcoholic poet. Able to down a bottle of mezcal in two swallows, Valderrama lived the Chicano dream as formulated by Martín-Rodríguez: permanently deterritorialized, eternally out to lunch, articulating ecstasy in song and pithy epigram, here today and gone tomorrow. Valderrama avoided inner dialogue with historical trauma, safe inside his aesthetic fantasy world meant to "relieve the memory's secret dungeons of their destructive work," just as the absinthe-loving French poet Jarry recommended (Conrad 1988, 73). Nevertheless, in reading anthologies of new Chicano and Chicana writers, we find they are indeed capable of melancholy, brooding fatalism, and long depressing dialogues with trauma (Tatum 1992, 1993; Heyck 1994). The real shift might be in the theories academics now subscribe to, criteria that privilege the manic over the depressive. It was exactly the opposite taste that led to arch-pessimist Juan Rulfo's canonization in the 1950s.

Fantasies of eternal indeterminacy might be the rave on campus, but how relevant are they to nonacademic demographic clusters or diasporic populations, or other expressions of cultural identity characterized by *the slow habituation of meaningfulness*? Following expulsion from Spain, Sephardic Jews carried popular fifteenth-century romance formats with them for several hundred years, vitually intact, even after final *settlement* in Israel or the United States (Armistead and Silverman 1979). Communities become diasporic not out of choice but necessity; their goal is to go somewhere and do a better job of just what they were doing before, if possible. "In Los Angeles, for example, thousands of Zapotec immigrants from Oaxaca, as well as transporting their local saints and Madonnas northward, have also transplanted their traditional village governments *en bloc* to inner-city Catholic parishes" (101). Stable or in transit, the actual phenomenological experience of identity is that of archaic authorization, however illusory, and creative impersonation, however unoriginal. A diasporic community can "reterritorialize" on the identity-confirming musical style itself. We are bound to find any number of creative adjustments and adaptations in this diasporic process — all made in the interest of replication. *Rancheros* are not amateur Thomas Kuhns inventing new paradigms. What they want is creative recontact with tried and true formulas of settlement, stabilization, and value-system replication. Their binge-drinking practices, likewise, can *initially* be described in Deleuzoguattarian terms of nomadism or the sudden return of war machines or the creative use of the death instinct; in this scenario, alcohol sets raw affects spinning and sweeping across the colonized psyche to incite revolt or resistance to hegemonic categories and knowledges. But this is not postmodern nomadism for the sake of nomadism, usually, but a perfectly premodern settling or reterritorialization at a less "civilized" level of the psyche. "Out-of-control" drinking commonly facilitates a kind of controlled civilizational collapse, probably back to the level of civilization first achieved via the alcohol trade in the first place (McGovern 2003).

Let us redefine "escapism" as the essential human need to not feel lost in the midst of urban chaos. Ecstatic rural memories temporarily trump sordid city realities, in sixteenth-century Tenochtitlán or twenty-first century Chicago. José Alfredo's universe of celebrants still exists, has indeed grown larger than ever due to demographic and migratory patterns. What good is a "cultural identity" if it doesn't include a reliable system of spatiotemporal arrangements that protects an individual's secret connections with *acaecimientos* or time-suspending events? When a cultural or ethnic identity is underwritten or protected in this way, the process of identity "change" can be defined as whatever onsite adjustments and repairs are needed to keep open the portals of archaic authorization. Poets need these portals just as much as drunkards do, as drunken poets like Valderrama or Baudelaire always understood. In her otherwise pitiless portrait of Mexican drinking buddies in Seguín, Texas, Sandra Cisneros has the battered wife realize that "each is nightly trying to find the truth lying at the bottom of the bottle like a gold doubloon on the sea floor" (1992, 48). Texan poet Gloria Anzaldúa does not favor alcoholic magic, but she understands its lure: "Living in the Borderlands means you fight hard to resist the gold elixir beckoning from the bottle" (1994, 401). Many resist, but many others give in, for good reason: alcoholic communitas remembers and reunifies what was misplaced in social flux, border crossing, and urban chaos.

Psychological adaptation to historical absurdity is not a trivial achievement, whenever it is achieved, whoever achieves it, and however it is achieved. Alienation has a nasty habit of showing up "everywhere in modern industrial society, irrespective of the ownership structure prevailing in each case" (Catephores 1990, 48). Christopher Bollas sees the construction of a "false self" as "absolutely essential to our life": "We retreat very subtly back to transformed dyadic affiliations, back into triangular structures . . . all unconsciously soothing — even when occasions of mental pain themselves — because the mentally objectifiable dilemma is always preferable to the complex that is beyond its mental processing" (1992, 244). The alcohol-assisted ritual resinstatement of such regressive Oedipal dilemmas or paradigm scenarios was the basic procedure of the "Jose Alfredo catharsis" discussed earlier. Today, in cultural products that are actually being consumed by the seminomadic peoples remaking American cities from within, socially conservative attitudes predominate: recalcitrant heterosexism, reliance on vows and words of honor, love of large families, the alcoholized living of courtship emotions, births, and funerals, and promiscuous *donjuanismo* that is sometimes emulated and reproduced by Mexican lesbians (Zavella 2003, 239), and not for purposes of postmodern irony. There is nothing here to feel guilty about. Many a hard-won sense of self is gained inside the "puppet theater" of traditional forms of representation; more vitally still, it is with the aid of melodramatic cultural systems that populations reproduce themselves. Naturally these heterosexist systems are easily mocked by those with greater cultural resources in Bourdieu's sense.

Bollas notes that some artists and philosophers do not retreat from the angst of complexity but "stay with it, to see if it can be accounted for or narrated, perhaps celebrated: but the risks to such adventurers are high" (242). When alcohol becomes a tool of creative chaos used by culturally privileged writers or artists, they can end up under the volcano (Lowry) or crucified during holy week (Revueltas). Artistic confrontations with complexity do not always end so sacrificially, but that is their general direction. Great works of twentieth-century Mexican writers are characterized by "an exquisite taste for failure" (Portal 1980, 264). In cultural elites we also find an exquisite taste for alienation, an avant-garde, pseudo-ethical preference for the very bleakest images of urban misery, and subsequent adulation of photographers who capture the same (e.g., Ortiz Monasterio 1995; Gifford and Perry 1998). Here the procedure is: skip the high and go straight to the hangover, and you can never have too many images of rotting dog carcasses. We first encountered this bizarre aesthetic of ugliness in Juan Rulfo, the writer/photographer of hellish village Mexico.

Far be it from me to dismiss any cultural practice that seeks to ameliorate rural or urban alienation by telling the truth, the whole truth, and so forth. But if paradigms must be subverted, why not target the academic penchant for defining the creative self solely in terms of uniqueness, radical originality, and endless generation of new paradigms? The musical folk-urban continuum we have examined, Limón's Tex-Sex-Mex romance, clearly facilitates aesthetic modes of self-construction for people who would never use the word "aesthetic." Richard Shusterman eloquently defends the unoriginal and the non-novel, "a sense of the art of living based on certain generic formulas and ideals already socially entrenched as appropriate" (1992, 254). Shusterman's perspective is precisely the opposite of intellectuals unwilling to part with their social leadership ambitions, their Gramsci-like desire to penetrate "the amorphous mass element" with their own seminal ideas and save the people from themselves. If creative coping or resistance were limited to art worlds, we would all be in big trouble. Sophisticated critical instruments developed to study the visible light emitted by said art worlds are not able to scrutinize the "dark matter" of non-elite, alcoholized forms of resistant coping. Put yourself in the huaraches of people tired of holding social pyramids on their shoulders. They too want to be extraordinary, and this need can be fulfilled ecstatically during time-warping events that implode dull, ordinary, practical slavery to the Aztec calendar (then) or the yankee dollar (now).

In the long run we are all dead. In this light, maybe the relevant question is not "How long did *Fulano* live?" but "How many deeply meaningful events did *Fulano* experience in the years he did live?" The actual number of years on earth (just over forty-seven in the case of José Alfredo) is meaningless in itself. This "universal mestizo" knew how to look at Guanajuato's Yuriria Lake by moonlight — after an ocular adjustment with rum and cola (Sánchez Pérez 1999, 10). The perfectly nomadic

Jiménez of the 1960s distilled the emotions of Mexico's alcoholized cosmology and they live on, quite literally, in every drinking episode they accompany. People can hardly be blamed for idolizing a quasi-shamanic culture creator who gave them musical spacecrafts, fixative dyadic or triangular fantasies to cling to as they migrate across a border or traverse the inevitable physical and mental destructuration wrought by time. Alcoholic aesthetics can be youthful, festive, manic; in later life they facilitate a love for ruins, ruinations, and ruminations. In these *kairos* echochambers, the most meaningful events of our humble lives reverberate forever, anchoring inalienable modes of self-construction in the midst of physiological collapse.

If pressed to define the essence of alcohol's power in Mexican culture, I would say that it serves to validate numerous modes of cultural confabulation, that it literally *closes the gap* separating internal repertoires of paradigm scenarios from their conscious mental representation or behavioral enactment. Perhaps the desire for such gaplessness would not be so pressing if familial, financial, and educational systems were perfect, but they are not, and never will be, and bodyminds of the real world libidinal economy cannot wait. Alcoholic stroking of preexisting cultural figuration is clearly an impatient way to pursue meaning; catharsis is the short-term achievement of emotional fluidity, not the long-term achievement of emotional fungibility. For better and for worse, a developmentally regressive, musically encoded romance plotline remains integral to the cultural meaning of alcohol use by Mexicans — what I undertook this book to clarify. I have not glossed over the harm and the hardships caused by this alcoholized system of self-organization, nor do I entertain any illusions that it is nearing its end. Brain by inebriated brain, the cultural spectrum will continue to be shifted into infrared or ultraviolet zones, back and forth between depression and fantasmatic plenitude. At least four hundred or four hundred million additional rabbits will emerge in the Valley of Yuriria or the newly enchanted gardens of Greater Mexico. New generations will discover that, in the midst of a proper fiesta, time is no longer money, stigma transmutes itself into glory, fireworks are likely, and borrachos always get the last word: *¡Viva México!*

Bibliography

Agraz García de Alba, Gabriel. 1963. *Historia de la industria del Tequila Sauza: Tres generaciones y una tradición.* Guadalajara: Departamento de Investigaciones Históricas de Tequila Sauza.

Aguilar Siller, Oscar. 1997. *¡Salud, por México! Alcohólicos Anónimos salva a sus hermanos.* Mexico City: Editorial Grijalbo.

Aguirre Beltrán, Gonzalo. 1963. *Medicina y magia: El proceso de aculturación en la estructura colonial.* Mexico City: Instituto Nacional Indigenista.

Ahearne, Jeremy. 1995. *Michel de Certeau: Interpretation and Its Other.* Stanford: Stanford University Press.

Alarcón, Norma. 2003. Traddutora, Traditora: A Paradigmatic Figure of Chicana Feminism. In *Perspectives on Las Américas: A Reader in Culture, History, and Representation*, eds. M. C. Gutmann, F. V. Matos Rodríguez, L. Stephen, and P. Zavella. Oxford: Blackwell, 33–49.

Alasuutari, Pertti. 1982. *Desire and Craving. A Cultural Theory of Alcoholism.* Albany: State University of New York Press.

Alfaro, Alfaro. 1994. El tequila y sus signos: Elogio del hidalgo campirano. In *El tequila: Arte tradicional de México*, ed. Alberto Ruy Sánchez. Mexico City: Artes de México, 10–15.

American Psychiatric Association. 1994. *Diagnostic and Statistical Manual of Mental Disorders*, 4th Ed. Washington, D.C.: American Psychiatric Association.

Anderson, Benedict. 1991. *Imagined Communities*, rev. ed. London: Verso.

Anderson, Carl M., and Arnold J. Mandell. 1996. Fractal Time and the Foundations of Consciousness: Vertical Convergence of 1/f Phenomena from Ion Channels to Behavioral States. In *Fractals of Brain, Fractals of Mind*, ed. E. R. Mac Cormac and M. I. Stamenov. Amsterdam and Philadelphia: John Benjamins, 75–126.

Anzaldúa, Gloria. 1994. "To live in the Borderlands means you. . . ." In *Barrios and Borderlands: Cultures of Latinos and Latinas in the United States*, ed. D. Heyck. New York: Routledge, 400–2.

Araúz de Robles, Santiago. 1978. *Sociología del toreo.* Madrid: Prensa Española.

Armistead, Samuel G., and Joseph H. Silverman. 1979. *Tres calas en el romancero sefardí (Rodas, Jerusalén, Estados Unidos).* Madrid: Castalia.

Artaud, Antonin. 1992. *Mexico y Viaje al país de los tarahumaras* [orig. 1936–1948], ed. L. Schneider. Mexico City: Fondo de Cultura Económica.

Aub, Max. 1969. *Guía de narradores de la Revolución Mexicana.* Mexico City: Fondo de Cultura Económica.

Azanza Jiménez, José. 1999. *Mis vivencias con José Alfredo Jiménez.* Mexico City: EDAMEX.

Azuela, Mariano. 1992. *Los de abajo* [orig. 1915], ed. John E. Englekirk and Lawrence B. Kiddle. Prospect Heights, IL: Waveland Press.

Bach, Sheldon. 1991. On Sadomasochistic Object Relations. In *Perversions and Near-Perversions in Clinical Practice: New Psychoanalytic Perspectives*, eds. G. I. Fogel and W. A. Myers. New Haven and London: Yale University Press, 75–92.

195

Bakhtin, Mikhail. 1984. *Rabelais and His World*, trans. H. Iswolsky. Bloomington: Indiana University Press.

Bantjes, Adrian A. 1994. Burning Saints, Molding Minds: Iconoclasm, Civic Ritual, and the Failed Cultural Revolution. In *Rituals of Rule, Rituals of Resistance: Public Celebrations and Popular Culture in Mexico*, eds. W. H. Beezley, C. E. Martin, and W. E. French. Wilmington, DE: Scholarly Resources, 261–84.

Bareham, Tony. 1989. *Malcolm Lowry*. New York: St. Martin's Press.

Barr, Andrew. 1999. *Drink: A Social History of America*. New York: Carroll & Graf.

Barragán López, Esteban. 1997. *Con un pie en el estribo: Formación y deslizamientos de las sociedades rancheras en la construcción del México moderno*. Zamora: El Colegio de Michoacán.

Barry III, Herbert. 1976. Cross-Cultural Evidence that Dependency Conflict Motivates Drunkenness. In *Cross-Cultural Approaches to the Study of Alcohol*, ed. M. W. Everett, et al. The Hague: Mouton Publishers, 250–64.

Bartra, Roger. 1987. *La jaula de la melancholia: Identidad y metamorfosis del mexicano*. Mexico City: Grijalbo.

Baudot, Georges, and Tzvetan Todorov, eds. 1990. *Relatos aztecas de la conquista*, trans. Guillermina Cuevas. Mexico City: Grijalbo.

Baumeister, Roy F. 1991. *Escaping the Self: Alcoholism, Spirituality, Masochism, and Other Flights from the Burden of Selfhood*. New York: Basic Books.

Becker, Ernest. 1973. *The Denial of Death*. New York: Free Press.

Becker, Marjorie J. 1993. Black and White and Color: *Cardenismo* and the Search for a Campesino Ideology. In *Constructing Culture and Power in Latin America*, ed. D. H. Levine. Ann Arbor: University of Michigan Press, 155–70.

Beezley, William H. 1994. The Porfirian Smart Set Anticipates Thorstein Veblen in Guadalajara. In *Rituals of Rule, Rituals of Resistance: Public Celebrations and Popular Culture in Mexico*, eds. W. H. Beezley, C. E. Martin, and W. E. French. Wilmington, DE: Scholarly Resources, 173–90.

Beezley, William H., Cheryl E. Martin, and William E. French. 1994. Introduction: Constructing Consent, Inciting Conflict. In *Rituals of Rule, Rituals of Resistance: Public Celebrations and Popular Culture in Mexico*, eds. W. H. Beezley, C. E. Martin, and W. E. French. Wilmington, DE: Scholarly Resources, xiii–xxxii.

Benítez, Fernando. 1967. *Los indios de México*, vol. 1. Mexico City: Ediciones Era.

Benítez, Fernando . 2000. "El Señor Maguey." In *Maguey*, ed. Dominique Dufétel [orig. 1977]. Mexico City: Artes de México, 8–17.

Benjamin, Thomas. 2000. *La Revolución: Mexico's Great Revolution as Memory, Myth, and History*. Austin: University of Texas Press.

Bennassar, Bartolomé. 1979. *The Spanish Character: Attitudes and Mentalities from the Sixteenth to the Nineteenth Century*, trans. B. Keen. Berkeley: University of California Press.

Berghold, Josef. 1991. The Social Trance: Psychological Obstacles to Progress in History. *Journal of Psychohistory* 19:221–43.

Bernal, S. V., M. A. Márquez, B. B. Navarro, V. C. Selser, and V. L. Berruecos. 1985. *El alcoholismo en México: Negocio y manipulación*. Mexico City: Nuestro Tiempo.

Birth, Kevin K. 1996. Trinidadian Times: Temporal Dependency and Temporal Flexibility on the Margins of Industrial Capitalism. *Anthropological Quarterly* 69:79–89.

Blanco, José Joaquín. 1977. *Se llamaba Vasconcelos: Una evocación crítica*. Mexico City: Fondo de Cultura Económica.

Blau, Judith R. 1988. Music as Circumstance. *Social Forces* 66:883–902.

Bock, Philip K. 1999. *Rethinking Psychological Anthropology: Continuity and Change in the Study of Human Action*, 2nd ed. Prospect Heights, IL: Waveland Press.

Bollas, Christopher. 1992. *Being a Character: Psychoanalysis and Self Experience*. New York: Hill and Wang.

Bollas, Christopher . 1995. *Cracking Up: The Work of Unconscious Experience*. New York: Hill and Wang.

Bonfil Batalla, Guillermo. 1996. *México Profundo: Reclaiming a Civilization*, trans. Philip A. Dennis. Austin: University of Texas Press.

Bourdieu, Pierre. 1990. *The Logic of Practice* [orig. 1980]. Stanford: Stanford University Press.

Bourdieu, Pierre . 1996. *The Rules of Art* [orig. 1992]. Stanford: Stanford University Press.

Bourdieu, Pierre and Loic J. D. Wacquant. 1992. *An Invitation to Reflexive Sociology*. Chicago: University of Chicago Press.

Boyatzis, Richard E. 1976. Drinking as a Manifestation of Power Concerns. In *Cross-Cultural Approaches to the Study of Alcohol*, ed. M. W. Everett et al. The Hague: Mouton Publishers, 265–86.

Boyer, Christopher R. 2003. *Becoming Campesinos: Politics, Identity, and Agrarian Struggle in Postrevolutionary Michoacán, 1920–1935*. Stanford, CA: Stanford University Press.

Brandes, Stanley. 1980. *Metaphors of Masculinity: Sex and Status in Andalusian Folklore*. Philadelphia: University of Pennsylvania Press.

Brandes, Stanley . 1988. *Power and Persuasion: Fiestas and Social Control in Rural Mexico*. Philadelphia: University of Pennsylvania Press.

Brandes, Stanley. 2002. *Staying Sober in Mexico City*. Austin: University of Texas Press.

Brass, Tom. 2002. Latin American Peasants — New Paradigms for Old. *Journal of Peasant Studies* 29:1–40.

Braudel, Fernand. 1980. *On History*. Chicago: University of Chicago Press.

Brewin, Chris R. 2003. *Post-Traumatic Stress Disorder: Malady or Myth?* New Haven: Yale University Press.

Brodman, Barbara. 1976. *The Mexican Cult of Death in Myth and Literature*. Gainesville: University of Florida.

Bruman, Henry J. 2000. *Alcohol in Ancient Mexico*. Salt Lake City: University of Utah Press.

Brysk, Alison. 2003. Recovering from State Terror: The Morning after in Latin America. *Latin American Research Review* 38:238–247.

Bunzel, Ruth. 1991. El rol del alcoholismo en dos culturas centroamericanas [orig. 1940]. In *Antropología del alcoholismo en México*, ed. E. Menéndez. Mexico City: Centro de Investigaciones y Estudios Superiores en Antropología Social, 201–46.

Burkhart, Louise M. 1996. *Holy Wednesday: A Nahua Drama from Early Colonial Mexico*. Philadelphia: University of Pennsylvania Press.

Burr, Ramiro. 1999. *The Billboard Guide to Tejano and Regional Mexican Music*. New York: Billboard Books.

Cairns, Ed, and Mícheál D. Roe, eds. 2003. *The Role of Memory in Ethnic Conflict*. New York: Palgrave Macmillan.

Campos Navarro, Roberto. 1992. Percepción y prácticas curativas de una curandera urbana respecto del 'alcoholismo.' In *Prácticas e ideologías "científicas" y "populares" respecto del "alcoholismo" en México*, ed. E. Menéndez. México, D.F.: Centro de Investigaciones y Estudios Superiores en Antropología Social, 79–90.

Careaga, Gabriel. 1984. *Mitos y fantasías de la clase media en México*, 2nd ed. México, D.F.: Ediciones Océano.

Carmichael, Elizabeth, and Chloe Sayer. 1995. *The Skeleton at the Feast: The Day of the Dead in Mexico*. Austin: University of Texas Press.

Caro Baroja, Julio. 1964. Honor y vergüenza. *Revista de Dialectología y Tradiciones Populares* 20:41–60.

Carrasco, Davíd. 1987. Myth, Cosmic Terror, and the Templo Mayor. In *The Great Temple of Tenochtitlan: Center and Periphery in the Aztec World*, ed. J. Broda. Berkeley: University of California Press, 124–62.

Carrasco, Davíd . 1991. The Sacrifice of Tezcatlipoca: To Change Place. In *To Change Place: Aztec Ceremonial Landscapes*, ed. D. Carrasco. Boulder: University Press of Colorado, 32–57.

Carrasco, Davíd. 2000. *Quetzalcóatl and the Irony of Empire: Myths and Prophecies in the Aztec Tradition*, rev. ed. Boulder: University Press of Colorado.

Carrillo Cázares, Alberto. 1993. *Michoacán en el otoño del siglo XVII*. Zamora, Mich.: El Colegio de Michoacán.

Carroll, Michael P. 1986. *The Cult of the Virgin Mary: Psychological Origins*. Princeton: Princeton University Press.

Caruth, Cathy. 1996. *Unclaimed Experience: Trauma, Narrative, and History*. Baltimore: Johns Hopkins University Press.

Castellanos, Rosario. 1957. *Balún-Canán*. Mexico City: Fondo de Cultura Económica.

Castellanos, Rosario . 1962. *Oficio de tinieblas*. Mexico City: Joaquín Mortiz.

Castro Gutiérrez, Felipe. 1998. Condición femenina y violencia conyugal entre los purépechas durante la época colonial. *Mexican Studies* 14:5–22.

Catephores, George. 1990. Alienation. In *The New Palgrave: Marxian Economics*, eds. J. Eatwell, M. Milgate, and P. Newman. New York and London: W. W. Norton and Company, 45–49.

Certeau, Michel de. 1988. *The Practice of Everyday Life*, trans. S. Rendall. Berkeley: University of California Press.

Chasseguet-Smirgel, Janine. 1985. *Creativity and Perversion*. London: Free Association Books.

Chasteen, John Charles. 2001. *Born in Blood and Fire: A Concise History of Latin America*. New York: Norton.

Christian Jr., William A. 1996. *Visionaries: The Spanish Republic and the Reign of Christ*. Berkeley: University of California Press.

Cisneros, Sandra. 1992. *Woman Hollering Creek and Other Stories*. New York: Vintage.

Claramunt, Fernando. 1982. Los toros desde la psicología. In *Los toros: Tratado técnico e histórico*, vol. 7. Madrid: Espasa-Calpe, 1–181.

Claramunt, Fernando . 1989. *Historia ilustrada de la tauromaquia*. 2 vols. Madrid: Espasa-Calpe.

Claramunt, Fernando. 1991. *Modas y epidemias psíquicas en España*. Madrid: Ediciones Temas de Hoy.

Cohen, Anthony P. 1994. *Self Consciousness: An Alternative Anthropology of Identity*. London and New York: Routledge.

Cohen, Anthony P. and Nigel Rapport. 1995. Consciousness in Anthropology. In *Questions of Consciousness*, eds. Anthony P. Cohen and Nigel Rapport. London and New York: Routledge, 1–18.

Cohler, Bertram J. 1992. Intent and Meaning in Psychoanalysis and Cultural Study. In *New Directions in Psychological Anthropology*, ed. T. Schwartz, G. M. White, and C. A. Lutz. Cambridge: Cambridge University Press, 269–93.

Cohn, Norman. 1961. *The Pursuit of the Millenium: Revolutionary Messianism in Medieval and Renaissance Europe*. New York: Harper.

Cohn, Norman . 1975. *Europe's Inner Demons*. New York: Basic Books.

Conrad III, Barnaby. 1988. *Absinthe: History in a Bottle*. San Francisco: Chronicle Books.

Cook, Noble David. 1998. *Born to Die: Disease and New World Conquest, 1492–1650*. New York: Cambridge University Press.

Cook, Scott. 1993. Toward a New Paradigm for Anthropology in Mexican Studies. *Mexican Studies/Estudios Mexicanos* 9:303–36.

Cope, R. Douglas. 1994. *The Limits of Racial Domination: Plebeian Society in Colonial Mexico City, 1660–1720*. Madison: University of Wisconsin Press.

Corcuera de Mancera, Sonia. 1994. *Del amor al temor: Borrachera, catequesis y control en la Nueva España (1555–1771)*. Mexico City: Fondo de Cultura Económica.

Corcuera de Mancera, Sonia . 1997. *El fraile, el indio y el pulque (1523–1548)*. Mexico City: Fondo de Cultura Económica.

Corcuera de Mancera, Sonia. 2000. El pulque, su uso y abuso. In *Maguey*, ed. Dominique Dufétel. Mexico City: Artes de México, 54–63.

Cordero, Víctor. 1998. *Juan Charrasqueado: Su historia y sus hazañas*. Mexico City: Editorial Diana.

Cortés, Beatriz. 1992. Instituciones médicas y 'alcoholismo', o de la inexistencia del paciente alcohólico. In *Prácticas e ideologías "científicas" y "populares" respecto del "alcoholismo" en México*, ed. E. Menéndez. Mexico City: Centro de Investigaciones y Estudios Superiores en Antropología Social, 91–136.

Cossío y Corral, Francisco de. 1986. *Los toros: Tratado técnico e histórico*, vol. 8. Madrid: Espasa-Calpe.

Coulombe, Charles A., ed. 2002. *The Muse in the Bottle: Great Writers on the Joys of Drinking*. New York: Citadel Press.

Craib, Ian. 1998. *Experiencing Identity*. London: SAGE.

Crump, Thomas. 1987. The Alternative Economy of Alcohol in the Chiapas Highlands. In *Constructive Drinking: Perspectives on Drink from Anthropology*, ed. M. Douglas. Cambridge: Cambridge University Press, 239–49.

Cruz Martínez, María Teresa. 1994. *Catálogo de documentos-carta de la Colección Porfirio Díaz*. Alvaro Obregón, D.F.: Universidad Iberoamericana.

D'Andrade, Roy G. 1992. Schemas and Motivation. In *Human Motives and Cultural Models*, ed. R. D'Andrade and C. Strauss. New York: Cambridge University Press, 23–44.

d'Aquili, Eugene G. 1989. Social Historians Entranced; or, The Medium Is the Message. In *Social History and Issues in Human Consciousness*, eds. A. E. Barnes and P. N. Stearns. New York and London: New York University Press, 128–34.

Dardis, Thomas A. 1989. *The Thirsty Muse: Alcohol and the American Writer*. New York: Ticknor & Fields.

Davis, Mike. 2001. *Magical Urbanism: Latinos Reinvent the U.S. City*, rev. ed. London and New York: Verso.

Davis, Murray S. 1993. *What's So Funny? The Comic Conception of Culture and Society*. Chicago: University of Chicago Press.

de Certeau, Michel [see Certeau, Michel de]

De la Fuente, Ramón, María Elena Medina-Mora, and Jorge Caraveo. 1997. *Salud Mental en México*. Mexico City: Instituto Mexicano de Psiquiatría.

Deleuze, Gilles and Félix Guattari. 1983. *Anti-Oedipus* [orig. 1972], trans. R. Hurley, M. Seem, and H. R. Lane. Minneapolis: University of Minnesota Press.

Deleuze, Gilles and Félix Guattari . 1987. *A Thousand Plateaus* [orig. 1980], trans. Brian Massumi. Minneapolis: University of Minnesota Press.

Deleuze, Gilles and Félix Guattari. 1994. *What is Philosophy?*, trans. H. Tomlinson and G. Burchell. New York: Columbia University Press.

Delgado-Iribarren, Manuel. 1982. Los toros en la música. In *Los toros: Tratado técnico e histórico*, vol. 7. Madrid: Espasa-Calpe, 573–679.

Delgado Ruiz, Manuel. 1986. *De la muerte de un dios: La fiesta de los toros en el universo simbólico de la cultura popular*. Barcelona: Península.

deMause, Lloyd. 1974. The Evolution of Childhood. *History of Childhood Quarterly* 1:503–606.

Dennis, Philip A. 1975. The Role of the Drunk in a Oaxacan Village. *American Anthropologist* 77:856–63.

Denzin, Norman K. 1987. *The Alcoholic Self*. Newbury Park, CA: SAGE.

De Sousa, Ronald. 1990. *The Rationality of Emotion*. Cambridge: The MIT Press.

Devereux, Paul. 1997. *The Long Trip: A Prehistory of Psychedelia*. New York: Arkana.

deVries, Marten W. 1996. Trauma in Cultural Perspective. In *Traumatic Stress: The Effects of Overwhelming Experience on Mind, Body, and Society*, eds. B. A. van der Kolk, A. C. McFarlane, and L. Weisaeth. New York and London: Guilford.

Díaz-Guerrero, R., 398–413. 1967. *Estudios de psicología del mexicano*. Mexico City: Editorial Trillas.

Dolar, Mladen. 1996. The Object Voice. In *Gaze and Voice as Love Objects*, ed. R. Salecl and S. Zizek. Durham and London: Duke University Press, 7-31.

Doremus, Anne T. 2001. *Culture, Politics, and National Identity in Mexican Literature and Film, 1929–1952*. New York: Peter Lang.

Dorosz, Kristofer. 1976. *Malcolm Lowry's Infernal Paradise*. Stockholm: Acta Universitatis Upsaliensis.

Douglas, Mary. 1987. A distinctive anthropological perspective. In *Constructive Drinking: Perspectives on Drink from Anthropology*, ed. M. Douglas. Cambridge: Cambridge University Press, 3–15.

Drewermann, Eugen. 1995. *Clérigos: Psicograma de un ideal*, trans. Dionisio Mínguez. Madrid: Editorial Trotta.

Dufétel, Dominique. 2000. The Maguey, the Rabbit, and the Moon. In *Maguey*, ed. D. Dufétel. Mexico City: Artes de México, 18–27, 84–86.

Durazo, Manuel. 1998. Beber: cultura y marginalidad. In *Creer, beber, curar*, ed. Cristóbal López. Monterrey, N.L.: Fondo Estatal para la Cultura y las Artes de Nuevo León, 313–51.

Dutton, Donald G. 1995. *The Domestic Assault of Women: Psychological and Criminal Justice Perspectives*. Vancouver: University of British Columbia Press.

Eber, Christine. 2000. *Women and Alcohol in a Highland Maya Town: Water of Hope, Water of Sorrow*, updated ed. Austin: University of Texas Press.

Echeverría, Bolívar. 1994. El ethos barroco. In *Modernidad, mestizaje cultural, ethos barroco*, ed. B. Echeverría. Mexico City: UNAM/El Equilibrista.

Eliade, Mircea. 1954. *The Myth of the Eternal Return*. Princeton: Princeton University Press.

Eliade, Mircea . 1969. *The Quest*. Chicago: University of Chicago Press.

Ellenberger, Henri F. 1958. A Clinical Introduction to Psychiatric Phenomenology and Existential Analysis. In *Existence*, ed. R. May, E. Angel, and H. F. Ellenberger. New York: Simon & Schuster, 92–124.

Englekirk, John E. 1935 El "descubrimiento" de *Los de abajo*. Mexico City: Imprenta Universitaria.

Erofeyev, Victor. 2002. "The Russian God," trans. Andrew Bromfield. *The New Yorker*, December 16, 2002, 56–63.

Ey, Henri. 1978. *Consciousness: A Phenomenological Study of Being Conscious and Becoming Conscious*, trans. J. H. Flodstrom [orig. 1963]. Bloomington: Indiana University Press.

Fabian, Johannes. 1983. *Time and the Other: How Anthropology Makes Its Object*. New York: Columbia University Press.

Fallaw, Ben. 2001. *Cárdenas Compromised: The Failure of Reform in Postrevolutionary Yucatán*. Durham: Duke University Press.

Farriss, Nancy M. 1995. Remembering the Future, Anticipating the Past: History, Time, and Cosmology among the Maya of Yucatan. In *Time: Histories and Ethnologies*, ed. D. O. Hughes and T. R. Trautmann. Ann Arbor: University of Michigan Press, 107–38.

Fein, Seth. 1999. From Collaboration to Containment: Hollywood and the International Political Economy of Mexican Cinema after the Second World War. In *Mexico's Cinema: A Century of Film and Filmmakers*, ed. J. Hershfield and D. R. Maciel. Wilmington, DE: Scholarly Resources, 123–63.

Fernández, James W. 1995. Amazing Grace: Meaning Deficit, Displacement and New Consciousness in Expressive Interaction. In *Questions of Consciousness*, eds. Anthony P. Cohen and Nigel Rapport. London and New York: Routledge, 21–40.

Field, Peter B. 1991. Un nuevo estudio intercultural sobre la embriaguez. In *Antropología del alcoholismo en México*, ed. E. Menéndez. Mexico City: Centro de Investigaciones y Estudios Superiores en Antropología Social, 87–122.

Finkler, Kaja. 1994. *Spiritualist Healers in Mexico: Successes and Failures of Alternative Therapeutics*, [orig 1985]. Salem, MA: Sheffield.

Fisher, Seymour and Rhoda L. Fisher. 1993. *The Psychology of Adpatation to Absurdity: Tactics of Make-Believe*. Hillsdale, NJ: Lawrence Erlbaum.

Fiske, John. 1991. *Reading the Popular*. London and New York: Routledge.

Florescano, Enrique. 1994. *Memory, Myth, and Time in Mexico: From the Aztecs to Independence*, trans. Albert G. Bork and Kathryn R. Bork. Austin: University of Texas Press.

Franco, Jean. 1986. The Incorporation of Women: A Comparison of North American and Mexican Popular Narrative. In *Studies in Entertainment: Critical Approaches to Mass Culture*, ed. T. Modleski. Bloomington: Indiana University Press, 119–38.

Franzer, Jerry P. 1993. Alcohol and Other Drugs Are Key Causal Agents of Violence. In *Current Controversies on Family Violence*, eds. R. J. Gelles and D. R. Loseke. London: Sage, 171–81.

French, William E. 1994. Progreso Forzado: Workers and the Inculcation of the Capitalist Work Ethic in the Parral Mining District. In *Rituals of Rule, Rituals of Resistance: Public Celebrations and Popular Culture in Mexico*, eds. W. H. Beezley, C. E. Martin, and W. E. French. Wilmington, DE: Scholarly Resources, 191–212.

French, William E . 2003. "*Te amo muncho*": The Love Letters of Pedro and Enriqueta. In *The Human Tradition in Mexico*, ed. Jeffrey M. Pilcher. Wilmington, DE: Scholarly Resources, 123–35.

Fromm, Erich and Michael Maccoby. 1996. *Social Character in a Mexican Village*, 2nd ed., [Orig. 1970.]. New Brunswick and London: Transaction Publishers.

Fromme, K., and E. J. D'Amico. 1999. Neurobiological Bases of Alcohol's Psychological Effects. In *Psychological Theories of Drinking and Alcoholism*, eds. K. E. Leonard & H. T. Blane. New York: The Guilford Press, 422–55.

Fuentes, Carlos. 1964. *The Death of Artemio Cruz*, trans. Sam Hileman. New York: Farrar, Straus and Giroux.

Fuentes, Carlos . 1992. The Barefoot Iliad. In *The Underdogs* by Mariano Azuela, trans. Frederick H. Fornoff, ed. Seymour Menton. Pittsburgh and London: University of Pittsburgh Press, 123–40.

Galenson, Eleanor. 1988. The Precursors of Masochism. In *Fantasy, Myth, and Reality: Essays in Honor of Jacob A. Arlow*, ed. H. P. Blum et al. Madison, CT: International Universities Press, 371–80.

García Cantú, Gastón. 1963. *Utopías mexicanas*. Mexico City: Ediciones ERA.

García Cubas, Antonio. 2000. El pulquero y la pulquería [orig. 1904]. In *Maguey*, ed. Dominique Dufétel. Mexico City: Artes de México, 70–73.

García Ferrero, Francisco M. 1984. Valor etnográfico de las "Guías de Forasteros": El caso de Sevilla. In *Antropología cultural de Andalucía*, ed. S. Rodríguez-Becerra. Seville: Publicaciones de la Universidad de Sevilla, 267–84.

García Riera, Emilio. 1969. *Historia documental del cine mexicano*. Mexico City: Ediciones Era.

García Rubial, Antonio. 2002. The Kingdom of New Spain at a Crossroads. In *The Grandeur of Viceregal Mexico: Treasures from the Museo Franz Mayer*. Houston: Museum of Fine Arts, 9–22.

Garibay Alvarez, Jorge. 1997. *Las cantinas, donde la palabra se humedece*. Mexico City: EDAMEX.

Geertz, Clifford. 1973. *The Interpretation of Cultures*. New York: Basic Books.

Gell, Alfred. 1992. *The Anthropology of Time: Cultural Constructions of Temporal Maps and Images*. Oxford: Berg.

Gelles, Richard J. 1993. Alcohol and Other Drugs Are Associated with Violence — They Are Not Its Cause. In *Current Controversies on Family Violence*, ed. R. J. Gelles and D. R. Loseke. London: Sage, 182–96.

Gelles, Richard J., and Murray A. Straus. 1988. *Intimate Violence*. New York: Simon & Schuster.

Gelven, Michael. 1991. *Why Me? A Philosophical Inquiry into Fate*. DeKalb, IL: Northern Illinois University Press.

Gifford, Barry, and David Perry. 1998. *Bordertown*. San Francisco: Chronicle Books.

Gil Calvo, Enrique. 1989. *Función de toros: Una interpretación funcionalista de las corridas*. Madrid: Espasa-Calpe.

Gillespie, Jeanne L. 1998. Gender, Ethnicity, and Piety: The Case of the *China Poblana*. In *Imagination beyond Nation*, ed. E. P. Bueno and T. Caesar. Pittsburgh: University of Pittsburgh Press, 19–40.

Gilmore, David D. 1987. *Aggression and Community: Paradoxes of Andalusian Culture*. New Haven, CT: Yale University Press.

Gilmore, David D. 2001. *Misogyny: The Male Malady*. Philadelphia: University of Pennsylvania Press.

Girard, René. 1978. *Des choses cachées depuis la fondation du monde*. Paris: Grasset.

Girard, René. 1982. *Le Bouc émissaire*. Paris: Grasset.

Goldman, Harvey. 1992. *Politics, Death, and the Devil*. Berkeley: University of California Press.

Goldman, M. S., F. K. Del Boca, and J. Darkes. 1999. Alcohol Expectancy Theory: The Application of Cognitive Neuroscience. In *Psychological Theories of Drinking and Alcoholism*, eds. K. E. Leonard and H. T. Blane. New York: The Guilford Press, 203–46.

González Casarrubios, Consolación. 1985. *Fiestas populares en Castilla-La Mancha*. Ciudad Real: Servicio de Publicaciones de la Junta de Comunidades de Castilla-La Mancha.

González Torres, Yólotl. 1985. *El sacrificio humano entre los mexicas*. Mexico City: Instituto Nacional de Antropología e Historia/Fondo de Cultura Económica.

González y González, Luis. 1998. *Modales de la cultura nacional*. Mexico City: Clío.

Goodman, Felicitas D. 1988. *Ecstasy, Ritual, and Alternate Reality: Religion in a Pluralistic World*. Bloomington: Indiana University Press.

Gossen, Gary H. 1999. *Telling Maya Tales: Tzotzil Identities in Modern Mexico*. New York: Routledge.

Gramsci, Antonio. 1971. *Selections from the Prison Notebooks*. London: Lawrence & Wishart.

Gruzinski, Serge. 1979. La Mère dévorante: alcoolisme, sexualité et déculturation chez les Mexicas, 1500–1550. *Cahiers des Amériques Latines* 20:5–36.

Gruzinski, Serge. 1989. *Man-Gods in the Mexican Highlands: Indian Power and Colonial Society, 1520–1800*, trans. E. Corrigan. Stanford: Stanford University Press.

Gruzinski, Serge. 1994. Del barroco al neobarroco: Fuentes novohispanas de los tiempos posmodernos. In *México: Identidad y cultura nacional*, ed. G. Lechuga Solís. Mexico City: Universidad Autónoma Metropolitana, Unidad Xochimilco, 13–21.

Gruzinski, Serge. 2001. *Images at War: Mexico from Columbus to Blade Runner (1492–2019)*, trans. H. Maclean. Durham, NC: Duke University Press.

Guerra Guerra, Armando. 1977. *El alcoholismo en México*. Mexico City: Fondo de Cultura Económica.

Gusfield, Joseph. 1987. Passage to Play: Rituals of Drinking Time in American Society. In *Constructive Drinking: Perspectives on Drink from Anthropology*, ed. M. Douglas. Cambridge: Cambridge University Press, 73–90.

Gusfield, Joseph . 1996. *Contested Meanings: The Construction of Alcohol Problems.* Madison and London: University of Wisconsin Press.

Gutmann, Matthew C. 1996. *The Meanings of Macho: Being a Man in Mexico City.* Berkeley: University of California Press

Guzmán, Martín Luis. 1930. *The Eagle and the Serpent,* trans. Harriet de Onís [orig. 1928]. New York: Knopf.

Hall, Peter. 1998. *Cities in Civilization.* New York: Pantheon.

Hamber, Brandon, and Richard A. Wilson. 2003. Symbolic Closure through Memory, Reparation and Revenge in Post-Conflict Societies. *The Role of Memory in Ethnic Conflict,* eds. E. Cairns and M. Roe. New York: Palgrave Macmillan, 144–68.

Hamill, Pete. 1994. *A Drinking Life.* Boston: Back Bay Books.

Hassig, Ross. 2001. *Time, History, and Belief in Aztec and Colonial Mexico.* Austin: University of Texas Press.

Hastrup, Kirsten. 1985. *Culture and History in Medieval Iceland: An Anthropological Analysis of Structure and Change.* Oxford: Clarendon.

Haynor, Priscilla B. 2001. *Unspeakable Truths: Confronting State Terror and Atrocity.* New York and London: Routledge.

Hazan, Haim. 1987. Holding Time Still with Cups of Tea. In *Constructive Drinking: Perspectives on Drink from Anthropology,* ed. M. Douglas. Cambridge: Cambridge University Press, 205–19.

Heath, Dwight B. 1987. A Decade of Development in the Anthropological Study of Alcohol Use, 1970–1980. In *Constructive Drinking: Perspectives on Drink from Anthropology,* ed. M. Douglas. Cambridge: Cambridge University Press, 16–69.

Héau, Catherine. 1995. Identidad y cancionero popular. In *El verbo popular: Discurso e identidad en la cultura mexicana,* ed. A. R. Sneff and J. Lameiras. Zamora, Mich.: El Colegio de Michoacán, 127–44.

Heimann, Jim, ed. 2002. *Mexicana: Vintage Mexican Graphics.* Cologne: Taschen.

Herren, Ricardo. 1991. *La conquista erótica de las Indias.* Barcelona: Planeta.

Hershfield, Joanne. 1999. Race and Ethnicity in the Classical Cinema. In *Mexico's Cinema: A Century of Film and Filmmakers,* ed. J. Hershfield and D. Maciel. Wilmington, DE: Scholarly Resources, 81–100.

Herzfeld, Michael. 1997. *Cultural Intimacy: Social Poetics in the Nation-State.* New York and London: Routledge.

Heyck, Denis Lynn Daly. 1994. *Barrios and Borderlands: Cultures of Latinos and Latinas in the United States.* New York and London: Routledge.

Hibino, Barbara. 1992. Cervecería Cuauhtémoc: A Case Study of Tecnological and Industrial Development in Mexico. *Mexican Studies/Estudios Mexicanos* 8:23–44.

Híjar, M., M. Flores, M. V. López, and H. Rosovsky. 1998. Alcohol Intake and Severity of Injuries on Highways in Mexico: A Comparative Analysis. *Addiction* 93(10):1543–51.

Horowitz, Mardi. 1979. *States of Mind.* New York: Plenum Press.

Horowitz, Mardi . 1988. *Introduction to Psychodynamics: A New Synthesis.* New York: Basic Books.

Hoyos y Vinent, Antonio de. 1914. *Oro, seda, sangre y sol.* Madrid: Renacimiento.

Infante, José María. 1998. Psicoanálisis de la fiesta mexicana. In *México en fiesta,* ed. H. Pérez Martínez. Zamora, Mich.: El Colegio de Michoacán, 135–52.

Ingham, John M. 1986. *Mary, Michael, and Lucifer: Folk Catholicism in Central Mexico.* Austin: University of Texas Press.

Islas Escárcea, Leovigildo. 2000. Las haciendas pulqueras. In *Maguey,* ed. Dominique Dufétel. Mexico City: Artes de México, 46–51.

Jankowiak, William, and Dan Bradburd. 1996. Using Drug Foods to Capture and Enhance Labor Performance: A Cross-cultural Perspective. *Current Anthropology* 37:717–20.

Jáuregui, Jesús. 1990. *El mariachi: Símbolo musical de México.* Mexico City: Instituto Nacional de Antropología e Historia.

Jiménez, Armando. 1995. *Cancionero mexicano: 4000 letras de canciones* (complilation), vol. 1. Mexico City: Editores Mexicanos Unidos.

Jiménez, Armando . 2000. *Lugares de gozo, retozo, ahogo y desahogo en la Ciudad de México.* Mexico City: Océano.

Jiménez, Ivette. 1998. La fiesta en México: Tiempos y espacios entre la vida y el espectáculo. In *México en fiesta,* ed. H. Pérez Martínez. Zamora, Mich.: El Colegio de Michoacán, 153–72.

Joffe, Alexander H. 1998. Alcohol and Social Complexity in Ancient Western Asia. *Current Anthropology* 39:297–322 [with replies].

Joseph, Gilbert M. 1994. *Everyday Forms of State Formation: Revolution and the Negotiation of Rule in Modern Mexico,* edited vol. Durham, NC: Duke University Press.

———. 1999. The Challenge of Writing Narrative Cultural History. *Mexican Studies/Estudios Mexicanos* 15:359–71.

Katz, Friedrich. 1998. *The Life and Times of Pancho Villa.* Stanford: Standord University Press.

Katz, Jack. 1988. *Seductions of Crime: Moral and Sensual Attractions in Doing Evil.* New York: Basic Books.

Kearney, Michael. 1991. Borrachera y conversión religiosa en un pueblo mexicano [orig. 1970]. In *Antropología del alcoholismo en México,* ed. E. Menéndez. Mexico City: Centro de Investigaciones y Estudios Superiores en Antropología Social, 329–51.

Kearney, Michael . 1996. *Reconceptualizing the Peasantry: Anthropology in Global Perspective.* Boulder, CO: Westview Press.

Kennedy, John G. 1991. El complejo del tesgüino: El rol de la bebida en la cultura tarahumara [orig. 1963]. In *Antropología del alcoholismo en México,* ed. E. Menéndez. Mexico City: Centro de Investigaciones y Estudios Superiores en Antropología Social, 251–81.

Kern, Robert W. 1974. *Liberals, Reformers, and Caciques in Restoration Spain, 1875–1909.* Albuquerque: University of New Mexico Press.

Kernberg, Otto. 1991. Aggression and Love in the Relationship of the Couple. In *Perversions and Near-Perversions in Clinical Practice: New Psychoanalytic Perspectives,* ed. G. I. Fogel and W. A. Myers. New Haven: Yale University Press, 153–75.

Kernberg, Otto . 1992. The Psychopathology of Hatred. In *Affect: Psychoanalytic Perspectives,* eds. T. Shapiro and R. Emde. Madison, CT: International Universities Press, 209–38.

Kiev, Ari. 1972. *Transcultural Psychiatry.* New York: Free Press.

Klor de Alva, J. Jorge. 1992. Nahua Studies, the Allure of the "Aztecs," and Miguel León-Portilla. In *The Aztec Image of Self and Society: An Introduction to Nahua Culture,* ed. J. J. Klor de Alva. Salt Lake City: University of Utah Press, vii–xxiii.

Klor de Alva, J. Jorge . 1997. Nahua Colonial Discourse and the Appropriation of the (European) Other. In *Borrowed Power: Essays on Cultural Appropriation,* ed. B. Ziff and P. V. Rao. New Brunswick: Rutgers University Press, 169–92.

Knapp, Caroline. 1996. *Drinking: A Love Story.* New York: Delta.

Knauft, Bruce M. 1996. *Genealogies for the Present in Cultural Anthropology: A Critical Humanist Perspective.* New York and London: Routledge.

Kramer, Joel and Diana Alstad. 1993. *The Guru Papers: Masks of Authoritarian Power.* Berkeley: Frog, Ltd.

Krauze, Enrique. 1997. *Mexico: Biography of Power: A History of Modern Mexico, 1810–1996,* trans. Hank Heifetz. New York: Harper-Collins.

Krauze, Enrique, and Fausto Zerón-Medina. 1993. *Porfirio: Vol. 4: El poder.* Mexico City: Editorial Clío.

Kreimerman Lew, Jessica. 1997. *La vida en rosa, el príncipe azul: Mujeres y amor en México.* Mexico City: Grupo Resistencia.

Kristeva, Julia. 1986. *The Kristeva Reader,* ed. T. Moi. Oxford: Basil Blackwell.

Krotz, Esteban. 1991. A Panoramic View of Recent Mexican Anthropology. *Current Anthropology* 32:183–88.

LaBarre, Weston. 1972. *The Ghost Dance: The Origins of Religion.* New York: Delta.

LaBarre, Weston . 1989. *The Peyote Cult* [orig. 1938]. Norman: University of Oklahoma Press.

Laing, R. D. 1972. *The Politics of the Family and Other Essays.* New York: Vintage Books.

Lambek, Michael. 1993. *Knowledge and Practice in Mayotte: Local Discourses of Islam, Sorcery, and Spirit Possession.* Toronto: U. of Toronto Press.

Lambek, Michael . 1996. Afterword: Spirits and Their Histories. In *Spirits in Culture, History, and Mind,* eds. J. M. Mageo and A. Howard. New York and London: Routledge, 237–49.

Lameiras, José. 1995. Tres relatos, tres interpretaciones y un asunto: La identidad popular en Payno, Altamirano y López Portillo y Rojas. In *El verbo popular,* ed. A. Roth Seneff and J. Lameiras. Zamora, Mich.: El Colegio de Michoacán, 91–126.

Lameiras, José . 1998. Impresiones literarias decimonónicas de lo festivo mexicano. In *México en fiesta,* ed. H. Pérez Martínez. Zamora, Mich.: El Colegio de Michoacán, 173–96.

Lang, A. R., C. J. Patrick, and W. G. K. Stritzke. 1999. Alcohol and Emotional Response: A Multi-dimensional-Multilevel Analysis. In *Psychological Theories of Drinking and Alcoholism*, eds. K. E. Leonard and H. T. Blane. New York: The Guilford Press, 328–71.

Leonard, K. E. and H. T. Blane, eds. 1999. *Psychological Theories of Drinking and Alcoholism*, 2nd ed. New York: The Guilford Press.

León-Portilla, Miguel. 1959. *Visión de los vencidos: Relaciones indígenas de la Conquista*. Mexico City: Publicaciones de la Universidad Nacional Autónoma de México.

León-Portilla, Miguel . 1968. *Quetzalcóatl*. Mexico City: Fondo de Cultura Económica.

León-Portilla, Miguel. 1992. *The Aztec Image of Self and Society: An Introduction to Nahua Culture*, ed. J. J. Klor de Alva. Salt Lake City: University of Utah Press.

Levine, Robert. 1997. *A Geography of Time*. New York: Basic Books.

Levy, Robert I., Jeannette Marie Mageo, and Alan Howard. 1996. Gods, Spirits, and History: A Theoretical Perspective. In *Spirits in Culture, History, and Mind*, eds. J. M. Mageo and A. Howard. New York and London: Routledge, 11-27.

Lewis, Oscar. 1959. *Five Families: Mexican Case Studies in the Culture of Poverty*. New York: Basic Books.

Lewis, Oscar . 1961. *The Children of Sánchez*. New York: Random House.

Limón, José E. 1994. *Dancing with the Devil: Society and Cultural Poetics in Mexican-American South Texas*. Madison: University of Wisconsin Press.

———. 1998. *American Encounters: Greater Mexico, the United States, and the Erotics of Culture*. Boston: Beacon Press.

Lockhart, James. 1991. *Nahuas and Spaniards: Postconquest Central Mexican History and Philology*. Stanford: Stanford University Press.

López Austin, Alfredo. 1980. *Cuerpo humano e ideología: Las concepciones de los antiguos nahuas*. Mexico City: Publicaciones de la Universidad Nacional Autónoma de México.

López Austin, Alfredo . 1996. *The Rabbit on the Face of the Moon: Mythology in the Mesoamerican Tradition*, trans. Bernard and Thelma Ortiz de Montellano. Salt Lake City: University of Utah Press.

Lorente-Murphy, Silvia. 1988. *Juan Rulfo: Realidad y mito de la Revolución Mexicana*. Madrid: Editorial Pliegos.

Lotman, Yuri M. 1990. *Universe of the Mind: A Semiotic Theory of Culture*, trans. Ann Shukmnan. Bloomington: Indiana University Press.

Lowry, Malcolm. 1965. *Under the Volcano* [orig. 1947]. Philadelphia and New York: J. B. Lippincott.

Lowry, Malcolm . 2000. *Un trueno sobre el Popcatépetl: Selected Poems*, trans. R. Vargas, J. E. Pacheco, and J. García Terrés. Mexico City: Ediciones Era.

Luna Zamora, Rogelio. 1999. *La historia del tequila, de sus regiones y sus hombres*, 2nd ed. Mexico City: Consejo Nacional para la Cultura y las Artes.

Lutz, Catherine. 1992. Motivated Models. In *Human Motives and Cultural Models*, ed. R. D'Andrade and C. Strauss. New York: Cambridge University Press, 181–96.

MacAndrew, Craig, and Robert B. Edgerton. 1969. *Drunken Comportment: A Social Explanation*. Chicago: Aldine.

Macuixtle García, Julio. 1992. La importancia del consumo de alcohol en Magdalena (Veracruz). In *Prácticas e ideologías "científicas" y "populares" respecto del "alcoholismo" en México*, ed. E. Menéndez. Mexico City: Centro de Investigaciones y Estudios Superiores en Antropología Social, 43–62.

Madera Ferrón, Héctor. 1993. *Silencio . . . genios trabajando: Los artistas que yo conocí*. Mexico City: Editores Asociados Mexicanos.

Madsen, William, and Claudia Madsen. 1991. La estructura cultural del comportamiento hacia el alcohol en México [orig. 1969]. In *Antropología del alcoholismo en México*, ed. E. Menéndez. Mexico City: Centro de Investigaciones y Estudios Superiores en Antropología Social, 309–28.

Magdaleno, Mauricio. 1937. *Resplandor*. Mexico City: Ediciones Botas.

Marco, Joaquín. 1977. *Literatura popular en España en los siglos XVIII y XIX*, vol. 2. Madrid: Taurus.

Martin, Cheryl English 1994. Public Celebrations, Popular Culture, and Labor Discipline in Eighteenth-Century Chihuahua. In *Rituals of Rule, Rituals of Resistance: Public Celebrations and Popular Culture in Mexico*, eds. W. H. Beezley, C. E. Martin, and W. E. French. Wilmington, DE: Scholarly Resources, 95–114.

Martindale, Colin. 1990. *The Clockwork Muse: The Predictability of Artistic Change*. New York: BasicBooks.

Martínez, José Luis. 1996. *Zapata iconografía*, 2nd ed. Mexico City: Fondo de Cultura Económica.

Martínez Limón, Enrique. 1998. *Tequila: The Spirit of Mexico*. Mexico City: Revimundo.

Martín-Rodríguez, Manuel. 2001. The Global Border: Transnationalism and Cultural Hybridism in Alejandro Morales's *The Rag Doll Plagues*. *Bilingual Review/Revista Bilingüe* 20:86–98.

Mathews, Holly F. 1992. The Directive Force of Morality Tales in a Mexican Community. In *Human Motives and Cultural Models*, ed. R. D'Andrade and C. Strauss. New York: Cambridge University Press, 127–62.

Mavor, Carol. 2003. Pulling Ribbons from Mouths: Roland Barthes's Umbilical Referent. In *Representing the Passions: Histories, Bodies, Visions*, ed. R. Meyer. Los Angeles: Getty Research Institute, 175–205.

McClenon, James. 1994. *Wondrous Events: Foundations of Religious Belief*. Philadelphia: University of Pennsylvania Press.

McGovern, Patrick E. 2003. *Ancient Wine: The Search for the Origins of Viniculture*. Princeton: Princeton University Press.

McGuire, Meredith B. 1990. Religion and the Body: Rematerializing the Human Body in the Social Sciences of Religion. *Journal for the Scientific Study of Religion* 29:283–96

McFarlane, Alexander C. and Bessel van der Kolk. 1996. Trauma and Its Challenge to Society. In *Traumatic Stress: The Effects of Overwhelming Experience on Mind, Body, and Society*, eds. B. A. van der Kolk, A. C. McFarlane, and L. Weisaeth. New York and London: Guilford, 24–46.

Medina Mora, María Elena, et al. 1999. Adicciones. In *Diez problemas relevantes de salud pública en México*, eds. J. R. de la Fuente and J. Sepúlveda Amor. Mexico City: Instituto Nacional de Salud Pública/Fondo de Cultura Económica, 247–91.

Mendoza, Vicente T. 1974. *El corrido mexicano: Antología*. Mexico City: Fondo de Cultura Económica.

Mendoza, Vicente T . 1982. *La canción mexicana: Ensayo de clasificación y antología*, 2nd ed. Mexico City: Fondo de Cultura Económica.

Menéndez, Eduardo. 1990. *Morir de alcohol: Saber y hegemonía médica*. Mexico City: Alianza Editorial Mexicana.

Menéndez, Eduardo . 1991. Alcoholismo y proceso de alcoholización; la construcción de una propuesta antropológica. In *Antropología del alcoholismo en México*, ed. E. Menéndez. Mexico City: Centro de Investigaciones y Estudios Superiores en Antropología Social, 13–32.

Menéndez, Eduardo. 1992. Trabajo, proceso de alcoholización y enfermedad laboral. In *Prácticas e ideologías "científicas" y "populares" respecto del "alcoholismo" en México*, ed. E. Menéndez. Mexico City: Centro de Investigaciones y Estudios Superiores en Antropología Social, 137–69.

Mészáros, István. 1989. *The Power of Ideology*. New York: New York University Press.

Milkman, Harvey and Stanley Sunderwirth. 1987. *Craving for Ecstasy: The Consciousness and Chemistry of Escape*. New York: Lexington Books.

Miller, William R. 1986. Haunted by the Zeitgeist: Reflections on Contrasting Treatment Goals and Concepts of Alcoholism in Europe and the United States. In *Alcohol and Culture: Comparative Perspectives from Europe and America*, ed. Thomas F. Babor. New York: Annals of the New York Academy of Sciences, 110–29.

Mitchell, Timothy. 1988. *Violence and Piety in Spanish Folklore*. Philadelphia: University of Pennsylvania Press.

Mitchell, Timothy . 1990. *Passional Culture: Emotion, Religion, and Society in Southern Spain*. Philadelphia: University of Pennsylvania Press.

Mitchell, Timothy. 1991. *Blood Sport: A Social History of Spanish Bullfighting*. Philadelphia: University of Pennsylvania Press.

Mitchell, Timothy. 1994. *Flamenco Deep Song*. New Haven: Yale University Press.

Mitchell, Timothy. 1998. *Betrayal of the Innocents: Desire, Power, and the Catholic Church in Spain*. Philadelphia: University of Pennsylvania Press.

Molina, P. V., V. L. Berruecos, and M. L. Sánchez. 1983. *El alcoholismo en México: Aspectos sociales, culturales y económicos*. Mexico City: Fundación de Investigaciones Sociales.

Monsiváis, Carlos. 1999. Cantinflas and Tin Tan: Mexico's Greatest Comedians. In *Mexico's Cinema: A Century of Film and Filmmakers*, ed. J. Hershfield and D. Maciel. Wilmington, DE: Scholarly Resources, 49–79.

Monsiváis, Carlos . 1998. José Alfredo Jiménez: "Les diré que llegué de un mundo raro." In *Y sigue siendo el rey: Homenaje a José Alfredo Jiménez*, ed. Sandra Azcárraga de Sepul. Mexico City: Fundación Cultural Artención, 13–38.

Muñoz, Rafael D. 1935. *¡Vámonos con Pancho Villa!* Madrid: Espasa-Calpe.

Moreno Rivas, Yolanda, with Alejandro Pérez Sáez. 1989. *Historia de la música popular mexicana*, 2nd ed. Mexico City: Alianza Editorial Mexicana.

Moreno Rivas, Yolanda, et al. 1979. *Historia ilustrada de la música popular mexicana* (11 albums, 22 discs). Mexico City: Promociones Editoriales Mexicanas.

Moses-Hrushovski, Rena. 1996. Remaining in the Bunker Long after the War is Over: Deployment in the Individual, the Group, and the Nation. In *Psychoanalysis at the Political Border: Essays in Honor of Rafael Moses*, ed. L. RAngell and R. Moses-Hrushovski. Madison, CT: International Universities Press, 165–88.

Muriá, José María. 1994. Momentos del tequila. In *El tequila: Arte tradicional de México*, ed. Alberto Ruy Sánchez. Mexico City: Artes de México, 16–25.

Musacchio, Humberto. 1999. *Milenios de México*, 3 vols. Mexico City: Hoja Casa Editorial.

Myerhoff, Barbara. 1974. *Peyote Hunt: the Sacred Journey of the Huichol Indians*. Ithaca: Cornell University Press.

Narro Robles, José R., et al. 1999. Cirrosis hepática. In *Diez problemas relevantes de salud pública en México*, eds. J. R. de la Fuente and J. Sepúlveda Amor. Mexico City: Instituto Nacional de Salud Pública/Fondo de Cultura Económica, 93–115.

Nazario, Sonia. 1999. Alcoholism Takes Devastating Toll on Latinos. *Houston Chronicle*, April 11, 1999, 24–25.

Negrón-Muntaner, Frances. 2003. Jennifer's Butt. In *Perspectives on Las Américas: A Reader in Culture, History, and Representation*, eds. M. C. Gutmann, F. V. Matos Rodríguez, L. Stephen, and P. Zavella. Oxford: Blackwell, 291–98.

Nevín, Jeff. 2001. *Virtuoso Mariachi*. Lanham, MD: University Press of America.

Noel, Eugenio. 1967. *Escritos antitaurinos* [orig. 1914]. Madrid: Taurus.

Nutini, Hugo G. 1997. Class and Ethnicity in Mexico: Somatic and Racial Considerations. *Ethnology* 36:227–38.

Oliver, Kelly. 1998. *Subjectivity without Subjects*. Lanham, MD: Rowman & Littlefield.

Oppenheimer, Andrés. 1996. *Mexico: En la frontera del caos*, trans. Isabel Vericat. Mexico City: Javier Vergara Editor.

Orellana, Margarita de. 1994, Microhistoria del tequila: el caso Cuervo. In *El tequila: Arte tradicional de México*, ed. Alberto Ruy Sánchez. Mexico City: Artes de México, 28–35.

Orozco, José. 2003. Gabriel Espíndola Martínez: Tequila Master. In *The Human Tradition in Mexico*, ed. Jeffrey M. Pilcher. Wilmington, DE: Scholarly Resources, 225–33.

Ortiz Monasterio, Pablo. 1995. *The Last City*. Santa Fe, NM: Twin Palms Publishers.

Osborn, Claire, and Andy Alford. 2003. A Troubling Trend: Hispanics and DWI. *Austin American-Statesman*, July 20, 2003, 1, 12–13.

Osorio, Rosa María. 1992. Usos, funciones y consecuencias de la alcoholización: El alcohol como instrumento de las relaciones familiares. In *Prácticas e ideologías "científicas" y "populares" respecto del "alcoholismo" en México*, ed. E. Menéndez. México, D.F.: Centro de Investigaciones y Estudios Superiores en Antropología Social, 21–41.

Paglia, Camille. 1991. *Sexual Personae: Art and Decadence from Nefertiti to Emily Dickinson* [orig. pub. Yale 1990]. New York: Vintage Books.

Paredes, Américo. 1993. *Folklore and Culture on the Texas-Mexican Border* [orig. 1958–1987], ed. R. Bauman. Austin: Center for Mexican American Studies, University of Texas.

Parker, Richard. 2003. The Carnivalization of the World. In *Perspectives on Las Américas: A Reader in Culture, History, and Representation*, eds. M. C. Gutmann, F. V. Matos Rodríguez, L. Stephen, and P. Zavella. Oxford: Blackwell, 213–28.

Parsons, Jeffrey R., and Mary H. Parsons. 1990. *Maguey Utilization in Highland Central Mexico: An Archaeological Ethnography*. Ann Arbor: University of Michigan Press.

Paz, Octavio. 1989. *Lo mejor de Octavio Paz: El fuego de cada día* [orig. 1935–1987], ed. Octavio Paz. Barcelona: Seix Barral.

Paz, Octavio . 2000. *El laberinto de la soledad* [orig. 1950, with *Postdata*, orig. 1969], ed. Enrico Mario Santí. Madrid: Cátedra.

Pérez, Ramona L. 2000. Fiesta as Tradition, Fiesta as Change: Ritual, Alcohol and Violence in a Mexican Community. *Addiction* 95(3):365–73.

Pérez Martínez, Herón. 1998. La fiesta en México. In *México en fiesta*, ed. H. Pérez Martínez. Zamora, Mich.: El Colegio de Michoacán, 11–63.

Pérez Montfort, Ricardo. 1998. La invención de lo "típico" en el imaginario: El México de charros y chinas poblanas. In *Identidad en el imaginario nacional*, ed. J. Pérez Siller and V. Radkau García. Puebla: Instituto de Ciencias Sociales y Humanidades, 371–85.

Pérez Siller, Javier. 1998. *Río Escondido*: El imaginario político de la Revolución hecha gobierno. In *Identidad en el imaginario nacional*, ed. J. Pérez Siller and V. Radkau García. Puebla: Instituto de Ciencias Sociales y Humanidades, 387–410.

Pernanen, Kai. 1991. *Alcohol in Human Violence*. New York: Guilford.

Phelan, John L. 1972. *El reino milenario de los franciscanos en el nuevo mundo*, trans. J. Vázquez. Mexico City: Universidad Nacional Autónoma de México.

Pilcher, Jeffrey M. 2001. *Cantinflas and the Chaos of Mexican Modernity*. Wilmington, DE: Scholarly Resources.

Piña Chan, Román. 1977. *Quetzalcóatl: Serpiente Emplumada*. Mexico City: Fondo de Cultura Económica.

Pozas, Ricardo. 1952. *Juan Pérez Jolote: Biografía de un tzotzil* [orig. 1948]. Mexico City: Fondo de Cultura Económica.

Ramos, Samuel. 1992. *El perfil del hombre y la cultura en México* [orig. 1934]. Mexico City: Espasa-Calpe.

Read, Kay Almere. 1998. *Time and Sacrifice in the Aztec Cosmos*. Bloomington: Indiana University Press.

Revueltas, José. 1990. *Human Mourning* [orig. 1943], trans. Roberto Crespi. Minneapolis: University of Minnesota Press.

Reyes García, Cayetano. 1998. *In altepeílhuitl*: La fiesta del altépetl 'pueblo' en el universo náuatl. In *México en fiesta*, ed. H. Pérez Martínez. Zamora, Mich.: El Colegio de Michoacán, 261–78.

Reyes Gómez, Laureano. 1992. Notas sobre el 'alcoholismo' entre los zoques de Chiapas. In *Prácticas e ideologías "científicas" y "populares" respecto del "alcoholismo" en México*, ed. E. Menéndez. Mexico City: Centro de Investigaciones y Estudios Superiores en Antropología Social, 63–77.

Ricard, Robert. 1947. *La conquista espiritual de México* [orig. 1933]. Mexico City: Editorial Juspolis.

Rivera Ayala, Sergio. 1994. Lewd Songs and Dances from the Streets of Eighteenth-Century New Spain. In *Rituals of Rule, Rituals of Resistance: Public Celebrations and Popular Culture in Mexico*, eds. W. H. Beezley, C. E. Martin, and W. E. French. Wilmington, DE: Scholarly Resources, 27–46.

Roach, Joseph. 1996. *Cities of the Dead: Circum-Atlantic Performance*. New York: Columbia University Press.

Robben, Antonius, and Marcelo Suárez-Orozco, eds. 2000. *Cultures under Siege: Collective Violence and Trauma*. Cambridge: Cambridge University Press.

Rodríguez Chicharro, César. 1988. *La novela indigenista mexicana* [orig. 1959]. Xalapa: Cuadernos del Centro de Investigaciones Humanísticas de la Universidad Veracruzana.

Rojas, José Luis de. 1998. El calendario festivo azteca. In *México en fiesta*, ed. H. Pérez Martínez. Zamora, Mich.: El Colegio de Michoacán, 241–54.

Romanell, Patrick. 1954. *La formación de la mentalidad mexicana (1910–1950)*. Mexico City: El Colegio de México.

Romanucci-Ross, Lola. 1973. *Conflict, Violence, and Morality in a Mexican Village*. Palo Alto: National Press Books.

Room, Robin. 1984. Alcohol and Ethnography: A Case of Problem Deflation [with replies by M. Agar, J. Backett, L. A. Bennett, S. Casswell, D. B. Heath, J. Leland, J. E. Levy, W. Madsen, M. Marshall, J. Moskalewicz, J. C. Negrete, M. B. Rodin, L. Sackett, M. Sargent, D. Strug, and R. Room]. *Current Anthropology* 25:169–91.

Room, Robin . 1998. Thirsting for Attention. *Addiction* 93(6):797–98.

Rorabaugh, W. J. 1979. *The Alcoholic Republic*. New York: Oxford University Press.

Rose, Gilbert J. 1987. *Trauma and Mastery in Life and Art*. New Haven: Yale University Press.

Rosenblatt, A., J. Greenberg, S. Solomon, T. Pyszczynski, and D. Lyon. 1989. Evidence for Terror Management Theory: I. The Effects of Mortality Salience on Reactions to Those Who Violate or Uphold Cultural Values. *Journal of Personality and Social Psychology* 57:681–90.

Rotker, Susana. 1998. Editor's Introduction. In *The Memoirs of Fray Servando Teresa de Mier*, ed. S. Rotker. New York: Oxford University Press, xxiii–lxiv.

Rubenstein, Anne. 1998. *Bad Language, Naked Ladies, and Other Threats to the Nation: A Political History of Comic Books in Mexico*. Durham and London: Duke University Press.

Rudgley, Richard. 1994. *Essential Substances: A Cultural History of Intoxicants in Society*. New York and Tokyo: Kodansha.

Ruiz Abreu, Alvaro. 1993. *José Revueltas: Los muros de la utopía*. Mexico City: Universidad Autónoma Metropolitana-Xochimilco/Cal y Arena.

Rulfo, Juan. 1983. Luvina [orig. 1953], trans. George Schade. In *Inframundo: The Mexico of Juan Rulfo*. Mexico City: Ediciones del Norte.

Rulfo, Juan. 1995. *Pedro Páramo* [orig. 1955]. Barcelona: Planeta.

Runyan, William M. 1993. Psychohistory and Political Psychology: A Comparative Analysis. In *Explorations in Political Psychology*, ed. S. Iyengar and W. McGuire. Durham and London: Duke University Press, 36–63.

Sahagún, Bernardino de. 1956. *Historia general de las cosas de la Nueva España*, 4 vols. Mexico City: Porrua.

Saldívar, José David. 1997. *Border Matters: Remapping American Cultural Studies*. Berkeley: University of California Press.

Salinas Pedraza, Jesús. 2000. Testimonios de un otomí. In *Maguey*, ed. Dominique Dufétel. Mexico City: Artes de México, 30–45.

Sánchez Garrido, José Luis. 1985. *Córdoba en la historia del toreo*. Córdoba: Publicaciones del Monte de Piedad y Caja de Ahorros de Córdoba.

Sánchez Pérez, Luis Aurelio. 1999. Prólogo. In *Mis vivencias con José Alfredo Jiménez* by José Azanza Jiménez. Mexico City: EDAMEX, 9–12.

Savater, Fernando. 1981. El torero como héroe. In *Las Ventas: Cincuenta años de corridas*, ed. M. Kramer. Madrid: Excma. Diputación Provincial de Madrid, 410–14.

Savater, Fernando . 1983. Caracterización del espectador taurino. In *Arte y tauromaquia*, ed. UIMP. Madrid: Turner, 111–25.

Sayette, M. A. 1999. Cognitive Theory and Research. In *Psychological Theories of Drinking and Alcoholism*, eds. K. E. Leonard and H. T. Blane. New York: The Guilford Press, 247–91.

Scardaville, Michael C. 1980. Alcohol Abuse and Tavern Reform in Late Colonial Mexico City. *Hispanic American Historical Review* 60:643–71.

Scheff, Thomas J. 1979. *Catharsis in Healing, Ritual, and Drama*. Berkeley: University of California Press.

Schneider, Carl D. 1977. *Shame, Exposure, and Privacy*. New York: Norton.

Schneider, Luis Mario. 1992. Artaud y México. In *México y Viaje al país de los tarahumaras* by Antonin Artaud, ed. L. M. Schneider. Mexico City: Fondo de Cultura Económica, 7–97.

Schultes, Richard Evans, and Albert Hofmann. 1992. *Plants of the Gods: Their Sacred, Healing, and Hallucinogenic Powers* [orig. 1979]. Rochester, VT: Healing Arts Press.

Scott, James C. 1990. *Domination and the Arts of Resistance: Hidden Transcripts*. New Haven: Yale University Press.

Segal, Boris M. 1986. The Soviet Heavy-Drinking Culture and the American Heavy-Drinking Subculture. In *Alcohol and Culture: Comparative Perspectives from Europe and America*, ed. Thomas F. Babor. New York: Annals of the New York Academy of Sciences, 149–60.

Seinfelt, Mark. 1999. *Final Drafts: Suicides of World-Famous Authors*. Amherst, NY: Prometheus Books.

Shapiro, David. 1981. *Autonomy and Rigid Character*. New York: Basic Books.

Sheehy, Daniel E. 2000. Nations and Musical Traditions: Mexico. In *The Garland Handbook of Latin American Music*, ed. D. A. Olsen and D. E. Sheehy. New York: Garland, 148–73.

Shengold, Leonard. 1992. *Halo in the Sky: Observations on Anality and Defense*. New Haven and London: Yale University Press.

Shengold, Leonard . 1995. *Delusions of Everyday Life*. New Haven and London: Yale University Press.

Shepherd, John, and Peter Wicke. 1997. *Music and Cultural Theory*. Cambridge, UK: Polity Press.

Sher, K. J., T. J. Trull, B. D. Bartholow, and A. Vieth. 1999. Personality and Alcoholism: Issues, Methods, and Etiological Processes. In *Psychological Theories of Drinking and Alcoholism*, eds. K. E. Leonard and H. T. Blane. New York: The Guilford Press, 54–105.

Shupe, Anson, William A. Stacey, and Lonnie R. Hazlewood. 1987. *Violent Men, Violent Couples: The Dynamics of Domestic Violence*. Lexington, MA: D. C. Heath.

Shweder, Richard A. 1991. *Thinking through Cultures: Expeditions in Cultural Psychology*. Cambridge, MA: Harvard University Press.

Shweder, Richard A. . 1999. Why Cultural Psychology? *Ethos: Journal of the Society for Psychological Anthropology* 27:62–73.

Siverts, Henning. 1973. Oxchuc Ceremonial Drinking: A Preliminary Survey of Responses to 120 Query Frames. In *Drinking Patterns in Highland Chiapas: A Teamwork Approach to the Study of Semantics through Ethnography*, ed. H. Siverts. Bergen: The Norwegian Research Council for Science and the Humanities, 147–75.

Slick, Sam L. 1983. *José Revueltas*. Boston: Twayne.

Smart, R. G. 1968. Future Time Perspectives in Alcoholics and Social Drinkers. *Journal of Abnormal Psychology* 73:81–83.

Smith, Gregg. 1998. *Beer in America: The Early Years, 1587–1840. Beer's Role in the Settling of America and the Birth of a Nation*. Boulder, CO: Siris Books.

Smith, Paul Julian. 1989. *The Body Hispanic*. Oxford: Clarendon Press.

Sommer, Doris. 1990. Irresistible Romance: The Foundational Fictions of Latin America. In *Nation and Narration*, ed. Homi K. Bhabha. London and New York: Routledge, 71–98.

Sotelo Inclán, Jesús. 1970. *Raíz y razón de Zapata* [orig. 1943]. Mexico City: Editorial CFE.

Spender, Stephen. 1965. Introduction to *Under the Volcano* by Malcolm Lowry. Philadelphia and London: J. B. Lippincott, vii–xxvi.

Stavans, Ilan. 1995. *The Hispanic Condition: Reflections on Culture & Identity in America*. New York: HarperCollins.

Stavans, Ilan . 1998. *The Riddle of Cantinflas: Essays on Hispanic Popular Culture*. Albuquerque: University of New Mexico Press.

Steele, C. M., B. Critchlow, and T. J. Liu. 1985. Alcohol and Social Behavior: 2. The Helpful Drunkard. *Journal of Personality and Social Psychology* 48:35–46.

Steele, C. M. and R. A. Josephs. 1990. Alcohol Myopia: Its Prized and Dangerous Effects. *American Psychologist* 45:921–33.

Stein, Howard F. 1987. Psychoanalytic Anthropology and Psychohistory: A Personal Synthesis. In *From Metaphor to Meaning: Papers in Psychoanalytic Anthropology*, eds. H. F. Stein and M. Apprey. Charlottesville: University Press of Virginia, 377–90.

Stein, Howard F. . 1994. *The Dream of Culture: Essays on Culture's Elusiveness*. New York: Psyche Press.

Steinglass, Peter, with L. Bennett, S. Wolin, and D. Reiss. 1987. *The Alcoholic Family*. New York: Basic Books.

Stern, Steve J. 1995. *The Secret History of Gender: Women, Men, and Power in Late Colonial Mexico*. Chapel Hill and London: University of North Carolina Press.

Stoller, Paul. 1989. *Fusion of the Worlds*. Chicago: University of Chicago Press.

Stoller, Robert J. 1985. *Observing the Erotic Imagination*. New Haven: Yale University Press.

Strathern, Andrew. 1995. Trance and the Theory of Healing: Sociogenic and Psychogenic Components of Consciousness. In *Questions of Consciousness*, eds. Anthony P. Cohen and Nigel Rapport. New York: Routledge, 117–33.

Stross, Brian. 1991. La cantina mexicana como un lugar para la interacción [orig. 1967]. In *Antropología del alcoholismo en México*, ed. E. Menéndez. Mexico City: Centro de Investigaciones y Estudios Superiores en Antropología Social, 283–307.

Sulkunen, Pekka. 1998. Images and Realities of Alcohol. *Addiction* 93(9):1305–12.

Taminiaux, Pierre. 1996. Sacred Text, Sacred Nation. In *Text and Nation: Cross-Disciplinary Essays on Cultural and National Identities*, ed. L. García-Moreno and P. C. Pfeiffer. Columbia, SC: Camden House, 91–104.

Tatum, Charles M., ed. 1992. *New Chicana/Chicano Writing*. Tucson: University of Arizona Press.

Tatum, Charles M.. 1993. *New Chicana/Chicano Writing*. Tucson: University of Arizona Press.

Taussig, Michael. 1992. *The Nervous System*. New York and London: Routledge.

Taussig, Michael . 1997. *The Magic of the State*. New York and London: Routledge.

Taylor, William B. 1979. *Drinking, Homicide and Rebellion in Colonial Mexican Villages*. Stanford: Stanford University Press.

Thomson, Guy P.C. 1994. The Ceremonial and Political Roles of Village Bands, 1846–1974. In *Rituals of Rule, Rituals of Resistance: Public Celebrations and Popular Culture in Mexico*, eds. W. H. Beezley, C. E. Martin, and W. E. French. Wilmington, DE: Scholarly Resources, 307–42.

Tierno Galván, Enrique. 1961. *Desde el espectáculo a la trivialización*. Madrid: Taurus.

Tusell Gómez, Xavier. 1976. The Functioning of the Cacique System in Andalusia, 1890–1931. In *Politics and Society in Twentieth-Century Spain*, ed. Stanley G. Payne. New York: Viewpoints, 1–30.

Twinam, Ann. 1999. *Public Lives, Private Secrets: Honor, Sexuality, and Illegitimacy in Colonial Spanish America*. Stanford, CA: Stanford University Press.

Uranga, Emilio. 1952. *Análisis del ser del mexicano*. Mexico City: Porrúa y Obregón.

Valverde, José Antonio. 1986. *El macho herido*. Madrid: Ediciones Iberoamericanas Quorum.

Valverde, Mariana. 1998. *Diseases of the Will: Alcohol and the Dilemmas of Freedom*. Cambridge: Cambridge University Press.

van der Kolk, Bessel. 1996a. The Complexity of Adaptation to Trauma. Self-Regulation, Stimulus Discrimination, and Characterological Development. In *Traumatic Stress: The Effects of Overwhelming Experience on Mind, Body, and Society*, eds. B. A. van der Kolk, A. C. McFarlane, and L. Weisaeth. New York and London: Guilford, 182–213.

van der Kolk, Bessel . 1996b. Trauma and Memory. In *Traumatic Stress: The Effects of Overwhelming Experience on Mind, Body, and Society*, eds. B. A. van der Kolk, A. C. McFarlane, and L. Weisaeth. New York and London: Guilford, 279–302.

van der Kolk, Bessel, Onno van der Hart, and Charles R. Marmar. 1996. Dissociation and Information Processing in Posttraumatic Stress Disorder. In *Traumatic Stress: The Effects of Overwhelming Experience on Mind, Body, and Society*, eds. B. A. van der Kolk, A. C. McFarlane, and L. Weisaeth. New York and London: Guilford, 303–27.

Vanderwood, Paul. 1998. *The Power of God against the Guns of Government: Religious Upheaval in Mexico at the Turn of the Nineteenth Century*. Stanford: Stanford University Press.

Vasconcelos, José. 1997. *The Cosmic Race/La raza cósmica*, trans. Didier T. Jaén. Baltimore: Johns Hopkins University Press.

Vaughan, Mary Kay. 1994. The Construction of the Patriotic Festival in Tecamachalco, Puebla, 1900–1946. In *Rituals of Rule, Rituals of Resistance: Public Celebrations and Popular Culture in Mexico*, eds. W. H. Beezley, C. E. Martin, and W. E. French. Wilmington, DE: Scholarly Resources, 213–45.

Velasco Fernández, Rafael. 1991. *Esa enfermedad llamada alcoholismo*. Mexico City: Trillas.

Vergara Figueroa, César A. 1997. *Apodos, la reconstrucción de identidades: Estética del cuerpo, deseo, poder y psicología popular*. Mexico City: INAH.

Viqueira Albán, Juan Pedro. 1999 *Propriety and Permissiveness in Bourbon Mexico* [orig. 1989], trans. S. Lipsett-Rivera and S. Rivera Ayala. Wilmington, DE: Scholarly Resources.

Voekel, Pamela. 2000. Piety and Public Space: The Cemetery Campaign in Veracruz, 1789–1810. In *Latin American Popular Culture*, eds. W. H. Beezley and L. A. Curcio-Nagy. Wilmington, DE: Scholarly Resources, 1-25.

Vovelle, Michel. 1990. *Ideologies and Mentalities*, trans. Eamon O'Flaherty. Chicago: University of Chicago Press.

Waddell, Jack O. 1980. Drinking as a Means of Articulating Social and Cultural Values: Papagos in an Urban Setting. In *Drinking Behavior among Southwestern Indians: An Anthropological Perspective*. Tucson: University of Arizona Press.

Waddell, Jack O . 1983. Sucking at the Father's Breast: Alcohol as Oral Magic in Algonquin-European Transactions. *Journal of Psychoanalytic Anthropology* 6:255–76.

Walker, Lenore E. 1979. *The Battered Woman*. New York: Harper & Row.

Wasson, R. Gordon. 1974. *María Sabina and Her Mazatec Mushroom Velada*. New York: Harcourt Brace Jovanovich.

Watson, C. W. 1995. The Novelist's Consciousness. In *Questions of Consciousness*, edited by Anthony P. Cohen and Nigel Rapport. London and New York: Routledge, 77–98.

Weiss, Michael J. 2000. *The Clustered World*. Boston: Little, Brown and Company.

Welldon, Estela V. 1992. *Mother, Madonna, Whore: The Idealization and Denigration of Motherhood*. New York: Guilford.

Wells, Samantha, and Kathryn Graham. 2003. Aggression Involving Alcohol: Relationship to Drinking Patterns and Social Context. *Addiction* 98:33–42.

Wetzler, Scott. 1993. *Living with the Passive-Aggressive Man*. New York: Simon & Schuster.

Whitrow, G. J. 1988. *Time in History: The Evolution of Our General Awareness of Time and Temporal Perspective*. Oxford and New York: Oxford University Press.

Wilson, Carter. 1966. *Crazy February*. Philadelphia: Lippincott.

Wilson, Carter . 1973. Expression of Personal Relations through Drinking. In *Drinking Patterns in Highland Chiapas: A Teamwork Approach to the Study of Semantics through Ethnography*, ed. H. Siverts. Bergen: The Norwegian Research Council for Science and the Humanities, 121–46.

Windle, M. and P. T. Davies. 1999. Developmental Theory and Research. In *Psychological Theories of Drinking and Alcoholism*, eds. K. E. Leonard and H. T. Blane. New York: The Guilford Press, 164–202.

Wolf, Eric. 1959. *Sons of the Shaking Earth*. Chicago: University of Chicago Press.

Wood, Andrew G. 2003. María Félix and Agustín Lara: A Public Romance. In *The Human Tradition in Mexico*, ed. Jeffrey M. Pilcher. Wilmington, DE: Scholarly Resources, 185–97.

Woodcock, George. 1978. The Own Place of the Mind: An Essay in Lowrian Topography. In *The Art of Malcolm Lowry*, ed. Anne Smith. London: Vision Press, 112–29.

Wroth, William. 1979. *The Chapel of Our Lady of Talpa*. Colorado Springs: The Taylor Museum of the Colorado Springs Fine Art Center.

Wroth, William . 1997. Miraculous Images and Living Saints in Mexican Folk Catholicism. In *Folk Art of Spain and the Americas: El Alma del Pueblo*, ed. M. Oettinger, Jr. New York: Abbeville/ San Antonio Museum of Art, 158–68.

Zaid, Gabriel. 1997. Reading Chance, trans. John Page. In *El arte de la suerte*, ed. Alberto Ruy Sánchez. Mexico City: Artes de México, 84–85.

Zamora, Lois Parkinson. 1998. Quetzalcóatl's Mirror: Reflections on the Photographic Image in Latin America. In *Image and Mirror: Photography from Latin America, 1866–1994*, eds. W. Watriss and L. P. Zamora. Austin: University of Texas Press, 293–376.

Zarauz López, Hector L. 2000. *La fiesta de la muerte*. Mexico City: Consejo Nacional para la Cultura y las Artes.

Zavella, Patricia. 2003. "Playing with Fire": The Gendered Construction of Chicana/Mexicana Sexuality. In *Perspectives on Las Américas: A Reader in Culture, History, and Representation*, eds. M. C. Gutmann, F. V. Matos Rodríguez, L. Stephen, and P. Zavella, 229–44. Oxford: Blackwell.

Zerubavel, Eviatar. 2003. *Time Maps: Collective Memory and the Social Shape of the Past*. Chicago: University of Chicago Press.

Zizek, Slavoj. 1997. *The Plague of Fantasies*. London and New York: Verso.

Zúñiga R., Rogelio. 1986. Tesgüinada en las montañas. *Antropología: Boletín Oficial del Instituto Nacional de Antropología e Historia*, 8:3–10.

Index